Building Library Collections

by

Mary Duncan Carter

Professor Emeritus of Library Science,

The University of Michigan

and

Wallace John Bonk

Professor of Library Science,

The University of Michigan

Third Edition

The Scarecrow Press, Inc.
Metuchen, N.J. 1969

Copyright 1969, by Mary Duncan Carter
and Wallace John Bonk

SBN 8108—0270—8

In Memory of
Rudolph H. Gjelsness, Litt.D., LL.D.
(1894-1968)

Late Professor Emeritus of Library Science
and
Former Chairman of the Department
The University of Michigan

Table of Contents

Table of Contents

Foreword

by

Ralph A. Ulveling
Professor of Library Science, Wayne State University,
Former Director, Detroit Public Library

Each year thousands of books are published by the general, the technical, the governmental and the university presses in this and other countries. From this overwhelming mass of new publications every library must, within the limit of its funds, select that small part which will be most beneficial to the community it serves. This is properly an awesome responsibility to the young inexperienced librarian. To the competent veteran it is a task which though carried on week after week never can approach the ease of a well mastered routine. Each book examined requires the exercise of careful judgment, integrity, emotional control at times, and scrupulous honesty, guided always by a sense of purpose.

Very fittingly the authors begin this book with a presentation of public library objectives. In the building of a library's book collection the determination of objectives is the most important fundamental in the selection process. The wisdom and judgment exercised at this point will ultimately determine whether a library five years hence will be little more than a subsidized mediocre book-store following the dictates of the natural popularity of some subjects plus the popularity induced by advertising campaigns of publishers, or will be an instrument in the public educational structure, which provides books that in a meaningful way are beneficial to the community.

Book selection, and guidance to readers, together are the

vii

professional apex in librarianship. All other library activities are no more than supporting functions. The fact that at times those auxiliary functions have been given disproportionate attention in our literature is to be deplored. This book therefore assumes immediate importance not merely because it provides a perspective on one of the most important aspects of library operations, but because it will incidentally re-direct our attention away from charging devices, systems of record keeping and management controls—all of which have their place in operating a library—and will guide that attention back to the hard core around which all library service must be built, the building of the book collections.

Introduction

In this third edition, a number of changes have been made as a result of the authors' experience in using this book with students, as well as the suggestions of colleagues in other schools, following from their use of the first and second editions. The order of chapters has been altered to make explicit what was formerly only implicit: the first major concern with principles of selection was displayed in the United States by public libraries. We have therefore named the first chapter "Principles of Selection for Public Libraries." It is now followed immediately by the chapter dealing with variations by type of library.

We have not gone into the same detail with principles in that second chapter. Our hope is that other teachers will find useful the device that we employed—e.g., to have the students look back at the principles discussed in the first chapter and consider how they would be interpreted as type of library changes. In this regard, may we note that we have not attempted to fulfill a request made by some students—and occasionally by colleagues. The request can perhaps best be put as follows: in Chapter One, you give us the varying points of view taken toward public libraries, their purposes, and the principles of selection. What we want is a statement of what you believe to be true. Or, to put it another way, some have asked that we hand down the ten commandments of book selection from our particular bibliothecal Mount Sinai—that we give, *ex cathedra*, principles of unwavering and eternal truth.

Our reason for avoiding this task is simple: we do not believe that there are such great, unshakable truths, which can be enunciated in such a form that the librarian as selector can be saved the difficulty of making judgments. Book selection principles are general guides, but they must always be put into the context of the particular clientele served and the purposes which have been outlined for a given institution. One cannot select books for the Huntington Library by quite automatically following the book selection statement of a small public library serving a rural community. We hope that no librarian—and no student of library science—will ever take any statement made in this book and apply it blindly, with a sublime faith that thought and judgment are made unnecessary by a Carter and Bonk dictum.

The treatment of titles in the chapter on national and trade bibliography has been extended from that given in the second edition. A number of our colleagues reported that they had found this treatment particularly useful, and they said they would welcome its extension to retrospective American, British, French, and German bibliography. There may be an advantage in having samples of entry available in the text during class discussions, especially in those places where it is inconvenient to bring the actual bibliographies to class. Where given titles are not owned by a library, the samples can give some indication of the treatment of individual entries.

The lists of the national and trade bibliographies and the book selection aids have been brought up to the cut-off date of early summer, 1968. This is a most necessary, but irksome task, particularly because one can be certain that by the time the text has been set in type some publisher will bring out a major new tool (as was the case with *Choice* and the second edition), or that major changes will occur in some old familiar companions. We know of no solution to this problem, and we have learned to accept its inevitability with whatever reluctant resignation we can muster.

Other sections have been enlarged, with an effort being made to acknowledge some of the newer developments in librarianship which have an effect on selection—the appearance of area study programs, the growing use of "standing order" or "block buying" plans on a grand scale, and the continued interest in non-book materials. The bibliography appended to that chapter has been considerably enlarged, but the authors still stand on their conviction that the principles of selection are no different whether one is selecting a book or a film. Non-book materials create administrative problems rather than selection problems. We realize that some of our colleagues, whose judgment and accomplishments we respect and admire, feel that there is something almost mystically different between books and other materials. We must report that after a careful examination of selection of conventional and non-book materials, we are left convinced that the principles of selection do not vary with the physical forms in which the materials are presented.

It may be worth noting that we undertook writing this text in the hope that it would have a certain definite impact on our classroom teaching. Freed of the necessity of lecturing on these topics, we would be able to spend much more of the class time discussing with students the problems involved in selection, bringing out into the open the varying points of view which are bound to be held by any class, and, in general, using the class periods to help demonstrate our conviction that there are no simple measuring sticks which one can use to select like automata. But, given this purpose, we wanted to permit the possibility of discussion by avoiding the presentation of rules which students would simply memorize and repeat to us on examinations. We have felt that this has led to more successful consideration of selection in our own classes; we can only hope that most of our colleagues prefer this method to the use of the text as a manual for the presentation of iron-clad rules.

We wish to extend our appreciation to Mr. Harold L. Hamill, City Librarian of the Los Angeles Public Library, Mrs. Mary Mitchell, Interim Associate Director of the Detroit Public Library, Mr. Clarence R. Graham, Director of the Louisville Public Library, Mr. Arthur S. Ricketts, Assistant Director of that Library, and Mrs. Helene S. Taylor, former Director of the Bloomfield Free Public Library, for their kind permission to use statements of book selection policy and acquisitions procedures. We wish also to thank Dr. Leroy C. Merritt (Dean of the Library School of the University of Oregon, former Chairman of the California Library Association's Committee on Intellectual Freedom, and editor of the ALA Intellectual Freedom Committee's *Newsletter*) for permission to use the materials from the CLA Freedom Kit; and Dr. Lester Asheim, Director of ALA's Office for Library Education, for permission to use his article, "Not Censorship, But Selection," which appeared in the *Wilson Library Bulletin* for September 1953. We would also like to acknowledge the permission given by Mrs. Pauline J. Love, Chief of the Publishing Department of the American Library Association, to reproduce the *Library Bill of Rights* and the *Westchester Statement on the Freedom to Read.*

The debt of gratitude we owe to our respective partners in the matrimonial adventure is one which can be understood only by those who have experienced the utter disorganization of home and social life which results from efforts to bring a piece of writing to a successful conclusion. Their patience and forebearance deserves chronicling among stories of the noble! May the misery of a fourth edition come not upon them soon.

Chapter I

The Principles of Book Selection for Public Libraries

Introduction

Public librarians are occupied in performing many different tasks each day. They open the library every morning, hasten to compile yesterday's statistics, straighten desks and clear them for the day's action, see that the process of returning books to the shelves gets under way, and greet the first users with the fresh enthusiasm which a new day brings.

The average person, viewing the day-to-day operations of a library, might well ask himself which of all the jobs being done is the most important one. Is it answering reference questions? helping some reader to understand the intricacies of the library's card catalog? receiving books from a dealer and checking all the invoices and order slips? cataloging books?

The fact is that the fundamental task of the librarian is so unobtrusive that the observer might miss it—or, seeing it being performed—might misinterpret what the librarian is about. The department head, sitting quietly at his desk with a copy of *Publishers Weekly*, the circulation librarian, turning over the pages of Virginia Kirkus' *Bulletin*, the head librarian reading through the review section of *Library Journal*: these unspectacular activities represent the most important job of the librarian— the selection of those books which he judges will be best for his library.

When all is said and done, the major task of any library is to supply books to people—to supply those books which the individual user will find valuable and useful. The amount of satis-

1

faction a reader finds in a library depends directly upon the kinds of books the librarian has available for his use. If the librarian manages consistently to choose books of no interest or use to his readers, he cannot expect them to be satisfied with his library.

The interpretation given to the phrase "the best books for his library" will vary, however, with the purpose which the librarian envisages his library as serving. He might feel that the dissatisfaction· of a reader would have to be borne if that dissatisfaction arose from the fact that he could not get books which he wanted, but which the librarian believed were unsuitable to the purposes of the library. Various librarians may arrive at contradictory judgments concerning the value of a given title, and these opposing views become understandable the moment one realizes that the disagreeing librarians hold differing views of the library's purposes. What is best for the amusement of the reader may not be best for his education or enlightenment, and individual librarians may emphasize one of these aims in their own library. Before a discussion of principles can be profitably embarked upon, it is necessary to consider the purposes which the principles are intended to implement and to consider the various ways in which librarians have interpreted these purposes.

Purposes of the Public Library

The public library's broadest purpose has been expressed in various ways. Perhaps it can be summarized best by calling it the educational or civilizing aim. This view sees the library as attempting to provide people with information and knowledge which it is hoped will lead to wisdom and understanding. The Reverend Thomas Bray felt that collections of books, spread about through a country, would "ennoble [people's] minds with principles of virtue and true honor, and file off that roughness, ferocity and barbarity, which are the never failing fruits of ignorance and illiterature." This view of the library sees it as an "open door," through which people can participate in all the accumulated wisdom of the race. Underlying this aim of the library is the faith accepted by our society that the reading of books is a good thing, that it leads to desirable ends, and that books have the power to alter people for the better. This educational aim has been advanced by leaders of the public library movement in the United States since its inception.

Another purpose of the library in our kind of society might be called the civic aim. The public library offers citizens of a democracy the means by which they may become informed and intelligent citizens. The emphasis here lies not so much on their improvement as "liberally educated" human beings as on their improvement as functioning parts of a free society. Thomas Jefferson believed that the people of a country would never consent to the destruction of their liberties if they were informed and that nothing could do more good toward making them informed than the establishment of a small circulating library in every county. Where the people have the responsibility for electing public officials, it becomes imperative that they do their voting from knowledge, not from ignorance. Furthermore, the individual citizen may be called upon to take some part in community affairs—even though it may be only as a member of some local committee—and it is certainly desirable that he be informed in order that he may act his part intelligently.

In addition to these aims, many people believe that the library justly serves very utilitarian purposes: that, in addition to improving the individual as a citizen and as a humanely-educated person, it should also help him improve himself in his job. Gerald Johnson summarized this view in the following way: "Its sole reason for being [in the minds of some] is to help people get along in the world, to help school children get better grades, to help business men make more money, to help preachers write sermons that will keep the congregation awake." Thus, some librarians will buy books which will enable the mechanic to improve himself so that he can become a foreman, which will enable the salesman to teach himself to become an accountant, which will enable people to improve their "occupational mobility."

The *Minimum Standards for Public Library Systems, 1966* gives the following statement of public library purposes: (1) facilitating informal self-education of all people in the community; (2) enriching and further developing the subjects on which individuals are undertaking formal education; (3) meeting the informational needs of all; (4) supporting the educational, civic, and cultural activities of groups and organizations; (5) encouraging wholesome recreation and constructive use of leisure time.

Candor demands that it be admitted that not all of these aims are subscribed to with equal enthusiasm by all librarians. As a consequence, one must expect a certain degree of variation in the interpretation of the book selection principles. In the discussion of the traditional principles which follows, this divergency of opinion will be illustrated.

The Traditional Principles of Book Selection

(1) *Select the Right Books for the Library's Readers.* The first question is, who are the library's patrons? Is the library to serve only those who actually come to it today? Or should the librarian attempt to provide books for all those who may come some day? Should the librarian, to put it another way, select for present clientele only, or also for some potential clientele (however that potential group may be defined)?

One of the underlying principles of the free public library is that it is open to all. This statement implies that the librarian has the responsibility for selecting for all the members of the community—even though they may not come to the library at the moment—since they are all welcome to come. Some librarians believe that this ideal is a central tenet to be observed in determining the library's book selection policies. They do not interpret this first principle—the right books for the library's readers—as requiring that the librarian serve only those who now come to the library. Rather they feel that it imposes on the librarian the responsibility for reflecting in the library collection all the manifold interests of this potential community-wide clientele.

Even if the librarian agrees with this view, there are still two approaches to carrying it out which could be taken. One is the passive approach: let those who come, come; the library will have a good collection to serve them so that any future reader will find the material he wants. The other is the active approach: buy through the whole range of subjects, but proselytize to increase the use of the library by those not now using it.

One of the arguments advanced for the inclusion in the library collection of a whole range of non-book materials has been that these materials will serve to attract to the library the person who is not interested in reading books. If the library is truly to serve the entire community, proponents of this view argue, then it must assume the task of providing access to ideas for those to whom books are not an effective medium for the communication of ideas.

Another traditional statement of principle which reflects this conviction that the library should serve the whole community—and not merely the group of present readers—runs as follows:

(2) *See to it that No Race, Nationality, Profession, Trade, Religion, School of Thought, or Local Customs is Overlooked.* Again, if one accepts this principle, it is argued that one buys in these areas even though members of these particular groups may not be active present users of the library. They are all potential users, and their possible future interests should be anticipated.

One can move from this broadening of the selector's range—which is based upon the make-up of the community—to an even wider principle:

(3) *Every Library Collection Should be Built up According to a Definite Plan on a Broad General Foundation.* The librarians who advocate this approach have advanced the view that the library collection has its own needs, apart from the needs of the community which it serves. These librarians feel that the selector has a responsibility to the collection itself and should attempt to round it out. Such a collection would have material on all subjects, whether or not there were any groups in the community interested in the various subjects, either as active or potential users.

There are some very practical problems involved in the acceptance of this principle, which have led many librarians to abandon any attempt to carry it out, even though in theory they consider it good. If the library is limited in funds, as most libraries are, if it is not one of the behemoth collections, the librarian may well have cause to hesitate before attempting to build the well-rounded collection. If book "A" is purchased because it has intrinsic worth, expounds its subject brilliantly, is the product of a highly authoritative writer, but does not represent a present reading interest in the community, then some book "B," which is of interest to the community, cannot be purchased. The librarian may then ask: Can one justify the use of limited funds to buy books which *may* some day be read? Can one justify spending limited funds to build the ideal, the well-proportioned, the balanced collection, when there is not enough money available to buy all the titles present readers want?

Some librarians have preferred to concentrate on the bird in the hand. They would accept the following principle as primary:

(4) *Demand is the Governing Factor in Selection.* Librarians who accept this principle would abandon the effort to complete a well-rounded collection, as they would also abandon the effort to buy for potential, rather than actual users. Although they would buy some books as part of the basic collection, they would concentrate on trying to supply those books which their present readers need. Other factors than demand would be considered, but demand would be the over-riding factor. In attempting to carry out this policy, continuing acts of judgment on the librarian's part would be necessary. If some books are to be bought for the basic collection—in addition to those in demand—the librarian would have to determine the percentage of the book budget which was to be allocated to building the general collection. This balancing of the two pressures would have to be decided by the librarian on the basis of a series of factors: knowing which way the decision had gone the previous week, and the week before that, and the month before that; knowing how much money was left in the book fund; knowing of any heavy seasonal buying which might lie ahead—the list could be extended considerably.

There is another set of principles to be considered. These are concerned more with the quality of the titles selected than with questions as to the group for whom one ought to buy. Basing selection on demand raises this issue: Will we apply some standard of excellence in selecting a book, or will we buy anything asked for, regardless of its quality? Melvil Dewey advocated the purchase of the best books. Emphasis on the best underlines a point of view which sees the library as the primary source in the community for serious, educational materials. It is a view held by those librarians who are interested in increasing the use of the library for sober ends, who feel that the library has an important role to play as pedagogue to the nation. These librarians, emphasizing as they do the educational purpose of the library, endorse the principle that

(5) *Materials Acquired Should Meet High Standards of Quali-*

ty in Content, Expression, and Format. Librarians committed to this view would emphasize authoritativeness, factual accuracy, effective expression, significance of subject, sincerity of the author's purpose, and responsibility of the author's opinions. They would resist buying a book which failed to meet these standards, even if the book were in heavy demand. Such a conviction has led to a de-emphasis in some libraries of fiction, particularly light fiction. Some libraries even limit the number of current fiction titles which will be purchased in a given year, regardless of the demand for additional titles. The classics of fiction would be stocked by these libraries even if demand for them were not great. Those librarians who feel strongly the importance of the library as an educational force rejoice in the increase in non-fiction reading reported in recent years.

The problem of fiction in the library is not a new one, and an effective statement of this issue was made in the 1875 report of the Examining Committee of the Boston Public Library:

> There is a vast range of ephemeral literature, exciting and fascinating, apologetic of vice or confusing distinctions between plain right and wrong, fostering discontent with the peaceful, homely duties which constitute a large portion of average men and women's lives, responsible for an immense amount of the mental disease and moral irregularities which are so troublesome an element in modern society—and this is the kind of reading to which multitudes naturally take, which it is not the business of the town library to supply . . . Notwithstanding many popular notions to the contrary, it is not part of the duty of a municipality to raise taxes for the amusement of the people, unless the amusement is tolerably sure to be conducive to the higher ends of good citizenship. The sole relation of a town library to the general interest is as a supplement to the school system; as an instrumentality of higher instruction to all classes of people.

It is interesting to note that the mid-twentieth century also sees much concern expressed over the deleterious social effects of the reading of certain kinds of novels, which are judged to be pernicious. Legislative committees—both at the national and state level—have held hearings which have discussed the degree to which certain paperback books could be held accountable for the immense amount of mental disease and moral irregularities which plague our age, as they apparently plagued Boston in 1875.

The view of the library as primarily an instrumentality of education is not universally accepted. At the other extreme are those librarians who see the public library as being largely a source of entertainment for people. They would enunciate their major principle, perhaps, in the following manner:

(6) *Our Purpose is the Same as the Park Department.* These librarians view the library as one of the recreational agencies of a city. They will buy heavily where there is public demand and will not be greatly interested in the quality of the material. They would probably agree with F. B. Perkins, who made the following statement in the 1876 report of the U.S. Bureau of Education:

> The first mistake likely to be made in establishing a public library is choosing books of too thoughtful or solid a character. It is vain to go on the principle of collecting books that people ought to read, and afterwards trying to coax them to read them. The only practical method is to begin by supplying books that people already want to read, and afterwards to do whatever shall be found possible to elevate their reading tastes and habits. Most of those who read are young people who want entertainment and excitement, or tired people who want relaxation and amusement.

This group might approve wholeheartedly of the traditional principle which asserts

(7) *Do Not Hesitate to Install a Mediocre Book Which Will Be Read in Preference to a Superior Book That Will Not Be Read.* This principle does not imply, of course, that all those librarians who accept it would buy books which are patently trash, but they will emphasize the demands of the community, as opposed to the demands of quality. They would assert as a principle that

(8) *Quality of Materials Must be Related to the Other Two Basic Standards of Selection—Purpose and Need.* Since their purpose is primarily to furnish recreational reading, and since their public expresses a need for such materials, they will abandon the building of an ideal collection.

In this matter, there are librarians who cannot embrace either extreme. They see the library as performing a variety of tasks, which in turn demands a variety of materials. They would argue that

(9) *The Collection is Inclusive and Contains Whatever Materials Contribute to the Purposes of the Library.* Such librarians would agree with William F. Poole that it is important to remember, if one is trying to select the best books, that there are as many kinds of best as there are kinds of readers. They might ask, as Charles Cutter asked, "Best in what? in style? in interest? in instructiveness? in suggestiveness? in power? Best for whom? for the ignorant? for people in general? for college graduates? for the retired scholar?" Since these librarians attempt to serve all those various categories of readers, they would be willing to accept a variety of materials, whose standards of quality might vary as the titles are seen to be useful for one group or another.

Such librarians will look carefully at each title in the process of selecting, decide for which type of reader it was intended, and then apply the appropriate standards of quality. A library built on this principle might indeed include the classics of fiction, but it might also include popular materials. The extent to which it will include books representing such disparate categories will depend upon the judgment of the librarian, who will have to weigh a whole complex of local factors. A librarian accepting this view might conclude that the statement "Our purpose here is the same as the Park Department," need only be changed to: "*One* of our purposes here is the same as the Park Department," to make it acceptable.

This middle-of-the-road position is not new. William I. Fletcher stated it ably in the 1876 report of the U.S. Bureau of Education:

> No question connected with public libraries has been so much discussed, or is of such generally recognized importance, as that of the kinds of reading to be furnished. On the one hand, all kinds of arguments—from the political one, that it is not the province of government to furnish the people with mere recreation, to the religious one, that it is wicked to read novels—have been urged against the admission of any but the very highest order of fictitious works; while, on the other hand, the sweeping assertion is made by some that the public library cannot refuse to supply whatever the public sentiment calls for. The mean between these two extremes is doubtless the true view of the case. The managers of public libraries are not less bound to control

and shape the institution in their charge so as to produce
the best result than are the managers of the school system.
To say that calls for books should be accepted as the
indications of what should be furnished, is to make their
office a merely mechanical and perfunctory one. In such
communities as we are especially considering [manufactur-
ing communitites], adherence to such a principle as this
would make the library a mere slop shop of sensational
fiction. But in avoiding the Scylla of unlimited trash, the
Charybdis of too high a standard must be equally steered
clear of.

While the judgments of the past are being called to bear
witness, let the following words of Charles Cutter—who also
summarized this problem in his colorful and effective rhetoric—
be introduced as evidence:

When you have a perfect people you can afford to have only
perfect books, if there are such things. When you have a
homogeneous public you can hope to have a stock of books
exactly fitted to them all, and no book shall be unfitted to
any one of them. But so long as there is a public of every
diversity of mental capacity, previous education, habits of
thought, taste, ideals, you must, if you are to give them
satisfaction or do them any good, provide many books
which will suit and benefit some and will do no good,
perhaps in some cases may do harm, to others. It is inevitable. There is no escape from this fundamental
difficulty. . . .

Select your library then, as Shakespeare wrote his plays, the
highest poetry, the deepest tragedy, side by side with the
comic and the vulgar ... To sum up, what I have been
trying to show is the great diversity in very many respects
of those who come to the library, the consequent diversity
of the best each can read, the necessity of providing many
different kinds, qualities, degrees of good books, the impossibility of limiting one's choice to any one degree of good,
lest it should be too high for some and too low for others.

The emphasis in the statements by both these gentlemen is on
service to the individual reader, pointing out that one cannot
select for some abstract mass of readers who are all statistically
alike. It contrasts strongly with a view held by many librarians

today, which makes of the library one of the media of mass communication, trying to reach large groups of readers with the same message, presented in the same form. This school of thought would envision book selection as a process of applying the results of reading studies of large groups to the groups which make up the reading public of a given library, rather than emphasizing and considering the individual differences among members of the groups. Ralph A. Ulveling, Former Director of the Detroit Public Library, commented on this tendency in 1959:

> But the public library is not one of the mass communication media and should not organize its fundamental services on a mass basis. Ten years ago, when I was a member of the United States National Commission for Unesco, I tried, within the limits of my persuasiveness, to have libraries so recognized. Eventually it became clear to me that a precise distinction which I now recognize as sound and proper, kept libraries out of the mass communication category. To that body a mass medium is one through which a message is distributed widely in a single form. All listeners hear identical words coming out of the radio or from the TV. The monthly magazine brings the same pictures and the same articles at the same time into all homes that subscribe for it, regardless of its usability at the time it comes. But the public library, unlike motion pictures or any of these, should provide an individualized service for every patron who comes to it. Thus it is not a mass medium providing one message for all, but it is rather a medium for serving masses of individuals with a prescription service whereby each gets the precise thing that is best suited to his particular needs, to his ability, to his interests, and to his background.

It may be well at this point to remark that there are two types of libraries to which the principles are addressed: (1) the ideal library, which exists as an abstraction (and to which the general principles apply directly and fully); and (2) the actual library which exists in a particular community (and to which the general principles must be adapted). It is this distinction which leads us to consideration of another factor of signal importance in effective book selection.

In any judgment of a book, the librarian has to consider not only the abstract principles of book selection, but the community of readers which his particular library serves. An informed and intelligent judgment cannot be made if there is insufficient knowledge of the community, either the general community (in the case of the librarian who tries to meet potential demand as well as present demand), or of the specific group of present readers (in the case of the librarian who tries to supply those books which present readers want). It is therefore most important that the librarian

(10) *Know the Community.* Knowledge of the community consists of two kinds of information: (1) general information which applies to any community; (2) the specific reading interests and needs of a particular community. The general information is the kind which can be gathered from general reading interest studies of adults—which it is assumed will apply, to some degree at least, to any community of adults. These studies are attempts to describe the general reader, who is, of course, a statistical abstraction. Many efforts have been made to outline the nature and needs of this statistical personage.

Douglas Waples and Ralph Tyler's *What People Want to Read About* (1931) made the first serious attempt to apply social science research methods to reading interests. They demonstrated that the factors which made for differences in reading interests were—in order of importance—sex, amount of schooling, occupation, environment, age, and time spent in reading. The more of these factors any two groups have in common, the more alike their reading interests will be. The book selector, armed with the data gathered by Waples and Tyler—and by other studies of special groups of readers—could then proceed to select books which would appeal to people fitting into the various categories outlined and could feel some certainty that the books chosen would be of interest to their readers—at least to the degree that their readers fitted into the categories.

Various other studies have revealed—as further clues to the book selector—that women read more fiction than men; that men tend to read more on business and public affairs; that women do more recreational reading, while men do more work-related reading; that the higher the level of education, the more reading that is done; that the largest single category of non-fiction reading is biography and autobiography, followed by social problems and self-help books; but that, taken as a whole, the question of reading interests of adults can be most simply answered by saying that readers delve into every conceivable subject, and that they read most heavily in what is readily available. The general information revealed by such studies will form a useful background for the librarian who is charged with selecting books, and will enable him to exercise a more informed judgment as to the potential usefulness of a given book.

In addition to the general studies, which apply in part to any community, the librarian has the task of determining what the readers of his community want or need. This task may also be divided into two parts: (1) a general study of the community, which will reveal its broad outlines—educational level, occupations, distribution by ages, sex, etc.—all of which will form a measure of the degree to which that community fits the pattern of the "general reader's community" as revealed by the various reading surveys; and (2) a study of the actual users of the library, which will reveal their particular reading interests and relevant sociological data. The actual techniques for determining these facts have been outlined in various places, and the Library-Community Project of the American Library Association has demonstrated them in selected libraries. A discussion of the details of community study will be presented in a subsequent chapter. At this point, it is only necessary to point out that intelligent book selection demands a reasonable knowledge of the community and of the library's readers.

The history of American librarianship shows clearly the emergence of tensions between those who profess the ideal and those who stress the realities of community service to particular readers, between the librarians who would select by intuition or some knowledge of the abstract general reader and those who want factual data on their own community and the individual readers who use their libraries. American library history also shows that librarians have come to believe that the library tries to accomplish a number of purposes. It is equally clear that the individual librarian may emphasize one or another of these purposes, either because the need is greater in his community or because of his own interests and temperament. The fact seems to be that two libraries of the same size, in two towns much alike, can be two very different institutions, reflecting the succession of judgments and choices made by librarians in selecting the materials which make up the collection. Some lament this lack of uniformity, some applaud this existence of many mansions in the house of librarianship. What seems most essential is that librarians recognize the causes of this variety and understand their own convictions—that they make judgments and choices from a clearly realized point of view and not from some nebulous, imprecise feelings which they have never translated into real understanding.

The best way of assuring that such clear realizations will be achieved is to have a written statement of book selection policy. This statement should include an outline of the general purposes that the library is attempting to serve, as well as a statement of those specific aims which arise out of the particular community's needs. The statement of purpose might well be followed by a determination of the standards of selection to be applied to books being considered for purchase. Such a statement should be prepared by the librarian and the Library Board, should be formally adopted by the Board, and—equally important—should be reviewed periodically. Some librarians, particularly those in small libraries, have questioned the need for such a written statement. Although its actual necessity in the small library may not be incontrovertible, its advisability seems obvious, since it cannot help but make clear the many areas in which it is easy to be vague.

The need for periodic revision is important. While it is true that the general purposes of the library are relatively stable, the particular aims arising out of the nature of the local community may very well alter with the passage of time. Librarians have the responsibility for being alert to changing populations, new community problems, and all the changes which come with the growth of communities.

In the course of this chapter, we have talked about public libraries as if they were all identical units. It is important to note, however, that size of library has an impact on selection problems, and that the interpretation of a given principle may vary as the size of the library changes. In addition, the procedure for selecting will vary as size of library changes. The following discussion attempts to point out some of the major variations.

The Large Public Library

The large public library serves the most heterogeneous public. It runs the gamut from children to the aged, from college graduates to those with little formal education (including a large number who are now students at one level or another, with their special curriculum-created demands), from those interested in the most utilitarian how-to-do-it books to those concerned with the most abstruse subjects. It must provide books in every Dewey class and must represent both the popularization for the uninitiated and the more advanced work for the knowledgeable. The general principles apply most directly and without modification to the large public library—conceived of as an abstract unit.

But it must be remembered that the metropolitan public library consists of both the large central collection and a group of smaller branch libraries, whose communities of readers form distinct reading groups. The selection of books for the branch will be governed by the nature of the community each branch serves. Neighborhood branches may vary from those located in upper-income, upper-educational level areas to those situated in low-income, low-educational areas. Thus there will be a variety of types of collections in the various branches. In general, branches will not try to maintain extensive reference collections, will stress the more popular type of reading, will not store little-used materials, and will not attempt to provide materials for scholarly research. The central library—in addition to its popular reading collection, which might be thought of as a branch library within the main building—may have very extensive collections serving special research interests, such as business reference libraries, historical collections, music departments, and the like, in which the materials would include the highly specialized and the scholarly.

The major problem of selection in the large metropolitan library is to create a method of book selection which will adequately reflect this variety of types of reader and types of materials. Generally speaking, large libraries have as their major decision the determination of which titles they do not want to buy. Their financial resources would enable them to buy annually the entire production of new trade titles, if they wished to have one copy of each of the titles issued in this country. It is

their central concern, then, to select out of the total available
output that part which will be found useful in their various
collections, branch and central.

Organization of Book Selection in Large Public Libraries

In metropolitan libraries there are large professional staffs,
heavy subject departmentalization and specialization, and large
branch systems with generalists in charge of the individual
branch libraries. In such systems it would be difficult to involve
each member of the professional staff in book selection simultaneously. Organization in the form of a book selection department is needed, therefore. This department is responsible for
checking and circulating reviews to staff members, acquiring
approval copies of books for review, and, after the selection is
made, compiling lists of the books approved for purchase, where
such lists are used.

Since the department heads are specialists in their respective
fields, they check the book selection aids for material related to
their subjects. These specialists have the advantage of knowing
their collections well and being able to concentrate upon a
relatively narrow area of subject material. The branch book
collections and the collection for popular or home reading in the
main library make up a large part of the selection. One system
for selecting employs rotating committees, representative of
both the departments and the branches. These committees hold
book meetings at regular intervals to consider titles on the lists
compiled by the book selection department. Books are reviewed
by members of the book committee, the reviews being based
upon examination of books sent to the library on approval and
also upon published reviews. Approval copies are usually secured from the wholesaler or bookshop which supplies the
library with the bulk of its books, or—more frequently—directly
from the publishers. The head of the book selection department
requests certain titles, selected in advance from publishers'
announcements or from such aids as *Publishers' Weekly* or
Virginia Kirkus' Service, Inc. Copies of the books discussed at
the book meetings are available for examination by the branch
librarians after each meeting. One plan for securing prepublica-
tion copies for review purposes is known as the Greenaway plan.

It originated in an agreement made by Emerson Greenaway, librarian of the Philadelphia Free Library, with Lippincott to receive one copy of each trade title at the same time as the general reviewers did. This facilitated staff reviewing and pre-publication ordering of multiple copies. Many other publishers agreed to adopt the plan, and many libraries have availed themselves of this service.

At a book meeting, a book that is not approved by the committee is marked accordingly on the list, and, if the committee vote has not been unanimous, a minority report is often given. A book which is not approved is not bought. This decision is not necessarily final, and the question can be reopened.

An alternate method used in some of the large public libraries is to have the books which have been sent to the library on approval evaluated by the department heads, who prepare reviews which are made available to the branch librarians. They in turn select from this master list of approved books. The branch librarians read the librarians' book notes prepared by the department heads, examine the approved books, and place orders for their individual branches.

The trend seems to be away from the book selection meeting with oral reviews. Although the Detroit Public Library continues to employ this method, such large libraries as the Chicago Public, Enoch Pratt, and the Los Angeles Public have given it up. It is, of course, very costly in terms of staff time. But its adherents believe that it is both an effective method for selecting and useful for informing the staff about new books. Kenneth S. Tisdel, in his "Staff Reviewing in Library Book Selection," concluded that the results of using either system will be the same, in terms of the book collection.

The Medium-Sized Public Library

Like the large public library, the medium-sized library deals with a wide variety of readers. The range of interests may not be as large as that of the metropolitan area, with its many industries, national groups, commercial and social organizations, and so forth, but the users of the library are still a much more heterogeneous group than those of a college, school, or special library. The librarians of a medium-sized public library have the

advantage of being able to know the individual users more
personally than the staff of a central library in a large city and
can thus be more immediate in selecting to meet reader interests.

The major problem of selection for the medium-sized library
arises from its more limited budget. It becomes imperative that
selection be very carefully done. By exercising judgment, the
medium-sized library can buy the significant titles issued in any
year, but any flagging of attention to selection will result in
wasteful choices. If a large library were to buy a few dozen titles
which turned out to be little used, the impact on the budget
would be minor, and the books could always be considered as an
investment in the research collection. The medium-sized public
library cannot afford to spend any of its limited funds on books
whose usefulness in that library is limited. A large part of its
collection must be built of books that will be used intensively.

Recently a new demand has been falling on these libraries,
and it has occasioned discussion among librarians as to the
extent of their responsibilities in book selection. With the development of junior colleges in communities, with the activities
of university extension centers, with the tendency of college
students to return home more frequently during the semester,
there has arisen a demand for books which will support the
courses these students are taking. The librarian of the medium-
sized library, already hard pushed to make his budget meet
present demands, pressed by the ever-growing number of high
school students crowding into the public library, now is asking
himself if he really must buy readings in sociology and history
and economics and linguistics, and all the whole range of
courses in the college curriculum, to satisfy the students who
come to the library asking for what are essentially assigned
readings for specific courses. In a sense, he is being asked to
make his library partly a reserve reading room for college
students.

As one might expect, the response to this demand has been
varied. Some librarians have decided against attempting to
provide such books. If a given book meets a demand by the
general reader, and also happens to be on a course reading list,
they will be glad that it serves a dual purpose. But even here,
problems arise. If there are many students taking a course for

which this book is required reading, will the librarian then duplicate copies to satisfy the extra demand, which is above and beyond the call by regular library patrons? Those librarians who are resisting this pressure feel that it is the college's responsibility to buy multiple copies of reserve books—or, at the least, to be willing to send copies on interlibrary loan to the besieged public library.

Other librarians have felt that this is a legitimate responsibility of their libraries. These students are part of the community; they have a special interest: why should this be any different from buying books for the special interests of the garden club, which may be studying nematodes, and for whom the library will buy titles? It has been argued that, if librarians buy for this year's Sociology I reading list, they will discover—as college librarians discover—that next year the list will have been changed, and the books which they bought will go unused. Proponents of such buying point out that this is essentially what happens to any book that is bought because it is in current heavy demand. The best-selling novel, for example, which may have been bought in multiple copies, will probably not be heavily read after a year—or perhaps two. But this obsolescence does not mean that one will refuse to buy the title, if it meets the standards of selection.

Organization of Book Selection in the Medium-Sized Public Library

In the medium-sized public library, all of the professional librarians on the staff participate in the selection of library materials. They bring to selection a knowledge of the existing collection as well as a knowledge of reader interests and preferences. Two methods of checking book selection aids are in common use. In some libraries, all the aids are checked by staff members according to their subject specialties. These specialties may reflect the formal educational background of the librarian or they may be based on hobbies or his own reading. In other libraries, one staff member is made responsible for checking a single book selection aid. In either case, the selections are coordinated by the chief librarian, who checks recommended books in the light of the overall collection and the budget.

Few libraries of this size have book selection meetings. Those which do are obliged to base their consideration of titles upon book reviews, rather than upon actual examination of the books, since approval copies are seldom available to libraries of this size. Cooperative selection might obviate this difficulty. It has been experimented with in several areas with some success. Some metropolitan libraries have opened their book meetings to the librarians in suburban areas. This method gives the librarians of medium-sized libraries a broader view on which to base their own selection. It also points the way to regional cooperation and extended interlibrary loan. Several large public libraries distribute their weekly or fortnightly lists to other libraries. The Detroit Public Library's weekly lists (of department books and of home reading books) are distributed throughout Michigan by the Michigan State Library.

The Small Public Library

The small public library—as a statistical abstraction—has been characterized as being largely a fiction lending library. It is usually staffed by a part-time person, often without any library training, open only on a part-time basis, and it has a very small budget. It will have few of the standard selection tools, and if the librarian is untrained, she may not be familiar with the range of aids available for her use—if, indeed, the library could afford to purchase them. The over-riding factor in selection will probably be demand, and the best-sellers are likely to be the library's main stock in trade. If the librarian has training, she may experience frustration because many of the principles of book selection simply cannot be implemented due to the budget limitations.

The need for some kind of program aimed at improving the library service of the small library has long been recognized. Many states provide workshops for the untrained librarians of these small libraries to help them learn about such matters as book selection. State agencies provide consultant service to aid the librarians in the solution of their problems, distribute lists of books selected by the state agency, and furnish loans of extensive collections of books to those libraries whose budgets are limited. Recently much emphasis has been placed on the federated system, regional libraries, or county library systems, to make available to the smallest library the resources commonly associated with only the large metropolitan libraries. A larger system will have the money to hire a full-time, professionally-trained headquarters staff and to buy the necessary selection aids. Thus it will be able to supply the expensive selection process for the small library.

Even with the best will in the world, a librarian who has $1,000 a year to spend on books cannot achieve the same results as one who has $100,000. The emphasis on library systems in the 1966 standards represents the official recognition of this inescapable fact.

Organization of Selection in the Small Public Library

Book selection in the small public library may be restricted to a single person, as there may be only one librarian on the staff. The librarian is obliged to check possible titles, select titles for purchase, and order them. In such a library members of the library board and patrons with special backgrounds and interests can help. The wishes of library borrowers are likely to carry more immediate weight in the small public library than in other types. The librarian relies entirely on the checking of selection aids. With a small budget, the aids are few. Heavier dependency is placed on the use of state library extension agency lists, one weekly book review (frequently the *New York Times Book Review*), and the "New Books Appraised" section in *Library Journal* and/or *The Booklist*.

Standards for Library Service

When variations in interpretation of the principles can result even in one type of library as size of unit varies, there is a danger that eventually the feeling may grow up that "anything goes," because nothing is really fixed, firm, and certain. As early as the ALA Midwinter Meeting of 1916, a committee was appointed to study the possibility of "grading" libraries as to the quality of service given, after having classified them by population served, amount of taxable property, size-of-area, etc. There was considerable controversy about this concept, but pursuit of the idea continued. In 1933, standards were written for public libraries. These consisted of a brief general statement including commentary on staff, book collection, measurement of the use of the library, and required income (a minimum of $1.00 per capita). The statement was endorsed by several state library associations.

As the depression continued into the thirties, it became evident that libraries needed more specific statements of standards in order to furnish them with the same type of guidelines used by other social service agencies. The National Planning Resources Board paved the way for the later *Post-War Standards for Public Libraries*, published by ALA. It was an ambitious and detailed statement. The 1956 standards announced that the effort to write standards for small libraries had been abandoned, and that the new standards were intended for systems of libraries large enough to provide a budget which would support the level of service defined as minimum by the standards. (Roughly put, it was the level of service of metropolitan libraries.) This did not meet with the complete approval of the librarians of smaller public libraries, who felt, one suspects, that they had been thrown to the city hall wolves with no defense for their service. One result of their dissatisfaction was the preparation of "interim" standards for small public libraries. The 1966 standards retained the emphasis on systems.

In the development of standards, there has been a growing effort to minimize purely quantitative measures and to establish some kind of qualitative measures. This effort did not meet with immediate acceptance despite the work of many committees, which spent many hours of devoted labor. If one attempts to move away from such quantitative measures as the size of the reference collection, or the number of reference staff and attempts to develop meaningful quantitative measures for *quality* of reference work he will soon discover the complexities involved in trying to find objective measures for operations evaluated by subjective judgments.

Whatever the difficulties involved in creating meaningful standards, the effort is bound to continue because there is a strongly-felt need for common benchmarks by which comparisons can be made among libraries of the same group. Thus, in the late 1960's, there were standards for public library systems, a set of interim standards for small public libraries standards for college, correctional institution, junior college, hospital, school, special, and state libraries. At this time, also, the Association of College and Research Libraries was discussing the creation of standards for university libraries. Standards have been written for individual services such as those to children and young adults and for bookmobile service. A number of these sets of standards were under revision, and the reader interested in them is reminded to seek out the latest edition. The standards include many more topics than selection of materials, but it is suggested that the sections on selection in each set of standards be read, and that the several statements be compared.

The next chapter will take up some of the differences among the other types of libraries, which have an effect on book selection.

Conclusion

This presentation of principles has attempted to stress the relationship of the librarian's conception of the library's purpose to his attitude toward book selection principles, the eternal need for judgment, and the continual balancing of one principle against another in terms of the immediate library situation. To be a good selector is not an easy job. It requires a great deal of time and thought and effort and intelligence. The librarian cannot avoid responsibility for constant judgments in the field of book selection because the principles do not furnish automatic machinery for deciding whether or not to buy a given book; they do not furnish a yardstick against which a title can be placed and a numerical reading of fitness taken; they cannot be applied blindly. There is no mathematical formula for successful book selection. There is no easy road to the building of book collections.

CHECK LIST OF STATEMENTS
ON BOOK SELECTION PRINCIPLES

In this chapter, a selected group of traditional statements of principles was used to illustrate various attitudes toward the problems of selection which librarians have taken. This checklist is a summary in topical array of statements by various authors on this subject. It is recommended that this checklist be read through as if it were in narrative form. Such a reading will reveal a number of facts of interest: (1) the repetition of a given principle without change through the years; (2) the slight—but sometimes highly significant—alteration of some of the principles by succeeding authors; (3) the flat contradiction of one author by another—or of one author by himself.

The author of each statement (and the date of the work from which it was taken) is given in parentheses following the statement. Complete bibliographical data will be found in the bibliography at the end of this chapter.

Purposes of the Library and Selection

1. Preceeding a determination of book selection policy, every library should have a statement of library philosophy and over-all objectives of the individual library system. (PLD Reporter, 1955. Group 14)
2. The functions of the library determine the character of the book collection. (Bowerman, 1930)
3. Materials should be selected, retained, and discarded in the light of conscious objectives of each' library. (Public Library Service, 1936)

Book Selection Policy Statements

4. Every library should have a written statement of policy, covering the selection and maintenance of its collection of books and nonbook materials. (Public Library Service, 1956)
5. Formulate a written book selection policy, prepared by the librarian and board jointly and adopted formally by the board. (PLD Reporter, 1955. Group 7)
6. Every library should have a concrete statement of book selection policy, as a basis for selecting material and for use in explaining the library's policy as well as the exclusion or inclusion of specific items of material. (PLD Reporter, 1955. Group 13)
7. The first four sections of the Library Bill of Rights make an excellent statement of broad principles of book selection. (PLD Reporter, 1955. Group 12)

8. A broad statement of book selection policy should be followed by (1) a determination of the criteria in each field; (2) a statement of limiting factors governing book purchase; (3) a listing of techniques and screening tools. (PLD Reporter, 1955. Group 14)

9. Fix upon a policy of selection and stick to it until it has proved wrong, buying consistently along the line of this policy, until a better one is found. (Drury, 1930)

The Library's Users—Actual and Potential

10. The high purpose of book selection is to provide the right books for the right reader at the right time. (Drury, 1930)

11. The best reading for the largest number at the least cost. (Dewey, 1876)

12. Fewer books, responsibly selected, for all the library readers, at any cost. (Drury, 1930. Quoting ALA Board of Education for Librarianship, 3d annual report, April 1927)

13. The first step in book selection should be to ascertain the reading interests of our readers. (Bonny, 1939)

14. As a responsibility of library service, books and other reading matter selected should be chosen for values of interest, information, and enlightenment of all the people of the community. (Library Bill of Rights, 1939)

15. Select books on subjects in which individuals and groups in the community have an interest. (Fairchild, 1903)

16. Select books on subjects in which individuals and groups in the community have a natural interest. (Bascom, 1922)

17. Book selection must be primarily in relation to the needs of the community which the library serves. (Bonny, 1939)

18. Study your community with care and try to provide something for all those who use or may be induced to use the library. (Bacon, 1907)

19. Study open-mindedly the community, endeavoring to analyze its desires, diagnose its ailments, provide for its wants, and satisfy its needs. (Drury, 1930)

20. Study your community and its needs. (PLD Reporter, 1955. Group 7)

21. The librarian should know the community to the extent of

being aware of all potential demands. (PLD Reporter, 1955. Group 3)

22. Provide for the entire constituency, not simply those using the library. (Fairchild, 1903)
23. Provide for all the people in the community, not merely for those who are enrolled as borrowers. (Bascom, 1922)
24. Provide for both actual and potential users. Satisfy the former's general and specific demands as far as possible; anticipate somewhat the demands which might or should come from the latter. (Drury, 1930)

Groups and Special Individuals

25. See to it that no race, nationality, profession, trade, religion, faith, or school of thought or local customs represented in the community is overlooked. (Fairchild, 1903)
26. So far as good books are obtainable and funds permit, represent in your selection every race, profession, trade, religious or political doctrine, interest, and local custom found in the community. Keep in mind, however, that the library is primarily an educational agent, and do not admit books containing harmful doctrines or teachings. (Bascom, 1922)
27. Purvey for recognized groups, reflecting every class, trade, employment, or recreation which develops a natural interest. (Drury, 1930)
28. Selection follows from conscious study of various groups. ... Sensitivity to interests, early recognition of needs before they are clearly expressed, and catholicity of contact and viewpoint mark the librarian who keeps the collection in tune with its owners. (Public Library Service, 1956)
29. No one group should be served at the expense of another. (PLD Reporter, 1955. Group 10)
30. Selection must go beyond the requests of particular groups who have come to use the library regularly and reach out to segments in the population which do not as readily turn to this facility. (Public Library Service, 1956)
31. The book selector should further have in mind many *individuals* who are making active use of his collection of

books and for whose special investigations he provides as occasion affords. (Drury, 1930)

32. Be willing to buy, as far as funds permit, the works asked for by specialists and community leaders. (Drury, 1930)

33. The public library is not to supply the specialist with his regular tools, but only with the general literature on his subject. (Bascom, 1922)

34. Select some books to meet the needs of only a few persons if by so doing society at large will be benefited. (Bascom, 1922)

35. Provide books which will be used by only a few people if they are likely, by the use of the books, to do original work of service to society. (Fairchild, 1903)

36. Sometimes buy a book wanted by a single reader. More often, borrow it for him from another library. (Bacon, 1907)

37. Do not sacrifice the interests of the student to those of the home reader. (Bascom, 1922)

38. If you have foreigners in your town, buy some books for them in their own language. (Bacon, 1907)

Standards of Selection

39. Erect suitable standards for judging all books, and strive to approximate them. (Drury, 1930)

40. Materials acquired should meet high standards of quality in content, expression, and format. (Public Library Service, 1956)

41. Books selected must be based on an established set of standards whether written or unwritten. (PLD Reporter, 1955. Group 11)

42. Select books which tend toward the development and enrichment of life. (Fairchild 1903; Bascom 1922; Haines 1950)

43. Select books that represent any endeavor aiming at human development—material, mental, or moral. (Drury, 1930)

44. Factual accuracy, effective expression, significance of subject, sincerity and responsibility of opinion—these and other factors must be considered and at times balanced one against the other. (Public Library Service, 1956)

45. Materials selected should be judged upon their authoritativeness and effectiveness of presentation. Each must be considered as a whole and not judged by any one of its parts. (PLD Reporter, 1955. Summary)
46. Secure any book which the library can use to advantage ... for knowledge and information, for power and inspiration, for amusement and recreation, either now or in the future. (Drury, 1930)
47. The standard appropriate for one community might not apply in another. (PLD Reporter, 1955. Group 12)
48. Within standards of purpose and quality, collections should be built to meet the needs and interests of people. (Public Library Service, 1956)
49. The collection of the public library is inclusive and contains whatever materials contribute to the purposes of the library. (Public Library Service, 1956)
50. Selection of materials should be determined by usefulness and should not be limited by format. (Public Library Service, 1956)
51. Buy volumes that are suitable for the library purpose in format as well as in contents, being attractive and durable in binding, paper, and printing. (Drury, 1930)

Completeness; Proportion; Balance
The "Well-Rounded Collection"

52. Do not strive for completeness. Select the best books on a subject, the best by an author. Do not get all of a series unless their merit or your need warrants it. (Bascom, 1922)
53. Do not buy an author's complete works if some of his books are worth your while to own and others are not. (Bacon, 1907)
54. Banish the idea of completeness except for an encyclopedic library or for a special collection. (Fairchild, 1903)
55. Do not strive for completeness in sets, series, or subjects unless convinced that it is necessary for real usefulness. (Drury, 1930)
56. Do not try to build up a "well-rounded" collection. Get what your readers need and want, or can be made to want. (Bacon, 1907)

57. Completeness is a practical impossibility. It is impossible to follow a scheme for balancing proportions of subject classes. (Drury, 1930)
58. Every library should be built up according to a definite plan on a broad general foundation. Its development must be flexible, but constant attention must be paid to the maintaining of just proportions as a whole, so that certain classes will not be overemphasized and others neglected. The needs of the library exist and should be met, as well as the needs of its readers. (Haines, 1950)
59. Keep a just proportion in the collection as a whole. (Bascom, 1922)
60. Have a good regard for proportion and balance, the most difficult task in a book selection. (Fairchild, 1903)

Demand

61. Quality of materials must be related to the other two basic standards of selection, purpose and need. (Public Library Service, 1956)
62. Representation must be comprehensive of and in proportion to demand and not subject. (McColvin, 1925)
63. Demand is a large governing factor in selection. (Drury, 1930)
64. Provide for actual demand and anticipate any reasonable demands which may be made upon the library's resources. (Bonny, 1939)
65. The value of the demand is gauged by the extent to which the subject fosters the purposes of human endeavor, i.e., human development and happiness. (Drury, 1930)
66. Variety of demand arises from the complexity of human nature and ability represented in the community and from the several different aspects of any subject. (Drury, 1930)
67. The demand theory is not a good basis for book selection, but it affects selection. (PLD Reporter, 1955. Group 10)
68. In book selection, popular demand must be recognized to the extent of maintaining community interest and support of the library. (PLD Reporter, 1955. Summary)
69. Study your community and compare its needs with its demands. Welcome its recommendations, but use your

judgment in following them. Be a leader, a guide, rather than a follower. (Bascom, 1922)

70. Restrain the unduly aggressive and recognize the inarticulate patron. Some demand that their every desire shall be satisfied and persist in recommending their hobbies; the unobtrusive also have rights. (Drury, 1930)

71. Buy no book without asking yourself whether in buying it you are not depriving your library of the chance to buy a better book that is in as·great demand. (Bacon, 1907; Drury, 1930)

72. As a rule, prefer an inferior book that will be read to a superior book that will not be read. (Bascom, 1922; Haines, 1950)

73. Aim at getting the best on any subject, but do not hesitate to install a mediocre book that will be read in preference to a superior one that will not be read. (Drury, 1930)

74. Duplicate the best rather than acquire the many. (Drury, 1930)

75. This is the secret of the art of selecting: few titles, carefully chosen for the community's need and freely duplicated. (Dana, 1908)

76. It is better to buy ten extra copies of a wholesome book wanted by the public than one copy each of ten books which will not be read. But even the very small library can wisely spend a little of its money each year on scholarly books. (Dana, 1920)

77. Because of basic standards of the public library, it is impossible to satisfy all popular demands. Popular demand may include two types of material: that of more permanent value and that of temporary or superficial value. We recommend that the emphasis in book selection policy be placed on securing a greater amount of worthwhile material, limiting the selection of other material as stringently as possible. (PLD Reporter, 1955. Group 8)

78. Popular demand must be considered, but should not serve as the primary criterion for purchase and duplication, for by so doing the library is selling short other interests in the community. (PLD Reporter, 1955. Group 3)

79. Do not think that because your library is tax-supported

you must buy every book for which the taxpayers ask. Encourage people to make their wishes known. But you are not bound to buy every book called for, if you think it is a book the library should not own, any more than your local school board is bound to give a course in Chinese in the high school because the daughter of a certain taxpayer is going to China as a missionary. (Bacon, 1907)

80. Select some books of permanent value not immediately interesting to readers. (Fairchild, 1903)

81. Select some books of permanent value, regardless of whether or not they will be much used. (Bascom, 1922)

82. While demand is primarily the basis and reason for supply, remember that the great works of literature are foundation stones in the library's own structure and therefore select some books of permanent value regardless of whether or not they will be widely used. (Haines, 1950)

83. Buy good editions of standard works. Even a very small library may own a few attractive editions of great authors. (Bacon, 1907)

84. Stock the classics and the standards, ever and always, in attractive editions. (Drury, 1930)

Controversial Issues

85. Let the basis of selection be positive, not negative. Select books which will be of service to somebody; do not exclude books because somebody thinks they will do harm. (Fairchild, 1903; Bascom, 1922; Haines, 1950)

86. Select for positive use. A book should not be simply good, but good for something. It must do service. Question its usefulness if the best that can be said is "It can do no harm." (Drury, 1930)

87. There should be the fullest practicable provision of material presenting all points of view concerning the problems and issues of our times, international, national, and local. (Library Bill of Rights, 1939)

88. All sides of issues should be presented insofar as possible, within budget limitations, with as much authoritative background as is available. (PLD Reporter, 1955. Group 3)

89. The library collection should contain opposing views on controversial topics of interest to the people. (Public Library Service, 1956)

90. Controversial books relating to the local community should be selected. (PLD Reporter, 1955. Group 11)

91. The collection must contain the various opinions which apply to important, complicated, and controversial questions, including unpopular and unorthodox positions. (Public Library Service, 1956)

92. If a public library does not provide the means to study the several sides of issues, it is failing in one of its unique reasons for existence. This does not necessarily imply numerical balance. Controversial materials kept in community libraries will naturally be limited to areas of controversy about which there is general concern. (Public Library Service, 1956)

93. The librarian should guard against taking the line of least resistance by avoiding issues, but meet them squarely. (PLD Reporter, 1955. Group 3)

94. The selection of all library materials should be as objective as possible. Selection which is affected by one's own beliefs is an act of censorship. (PLD Reporter, 1955. Summary)

95. Books or other reading matter of sound factual authority should not be proscribed or removed from library shelves because of partisan or doctrinal disapproval. (Library Bill of Rights, 1939)

96. In no case should any book be excluded because of the race, nationality, political or religious views of the writer. (Library Bill of Rights, 1939)

97. Care must be exercised that parts of the community do not unduly influence the collection, either positively or negatively. Selection must resist efforts of groups to deny access to materials on the part of other sections of the community, whether in the name of political, moral, or religious beliefs. (Public Library Service, 1956)

98. The library should not abdicate its responsibility for book selection to any individual or organization issuing restrictive lists. (PLD Reporter, 1955. Group 3)

99. Censorship of books, urged or practiced by volunteer arbiters of morals or political opinion, or by organizations that

would establish a coercive concept of Americanism, must be challenged by libraries. (Library Bill of Rights, 1939)

100. If materials serve the purpose of the library, are of required quality, and relate to an existing need or interest, they should not be removed from the collection because of pressure by groups or individuals. (Public Library Service, 1956)

101. Do not refuse to buy a book because one or more people object to it. What no one objects to is probably valueless. A vital book, like a person of any vitality, is sure to antagonize someone. (Bacon, 1907)

102. No political or sectarian bias should influence the exclusion of good books. (Brown, 1937)

103. Do not pander to any sect, creed, or partisan taste. (Dana, 1920)

Sex and Morality

104. Questions of sexual morality are very difficult. If the librarian exercises the censorship of exclusion, he will be accused of prurience; if not exercised, he will be accused of exposing impressionable youth to immoral suggestion. (Brown, 1937)

105. What is immorality and what is immaturity every library authority will determine for itself. (Brown, 1937)

106. In selection, judgment should be based on the total effect of the piece of material and not on the presence of words, phrases, or situations which in themselves might be objectionable. (PLD Reporter, 1955. Group 13)

107. Do not reject a book on the opinion of a few narrow-minded people who think it harmful or even bad. (Bascom, 1922)

108 The hypersensitive objections of the narrow-minded (in matters of sex) must not be mistaken for genuine expressions of community views. (Brown, 1937)

109. The underlying principle of my own selection of books, for a library which is essentially for the people (as contrasted with a university library) is that books which speak truth concerning normal, wholesome conditions may be safely bought, however plain-spoken. While, on the other hand,

books which treat of morbid, diseased conditions of the individual man, or society at large, are intended for the student of special subjects. Such are bought only after due consideration of the just relation of the comparative rights of the students and general readers. (West, 1895)

110. Avoid without censoring the ethically dubious. (Drury, 1930)

111. Buy few, if any, books that the majority of your clients would consider ethically dubious. If you buy any, restrict their circulation so that boys and girls will not draw them out. (Bacon, 1907)

112. One can always refuse to buy what is doubtful on the score of lack of funds. (Bacon, 1907)

113. There seems to be no reason why works which offend the current common views of morality should be purchased out of community funds. (Brown, 1937)

114. In the case of books with a sexual theme or treating of sex in an outspoken manner, if there are strong local opinions antagonistic to this type of book being on the public library shelves, the librarian should refrain from stocking such books. If, on the other hand, the books are of definite literary or other value, the librarian would be justified in taking a firm stand and insisting that they be kept in stock but supplied only upon special request to approved borrowers. (Bonny, 1939)

Religious and Political Problems

115. With political materials, librarians without being censors should still look for accuracy, integrity, and authority, always attempting to be aware of their own difficulty in being objective in such an emotionally charged field, particularly in regard to books covering recent happenings and current problems. (PLD Reporter 1955. Group 12)

116. About religious materials, it was agreed that the library should try to keep a balance, representing all religions and denominations as adequately as possible in its collection, that they should not buy and perhaps not even accept as gifts, books which were specifically denominational and not of general interest. (PLD Reporter, 1955. Group 12)

117. Of sectarian books get only those that are truly representative and likely to be used by the general reader, or at least by a considerable number of readers, and treat all sects alike. (Bascom, 1922)

Popular Materials and Fiction

118. We cannot justify swamping the library with ephemeral literature. When the supply of ephemeral books encroaches upon the satisfaction of the needs of the student and the searcher after information, it should be stopped. (Bonny, 1939)
119. When legal, the rental collection may be used to provide ephemeral materials, reserving book funds for those of more enduring value. (PLD Reporter, 1955. Group 10)
120. Do not buy novels simply because they are popular. To follow that line is to end with the cheapest kind of stuff. Some librarians claim, erroneously, that they must buy to please the public's taste; that they can't use their own judgment in selecting books for a library which the public purse supports. Librarians are charged with getting the best . . . not with suiting everybody. (Dana, 1920)
121. Do not aim too high—avoid trash, but do not buy literature which will not be read simply because it is "standard." Remember that the public library is popular in every sense of the word. (Dana, 1920)
122. No library could afford to set its standard of selection so high that it would reduce community interest in and support of the library, and there are important groups in the community to which light fiction means much. (PLD Reporter, 1955. Group 12)
123. Do not look down on fiction. Buy a good deal of it in a place where you are trying to induce people to use the library. It is good bait. Choose the best and duplicate. (Bacon, 1907)
124. In fiction, get the more popular of the wholesome novels found on the shelves of larger libraries. (Dana, 1920)
125. Do not be intolerant of fiction if it measures up to standard; it has educational as well as recreational value. (Drury, 1930)

126. It must be recognized that most public libraries find it necessary to buy some fiction and popular reading which is below the library's quality standards. (PLD Reporter, 1955. Group 1)

127. Perhaps it is a question of degree and gradualness of approach, and elimination gradually and consistently from the lower levels throughout the years. Some libraries, following this policy, have found themselves buying more copies of fewer and fewer novels. (PLD Reporter, 1955. Group 12)

128. Popular demand for fiction, not always of acceptable standards, creates a real problem. Librarians should try to meet demand but should not yield to popular pressure when books have been refused for definite reasons consonant with the library's objectives. (PLD Reporter, 1955. Group 12)

Children and Young People

129. Buy largely for children. Notice that I do not say: buy largely of juvenile books. There is too much pre-digested mental food for babes on the market today. Shun all but the best of it, and give the children some of the great books of all times. (Bacon, 1907)

130. Buy largely for children. They are the library's best pupils. They are more easily trained to enjoy good books than their elders. (Dana, 1920)

131. Since guidance is implicit in selection of materials for children and young people, book selection policy may differ among these and the adult groups. (PLD Reporter, 1955. Summary)

132. Teen-agers should participate in selecting their own materials and in deciding on the purchase of controversial materials for their own department. (PLD Reporter, 1955. Group 10)

Gifts

133. Gifts to the library should be judged upon the same basis as purchased materials. (PLD Reporter, 1955. Summary)

134. In controversial and sectarian subjects, gifts may be accepted when purchase is undesirable. (Haines, 1950)

Local History

135. Buy, or better, beg all books or pamphlets relating to your town or written by townspeople. Secure church and town reports, club programs, etc. Build up a little local history collection no matter how small your library. (Bacon, 1907)
136. Local interest should be fostered by buying freely books on local history and books by local authors. (Dana, 1920)
137. Develop the local history collection; the items will be sought for in the library if anywhere in the world. (Drury, 1930)
138. Make your collection of local history as extensive and useful as possible. (Haines, 1950)

Nonbook Materials

139. Nonbook materials should be an integral part of the collection, and, within limits of availability and usefulness, should be provided to the same degree of range and inclusiveness as books. (Public Library Service, 1956)
140. For nonbook materials, considerations of physical and technical excellence, as shown in quality of photography and sound, must be considered. (Public Library Service, 1956)

Relationship to Other Libraries

141. The character and emphasis of the public library collection should be influenced by the existence of other library collections in the community and area. (Public Library Service, 1956)
142. The ability of any library to meet all demands from its own holdings is limited. Needs beyond the resources of a given library can be met from those of other libraries. (PLD Reporter, 1955. Group 6)
143. Do not duplicate valuable books in other libraries in your

town, if these are easily accessible to the public. (Bacon,
1907)
144. Extensive use of interlibrary loan is recommended for
books of limited use. (PLD Reporter, 1955. Group 4)
145. Husband resources through cooperation, local, regional,
and national. (Drury, 1930)

Weeding

146. Systematic removal from the collection of material no
longer useful is essential to maintaining the purposes and
quality of resources. (Public Library Service, 1956)
147. The discarding of materials requires the same degree of
attention as initial selection and deserves careful study.
(PLD Reporter, 1955. Group 13)
148. Discard or refrain from adding books (other than the
classics and standards) for which there is no actual or
anticipated demand. (Drury, 1930)
149. Annual withdrawals from the collection should average at
least 5 per cent of the total collection. (Public Library
Service, 1956)

Administration of Selection

150. Selection must be an orderly, co-ordinate process. (Public
Library Service, 1956)
151. Maintain, so far as possible, promptness and regularity in
supplying new books. (Haines, 1950)
152. So apportion the library funds as to obtain books of the
highest quality for the greatest number of people. (Drury,
1930)
153. Keep within the budget, knowing the total amount available and maintaining a just but not rigid proportion among
the allotments. (Drury, 1930)
154. It is very important for the selector to have at hand at all
times a record of the amount of money available for purchases. (Drury, 1930)

Bibliography of Sources of Book Selection Statements

A.L.A. *Library Bill of Rights.* [See Appendix A]

Bacon, Corinne. "Principles of Book Selection." *New York Libraries,* v. 1, Oct. 1907, p. 3-6.

Bascom, Elva Lucille. *Book Selection.* Chicago, ALA, 1922.

Bonny, Harold Victor. *Manual of Practical Book Selection for Public Libraries.* London, Grafton, 1939.

Bowerman, George Franklin. *Censorship and the Public Library.* New York, Wilson, 1931

Brown, James Duff. *Manual of Library Economy.* 5th ed. London, Grafton, 1937.

Dana, John Cotton. *A Library Primer.* New York, Library Bureau, 1920.

Dana, John Cotton. "Selection and Rejection of Books." *Public Libraries,* v. 13, 1908, p. 177-8.

Dewey, Melvil. "The American Library Association." *Library Journal,* v. 1, 1877, p. 247.

Drury, Francis K. W. *Book Selection.* Chicago, ALA, 1930.

Fairchild, Mary Salome (Cutter). "Book Selection." *Public Libraries,* v. 8, 1903, p. 281.

Haines, Helen. *Living with Books.* 2d ed. New York, Columbia Univ. Press, 1950.

McColvin, Lionel Roy. *The Theory of Book Selection for Public Libraries.* London, Grafton, 1925.

PLD Reporter No. 4, 1955. "Book Selection; Proceedings of a Work Conference, 1955." Ed. by S. Janice Kee and Dorothy K. Smith. Chicago, ALA, 1955.

Public Library Service; a Guide to Evaluation with Minimum Standards. Chicago, ALA, 1956.

West, Theresa H. "Improper Books; Methods Employed to Discover and Exclude Them." *Library Journal,* v. 20, 1895, p. C32.

Bibliography

Altick, Richard. *The English Common Reader.* Chicago, Univ. of Chicago Press, 1957.

Asheim, Lester. "What do Adults Read?" *In* Adult Reading; 55th Yearbook of the National Society of Education. Part 2. Chicago, Univ. of Chicago Press, 1956)

Berelson, Bernard. *The Library's Public.* N.Y., Columbia Univ. Press, 1949.

Blackshear, Orilla T. "Building and Maintaining the Small Library Collection." (American Library Association Small Libraries Project, Pamphlet No. 5). Chicago, ALA, 1962.

Broderick, Dorothy. *An Introduction to Children's Work in Public Libraries.* N.Y., Wilson, 1965.

Bundy, Mary Lee. *The Library's Public Revisited.* Univ. of Maryland, School of Library and Information Service, 1967.

Ennis, Philip E. *Adult Book Reading in the United States.* Chicago, National Opinion Research Center, Univ. of Chicago, 1965.

Enoch Pratt Free Library. *How Baltimore Chooses; Selection Policies of the Enoch Pratt Free Library.* 4th ed. Baltimore, 1968.

Goldhor, Herbert. "A Note on the Theory of Book Selection." *Library Quarterly,* XII, 1942. p. 151-74.

Goldhor, Herbert, ed. "Selection and Acquisition Procedures in Medium-Sized and Large Libraries." (Allerton Park Institute No. 9) Champaign, Ill., 1963.

Gray, William S., and Monroe, Ruth. *Reading Interests and Habits of Adults.* N.Y., Macmillan, 1929.

Gross, Elizabeth. *Children's Service in Public Libraries.* Dobbs Ferry, N.Y., Oceana, 1968.

Haines, Helen. *Living with Books.* 2d ed. N.Y., Columbia Univ. Press, 1950.

Kelley, Grace O. *Woodside Does Read; A Survey of the Reading Interests and Habits of a Local Community.* Jamaica, N.Y., Queens Borough Public Library, 1935.

Schramm, Wilbur. "Why Adults Read." (*In* Adult Reading; 55th Yearbook . . . Chicago, 1956. See Asheim, above, for citation)

Shaffer, Kenneth R. *The Book Collection: Policy Case Studies in Public and Academic Libraries.* Hamden, Conn.; Shoestring, 1961.

Smith, Lillian H. *The Unreluctant Years; A Critical Approach to Children's Literature.* Chicago, ALA, 1956.

Smith, Ray. "Book Selection and the Community Library." *Library Quarterly,* XXXIII, 1963. p. 79-90.

Strout, Donald E., and Eaton, Thelma, eds. *The Nature and Development of the Library Collection, with Special Refer-*

ence to the Small and Medium-Sized Public Library. Urbana,
Ill., Univ. of Illinois Library School, 1957.
Waples, Douglas, and Tyler, Ralph. *What People Want to Read
About.* Chicago, ALA, 1931.
Wellard, James H. *Book Selection; Its Principles and Practice.*
London, Grafton, 1937.
Wheeler, Joseph L., and Goldhor, Herbert. *Practical Adminis-
tration of Public Libraries.* N.Y., Harper & Row, 1962. (Chapters
1;2;27.)
White, Ruth M. "Public Library Policies—General and Spe-
cific." Chicago, ALA, 1960. (Public Library Reporter No. 9)
Williams, Reginald G. *A Manual of Book Selection for the
Librarian and Booklover.* London, Grafton, 1920.
Wilson, Louis R., ed. *The Practice of Book Selection.* Chicago,
Univ. of Chicago Press, 1940.

Standards

American Association of State Libraries. *Standards for Library
Functions at the State Level.* Chicago, ALA, 1963.
Public Library Association. *Interim Standards for Small Public
Libraries: Guidelines toward Achieving the Goals of Public
Library Service.* Chicago, ALA, 1962.
——. *Minimum Standards for Public Library Systems, 1966.*
Chicago, ALA, 1967.
——. *Standards for Children's Services in Public Libraries.*
Chicago, ALA, 1964.
——. *Standards of Quality for Bookmobile Service.* Chicago,
ALA, 1963.
——. *Young Adult Services in the Public Library.* Chicago,
ALA, 1960.

Chapter II

Variations by Type of Library

Sooner or later at almost any meeting of librarians, one is bound to hear a librarian declare: "But in our situation. . . ." This phrase usually heralds an invocation of that great truism, "Circumstances alter cases," to justify some practice which other librarians have questioned. There is always the danger, of course, in being so far influenced by local demands that generally accepted professional standards may be ignored. It is tempting to use the appeal to "our situation" to justify a departure from sound practice, and the librarian must be eternally on guard to prevent informed professional judgment from descending to a standardless, rootless, spineless bending before each local wind. This appeal to local conditions has been used on occasion as a defense of unwillingness to change, to grow, to depart from the old ways. Nevertheless, much as this appeal to local conditions may be misused, it is essential to have a close knowledge of and a respect for the local factors which must be taken into account in building a book collection.

There are legitimate adaptations of the general principles which must be made as libraries vary by size and type. They are not departures from professionally accepted standards, but necessary modifications, amplifications, or variations of them.

One of the primary factors influencing the building of a collection is the type of library. Public, college, university, school, and special libraries must all gathered into the same mansion of principles. The objectives of each of these three types of libraries are not identical. These libraries serve different groups of people so they are interested in different types of materials. This chapter covers some of the variations created by difference in type of library.

The College Library

The library of the liberal arts college has three major functions: (1) to support the curriculum with materials in those subjects taught by the college; (2) to provide a basic collection aimed at the development of the "humane," the "liberally educated" person—apart from the curriculum requirements; (3) to support a degree of faculty research.

The college library will have a more homogeneous community of users than the public library. It does not encompass an age spread from pre-kindergarten to senescence; all of its readers will be high school graduates; they will have similar aspirations and occupational interests; they will be there to achieve the same kind of education.

Since the college library is not primarily intended for research, but for use of the student in his undergraduate education, it will not require the expenditure of funds for the more remote materials of narrow subject scope and intense specialization. Since it does not support a curriculum encompassing the special technical fields (medicine, engineering, agriculture, nursing, dentistry, etc.), it will not need the highly specialized books of these fields. Since it is not a public library, serving a wide variety of publics, including those interested only in light recreational reading, it can base its selection on the value and authority of a given title, rather than on its popular appeal. In the various subject fields, it need not emphasize the popularization, intended for the less skilled or less informed reader, although it may feel a responsibility for general works, introductory to a field, intended for the college student who is not specializing in that field, but who wishes some knowledge of it as part of his general education.

Organization of Book Selection in College Libraries

In the college library responsibility for selection is more widely dispersed than in the public library. In addition to the library staff, the members of the faculty are given responsibility for selecting in their subject fields. Because of the larger group involved, it is important that overall planning be done and that the decisions on selection policy be set down. A written book selection policy is just as important in a college as in a public library, although rarely encountered. In order to carry out this policy, library staff and faculty members must work together. College book selection should lean heavily on all faculty members, and full participation should be encouraged by the chairmen of departments.

As it would be unwieldly to have all the faculty participating in this activity without direction or coordination, it is advisable to have each faculty member make recommendations to the chairman of his department, or to the departmental library committee. The general college library committee should be made up of members of the faculty who are genuinely interested in books and who represent the college faculty as a whole.

Although the ideal situation is to have intelligent faculty participation in the selection of books in general fields, ultimate responsibility lies with the librarian and his professional staff. In certain college libraries, the selection of general materials is made by the professional library staff who meet at regular intervals after perusal of the various book reviewing media. The college administrator also has his place in the process of college book selection. It is his responsibility to provide a book fund which is adequate to the library's needs and to select faculty and a librarian who are able to carry out the book selection process.

It is assumed that the college librarian will have expert knowledge of sources for selection. He will have a knowledge of the overall collection and will consider every book order in the light of the needs of the library as a whole and its place as part of the total educational apparatus of the institution he serves.

The University Library

The task of the university library includes that of the college library, plus some additional responsibilities. It also attempts to build a collection to support the curriculum; but the curriculum is much broader than that of the liberal arts college. The university will include not only a liberal arts college but also special and professional schools and colleges. The range of subjects will therefore be much broader. In addition to the training of undergraduates, the university will support a program of graduate education, involving not only advanced courses, with their special reading requirements, but also graduate research. Furthermore, the university is ordinarily committed heavily to support faculty research.

This emphasis on research will lead to the collecting of much that is scholarly, little-used, and expensive. Selection will reach far beyond the ordinary trade materials, as the librarians hunt out the publications of scientific institutions of every country— foreign languages and knowledge of foreign bibliography become imperative. It will involve a knowledge of such non-book materials as the microfilm collections of books listed in the *Short-Title Catalogue,* the microfilm edition of the titles in Evans, the Human Relations Area Study files, technical reports of the various government agencies dealing with atomic energy, and a wide assortment of other special scholarly or scientific materials.

Organization of Selection in University Libraries

Generally speaking, the organization of university book selection resembles that of the college; the various departments of schools and colleges are theoretically responsible for selection in their subject areas, while the library staff remains responsible for the fields of general bibliography, for those areas not covered by departments, for special materials such as periodicals and documents, and for overseeing the general development of the collection. The factor which complicates the organization of selection in a university is size. As the university moves from a collection of a million volumes to one of two or three million; as the student body grows from 15,000 to 20,000 to 30,000; as the faculty increases in numbers to keep pace with the increasing enrollment, complications in all aspects of the institution increase in a geometric progression. And book selection, which could be fairly informal in the small liberal arts college, becomes difficult to organize efficiently, to oversee accurately, and to control adequately. The large university will be forced to abandon the effort of having the head librarian work with the departments in coordinating book selection. A "selections officer," "chief bibliographer," or "head of book selection and bibliography" will assume the responsibility for directing his own corps of workers, who will attempt to see to it that the general collection is kept sound in all of its many constituent subject parts. They will watch the buying of the departments, trying to prevent unnecessary overlapping, suggesting titles for purchase which the departments may have missed, or buying titles which they feel must be procured. This book selection group will work with dealers' catalogs, trying to pick up out-of-print items which should be in the collection. In general, the selections officer will be responsible for the development of the collection as a whole, and for the coordination of all the widely-dispersed sources of book orders. Let us take an imaginary example of a large university to illustrate the problems which arise in attempting to build the mammoth collection under a system of divided responsibility for selection.

Take subject department A. It has only six teachers, all actively interested in the publications in their field. They read their current literature avidly, watch all the new book announcements, receive piles of publishers' blurbs, and scan the book reviewing magazines in their field. They watch not only the output of the United States and Great Britain, but of France, Germany, and Russia. They continually spend all of their allotted money and are usually pleading for more. It happens that of the twelve divisions into which the subject of department A falls, the six people are really interested in only three. And, as might be expected, any check of their subject holdings in the library against a standard list would reveal that these three divisions of the subject are brilliantly represented in the collection. The remaining nine divisions of the subject? Ah, here we are not so fortunate. The selection officer knows that department A is bibliographically alive, that the department members are working hard at building up the collection in their subject. He is willing to let them go their own way, and, indeed, he is so busy with a dozen other departments and with the general collections that he really doesn't have time to check closely to see what they are not buying. With each passing year, the three parts of subject A in which the faculty are interested get more and more complete, as they buy not only current materials, but comb the past centuries for useful titles. The department is proud of its lopsided collection. It represents beautifully the interests of the people working in the department.

If one shifts the focus to department B, subject B, one finds that for years there has been a specialist in one aspect of the subject taught by department B, who has diligently added to the collection in his subject. The other members of the department, alas, have not been as interested in the library, and the selection officer, although not a specialist in this field, has tried to assure that important current publications in this field were added to the collection. Of course, he was not intimately familiar with all the societies and institutions, committees, commissions, laboratories, etc., issuing material, and some important aspects of contemporary publishing in this field have escaped him. As for building up the collection in retrospective works—this is beyond his time and knowledge. In addition, the diligent worker is to retire this year, and he will not be replaced by a subject specialist in his particular field, so that the fine collection which he built up will not be directly exploited. Interestingly enough, his replacement resembles the rest of the department: he is not avidly interested in the library and has no familiarity with the process of keeping up with current publishing in his field outside of the very prominent monographs and the usual flood of periodical articles in the better-known journals in the field.

Department C, subject C: in the rather long history of this department, it has varied from a very conscientious group of research men, through a mixture of scholars and teachers equipped to handle undergraduate level work, to its present status: a group of excellent teachers, who do very little research. They are acquainted with the significant books in their field, are sure to be asking for the latest titles, but they pay no attention to more remote materials.

One could proceed through an analysis of the forty or fifty departments, schools, and colleges which make up the various components of this particular university. We have played the novelist's role and depicted facts not generally known, not all laid out in a report to guide the daily buying of the university. Some of these facts are well enough known, some are felt intuitively, some are buried out of the sight of the selections officer, and, indeed, not realized by the individual departments concerned. After all, they function from day to day, they run their classes, direct their graduate students' research, have made no comparison of their library buying with that of other departments, are not perhaps aware that they have a real policy, unexpressed though it may be. They may never have thought of the possibility that they were not representing other interests than their own in their buying. Indeed, they might not consider this a valid objection if it were pointed out to them.

Given this wide participation in the selection process, coupled with frequent changes in faculty and library personnel, it is advisable to have a written book selection policy statement for the university library in order to assure some continuity in building the collection. This policy involves a knowledge of the resources of other libraries in the area, as well as a knowledge of the university's own book collection and the objectives of the university itself. Although its advisability has been widely recognized, the difficulty of drawing up a policy statement which will represent fully such a disparity of aims, subject matter, and types of materials has militated against the widespread appearance of full and complete statements. It would certainly be desirable if such a statement could be worked out in cooperation with all of the schools and departments of the university, since they will be responsible for implementing any selection policy in their own subject fields.

Although this process may suggest great attention to the individual title, it is not, in fact, very likely to be the case in much buying for large university collections. Large research libraries are apt to practice "block buying"—as, for example, by placing a standing order for all the products of a given publisher with no effort to investigate individual titles. Some librarians have criticized this method of purchasing because, they say, it abdicates the librarian's central responsibility—selecting each book to fit the library's needs. But even some of the librarians who shudder at the thought of buying all a publisher's titles sight unseen may on other occasions describe proudly their library's collection of—let us say—contemporary American poetry. They will wax enthusiastic as they recount the searches they make to discover the existence of all the privately printed volumes of verse, their unceasing efforts to make sure that they get one copy of every contemporary poet's works, no matter how obscure the author or unknown the printer. They are block buying—by subject.

When a library decides that it will finally follow the dictum so often enunciated and begin collecting local history as it is supposed to do, there is going to be a natural alteration in the librarian's "evaluation" of the materials for that collection. He will not be interested in the literary quality of the diaries and letters of early settlers—he wants them all. He will gather up bushelbaskets of play bills, yards and yards of the account books of early businesses, acres of old newspapers . . . and these are all justifiable, for they are meeting a different kind of purpose than that envisioned in the selection of individual titles for the general reader.

Take, as another example, a library that decides that it is going to build a special collection dealing with labor-management relations in a given industry. The focus of attention is again suddenly changed—one is no longer concerned with getting *only* the best books on the subject. One wishes to build a *comprehensive* collection, reflecting all the varied aspects of labor-management relations. Certainly one will want the objective histories and analyses written long after the fact, but one will also want the contemporary record, no matter how biased, violent, or partisan the accounts may be. The library will try to build files of union newspapers, management serials, the pamphlet publications of both, and will, of course, try to acquire any archival material which either side will surrender. The letters, diaries, journals, memoranda of the leaders of the labor and management groups, of individual workers and minor executives—all these materials will be sought to provide the background for researchers into the history of the subject. When such a library's selection officer reads *Publishers' Weekly,* he will gleefully order anything new that he sees listed, without waiting for reviews—for this collection is to be as extensive, inclusive, and as full as possible. The books and other materials derive their value—not just from intrinsic worth—but from their relationships to other materials in the collection and for the light they may shed on minor—as well as major—points. The assumption underlying the building of such a collection is that it is not intended for the use of the "general reader," but for the specialized researcher. The definitive studies whose writing such collections are created to assist cannot be based on a few general, even if excellent, popularizations.

Another example may perhaps be allowed. On the University of Michigan campus, there is a special library of early American history, the William L. Clements Library. It is a collection of *source* materials, not of secondary sources. That is, the books on its shelves describing, let us say, a battle in the American Revolution, were written *at that time*. The library is not interested in collecting modern books about the battle—it wants the eye-witness reports. Similarly, it is not interested in collecting modern works about the social customs of early America, it tries to buy the books printed in early America which reveal social customs. It does not refuse to buy a book because the author's style is defective—it is interested in collecting all it can find that was published in the period it covers. It is block buying—by period.

The only limiting factor for such libraries is the amount of money they have to spend, and, of course, availability of material. In large research libraries, or the smaller, but highly specialized collections, identification of the existence of an item is tantamount to selection. This procedure is perhaps most aptly described as the vacuum cleaner method of collecting. One sweeps into the library everything one can lay his hands on. Of course, even the largest and richest of our great university libraries have discovered that they cannot buy everything. But it is instructive to note what their procedure is likely to be when they cannot buy all. They are not so likely to resort to screening individual titles to get only the best in all subjects— they are much more likely to start dropping subjects in which they will no longer try to build special collections. (In such subjects, then, they can revert to selecting only the best titles for their more limited collection.) But, in the areas in which they are determined to build strong research collections, the acquisitions vacuum cleaner will continue to operate full blast.

This type of buying is not restricted to any one type of library, nor is it only characteristic of large libraries. The smaller college and public libraries may have only one single special collection, but as much care, love, and time may be lavished on it as on the dozens of special collections of the largest institutions. The special library serving business or industry may resemble the special collection in a university library in the type of acquisitions policy which is followed. Even the smallest public library may make some attempt at collecting local history.

Doubtless some librarians will still be disturbed by such a procedure carried on under the name of "book selection." Perhaps many unnecessary disagreements could be avoided by applying another term to such a method of building special collections. When one sets selection policy, he creates some standards by which he will judge individual titles. When one starts limiting or describing the areas in which one will purchase, he is setting acquisitions policy. If one says in that policy, "No books in Japanese will be bought," then one never applies the standards of selection to Japanese books—no matter how authoritative, elegant, or famous they may be. They have been ruled out by the acquisitions policy. Conversely, when the acquisitions policy states that the library will acquire *all* American books published before 1800, standards of selection also no longer apply. Or, if one prefers, he can think of two kinds of selection criteria—those which apply to individual titles (is it authoritative? is it well-written? etc., etc.) and those which apply to whole categories of titles (does this group of books contribute to the research needs of the users? is this subject of sufficient importance to warrant building a collection in it? etc., etc.) Both types aim at meeting the purposes of the library—but they are aimed at different purposes. Both procedures have their legitimate place in building collections—one must only remember that they do different things, that one must not expect block buying to produce the same kind of collection as individual selection of the best would do.

The organizing of area study programs in American universities after the Second World War provides an example of a development which forces block buying on even the reluctant library staff. The library—if it is lucky—will be given notice that in twelve months a staff of experts in, say, Asian studies will start giving courses and supervising master's and doctoral programs in this new specialty. The decision to begin such a program may not result from the fact that the University has a splendid collection of research materials in the area. Indeed, the University may never have collected in the area before.

What alternative does the library have but to begin buying

everything that it can to support such a program? It must buy language books, history, art, philosophy—well, one can go down the list of Dewey classes as a guide to what an *area* program will need. Many of the countries which will need to be represented do not have anything that could be called an organized book trade, and even the identification of the existence of the needed items is difficult. Furthermore, there will not normally be librarians on the staff who can read the 20 or 30 exotic languages which will be needed if the materials are to be processed.

The fact that developing such collections and organizing them will be extremely difficult has rarely been known to deter a university administration which is determined to embark on an area studies program.

Junior College and Community College Libraries

The junior colleges or community colleges serve a dual purpose. They prepare some students for the third and fourth year of college, and they also give a two-year terminal course. The terminal course may be intended to give the student a "general" education, or it may be intended to prepare him for some technical job below the professional level.

This diversity of purpose leads to a diverse curriculum. The junior college or community college faces the university or liberal arts college's selection problems, for it must buy to support a number of different curricula. Often the program will be heavily vocational, and the library will have to buy heavily to support the vocational course, while it continues to support a general college preparatory program.

In addition to diversity of purpose, the junior college—and especially the community college type—will have a more heterogeneous student body, representing varying degrees of academic intention and academic backgrounds. As a result, there may be much less rigidity in admission standards, which will have an effect upon the materials purchased, in that many of them may have to be fairly elementary. The selection process, as in the four-year college or university, should represent a cooperative effort of both the librarians and the faculty.

There was a rapid proliferation of junior colleges in the 1960's. By 1967, the *American Library Directory* reported a total of 858 such institutions. The rapid growth in the number of junior colleges led to difficulties as far as their libraries were concerned. One state discovered—early in the 1960's—that not one of its junior colleges met the standards for minimum library service. Enrollments had grown faster than collections. It may be of interest to note that when it was proposed that the state legislature make a special appropriation of some $250,000 for books, to bring all these libraries up to minimum standards, the movement failed because of opposition from the association of junior college presidents.

A happier effect of the newness of many of these institutions has been their ability to experiment with new types of library service, and to work toward closer integration of library materials with the instructional program. One such experiment stresses integration of books, films, filmstrips, tape recorders and other of the newer media into a single instructional program, with the student spending much of his time in the individual "learning stations." The impact on the selection process of widespread use of non-book materials is obvious. It is hoped that there will be studies comparing the effect of such practices with traditional library services.

School Libraries

School libraries, like their academic counterparts in college and university libraries, have a responsibility to both faculty and students. For the students, they must supply materials related directly to course needs, but they must also provide what are sometimes called "enrichment" materials. The latter form that part of a collection which aims at the liberal education of the student; which goes beyond strictly curricular needs to provide materials which will educate in a broader sense. They need also to provide materials for the use of the faculty; buying materials for the professional improvement of teachers as well as curriculum materials—i.e., those related to the teaching of specific courses.

Whereas the student body in colleges and universities is relatively homogeneous (all sharing at least a high school education, all having met the entrance requirements of the college or university, all being reasonably adequate readers), the school librarian is faced with much less uniformity in the student body.

The spread in the elementary schools is staggering—from those who are just learning to read, through those who are skilled and practiced readers. In junior and senior high, there are students who have moved a good distance into intellectual maturity and those who are still developing. Thus an elementary school librarian would not only need to provide materials supporting science study, for example, she would have to provide a much greater variety of levels of treatment of the subject than either college or university librarians.

The school librarian is also directly charged with teaching students to use the library in addition to operating the library. School librarians are seen first as teachers (the teaching certificate is a primary requirement; the master's degree in library science is not always a prerequisite for employment). Since few school libraries are overstaffed, the librarian finds it difficult to perform all the necessary duties. One result has been a need for selection tools which have already winnowed out the large number of general titles not useful for school purposes and which have graded the level of the materials. There are a large number of such special aids, (see the bibliography appended to Chapter V) which enable the librarian to use her time more efficiently.

Although selection principles are generally the same for the school library as for other types, there is a special problem in selecting books for the school library. The books chosen are supposed to support the socially acceptable (indeed, the socially demanded) indoctrination of the child into the ways of our society. Where censorship of books for adults is considered pernicious, censorship of books for children is demanded. The books selected are supposed to have positive qualities, to serve high purposes. In the lower grades, at least, children are not considered ready to deal with complex and difficult social questions. They must also be taught to accept those basic principles upon which our society rests, for, without a sharing of those beliefs by most members of society, society could not exist. On some occasions, however (and we trust they are rare), school administrators have become so impressed with this doctrine of social seriousness that reading for pleasure has become suspect. Some school librarians, as well as some children's librarians in public libraries, have reported difficulty in moving the award-winning children's books off the shelves. It seems that the standard for judging excellence had moved out of the child's world of pleasure into the sober and demanding adult world, and that these selectors for children had actually read these books for qualities sought for in adult literary giants.

Whatever weight is given the sober educational factor in selection, it should be remembered that, in general, the principles of selection for the school library are the same as those for other libraries. They are only applied to a different body of materials and a different clientele.

Organization of Book Selection in the School Library

In many school libraries it is difficult to organize selection since there is only one librarian, who must perform all parts of the library's work, to whom selection will be only one of many pressing duties. It is desirable to obtain faculty cooperation in selection (which, in itself, may be a very time-consuming task!). Sometimes a library committee may be appointed by the principal, or a few book-minded teachers have been known to volunteer to assist the librarian in selection. In larger systems, book evaluation centers have been set up, where librarians can come to inspect the books. Some school systems hold monthly book meetings at which books are reviewed and discussed.

The Role of the Faculty in Selection

In all academic libraries (college, university, and school), it has been customary for the faculty to take part in selection. Indeed, in some libraries, the librarians are restricted to selecting only general reference materials and those items not covered by departmental subject lines. The arguments for giving the faculty a prominent role in selecting materials seem good ones: (1) after all, they are the subject experts. They have degrees in their fields, which represent considerable reading and study. They know the past and present scholars in their respective fields; they know the major works and can evaluate a new contribution to the subject. (2) They teach the courses, so they know which readings will be required for the students, they know what kinds of materials will be needed for term papers, they know when they change the emphasis in a course or add new units.

One can then visualize the ideal faculty selector: he knows the currently productive scholars; he is thoroughly conversant with past scholarship; he knows fully what the library has in his field; he knows the sources of information for new materials and uses them; he is accurate in transcribing information about a title in requesting its purchase, and he even checks to see that the book is not already in the library; he is not narrow in his interests, but catches important related material; he has some interest in selecting for students as well as himself, and so he orders materials with a wide range of complexity for different groups of students—the major in the subject, the minor, the interested layman.

He is, like all ideal creatures, something of a rare bird. The realities of experience have taught us that not all faculty members will participate in book selection. Some are interested but do not have the time. They try to do a good job in the classroom, which means many hours each week spent in preparation; they are free with time for interviews with students; they participate in departmental and college committees; they have families which demand some time; they take part in community activities; they read their professional literature and try to keep up with the world outside their field. They simply do not find enough hours to do systematic and continuing work on building the collection.

There are those who do not participate because they are not interested. Some are indifferent, some are lazy. Others have come to rely on the library to have what they want and see no need of making an effort which would only duplicate the work already being done by the librarian. Some adhere to the practice of lecturing and asking the student to do their reading in a list of books which will be reserved for that purpose, and so they are not concerned with building the collection for independent study.

It is true, too, that it is growing very difficult for any working professor to find enough time to keep up with his literature. Many readers find that reviews must substitute for the books they will never have time to read; much journal reading becomes a scanning of title pages, with only occasional dipping into selected articles.

There is some reason to feel that some of the difficulty in

building general collections is attributable to a narrowing tendency of advanced education. The expertise becomes more and more restricted in scope. As a college sophomore, for example, the student may have taken the survey course in English literature, which sweeps from the Anglo-Saxons to modern times in two brief semesters. As a senior, he may take a survey course in eighteenth century literature, which covers the century in two semesters. As a graduate student, he may take two semesters to study the criticism of the Age of Queen Anne. As a doctoral student, his dissertation commonly will devote itself to one very small segment of that microcosm. Such narrowing of interest may lead to a somewhat parochial view, so that the professor may be truly interested in only a small part of his field.

There may be some tendency on the part of faculty members to tie their buying too closely to present curricular needs—and for a research library, this can be disastrous. It can also be unfortunate for the liberal arts college because it would fail to provide background for the general education of the students.

Surveying the realities of much faculty book selection in practice (at any level of education), some have argued for giving librarians the major responsibility for selection. Indeed, this has actually happened without planning at many institutions. It is asserted that librarians are not so inexpert in subject fields, after all. They will have had at the least one subject major and a good general liberal education and many are dedicated readers, who have been known to use their own collections to expand their own educations.

Furthermore, librarians are trained in using sources of information about new materials, and can often identify needed books before the faculty hears of them. This is true primarily because faculty are likely to rely on their professional journals, all of which are notoriously late in reviewing books. Librarians watch publishers' announcements, which come into the library in great tidal waves, issues of library periodicals which list forthcoming books, and all the multitude of specialized sources which are part of the librarian's armamentarium. It is this kind of knowledge which has enabled librarians with masters' degrees in a field like history to give good service as heads of chemistry libraries. They know how to find information; this is their stock in trade.

The librarian is also likely to watch the whole range of demands and needs. He will see where gaps exist or are being created. He sees the collection in a way that the individual faculty member or department is not likely to see it. And he will try to insure that all interests are represented, even if those interests are not loudly expressed.

Among librarians, as among faculty, not all are purer than Caesar's wife. If faculty are busy with their daily tasks, so are the hard-pressed librarians, whose libraries are under-staffed in the face of increases in demand for service. Simply trying to get the daily work done, or perhaps last week's, keeps them running desperately. They may simply not have all the time they need for the careful job of selection they want to do. And they may go home at night so exhausted that that pile of necessary reading just can't be faced—so their continuing education suffers.

Librarians are also most likely to have taken majors in the humanities (especially English and history) or the social sciences. They may feel inadequate in selecting materials in the sciences, or indifferent to them—or even, perhaps, a little hostile. They are more likely to respond favorably to the arguments in favor of more books for humanities or social sciences than those in favor of science books.

Some librarians—may the number be minuscule!—may not have any interest in building collections, or in intellectual pursuits of any kind.

Clearly, however, it is desirable that both faculty and librarians should cooperate in building the collection, each bringing to the task his special skills and knowledge. There should be constant and continuing communication across the barriers separating the library staff from the faculty and departments from each other. Unfortunately, there are some blocks to easy cooperation which have grown up with time.

There are occasional faults on the faculty side which lead librarians to suspicion of faculty suggestions—and sometimes to openly expressed hostility. One university librarian received a request from a very powerful department, asking that the library purchase a very expensive reprint of a massive set of source materials originally published in the 1880's. The purchase involved several thousand dollars, so the librarian sent the request to the book selection officer for checking. The selection officer first went to the catalog—to discover what one can guess: the library had bought the set in 1880. Chalk up one cause of doubt concerning the faculty's judgment.

In another university, a chemical experiment supported by a grant had reached a point at which the researchers needed a certain piece of information. A literature search did not turn it up, and so the main experiment was side-tracked while special equipment was built to run a subsidiary experiment to determine the data needed. It had been completed before the chemistry librarian got wind of the whole affair and had the sad duty (or satisfaction?) of reporting that the results had been obtained in Germany 40 years earlier, and were available in the library but had not been found by the experts.

The faculty have sometimes hardly endeared themselves to the librarian, or encouraged cooperation, by the sometimes openly expressed belief that librarians are really pretty low-powered clerks, without much in the way of brains or training, who were competent enough to stamp a date due card or collect a fine, but hardly able to make an informed judgment. This may certainly be true of some librarians, but it is hardly the way for faculty to obtain whole-hearted support from the library staff.

The faculty do individually sometimes take a very parochial view of the library. They see only their own needs, and are not at all concerned with other parts of the collection. This is a natural enough state of affairs but it may lead them to condemn the librarian for trying to ensure that the needs of all parts of the faculty and student body are satisfied.

It is also true that there is usually a small group of very vocal and active faculty members who demand materials, but there is a larger group who never order anything and, yet, will criticize the library staff at faculty meetings for not having what they need.

Librarians have made their contribution to the problem with a few faults of their own. They sometimes tacitly hold, or openly express, the belief that the faculty are really a pretty ignorant bunch when it comes to knowing anything about selecting books; that they are a selfish lot, not caring a whit whether any other faculty member or student need is met; that when they are not ignorant, they are lazy, and are careless as well. Librarians ask how else one can explain the books ordered under sub-title (by the expert, no less!); the authors all garbled—misspelled, or with works wrongly attributed to them; they point to the agonized screams for purchase of titles already in the collection, or point to the large number of order requests for books which have been in the library for months. Some librarians have concluded that faculty cannot be trusted at all.

There is sometimes a false assumption made by some librarians that because they know about sources of information, they know everything. This has led in some people to an unfortunate arrogance, which leads them to tell the specialist in nuclear physics that he may not buy a certain book because the librarian judges it as unimportant. It leads sometimes to the rejection of an order from a new member of the English department for the *Middle English Dictionary* because the library's "dictionary expert" considers it too specialized (but has not bothered to learn that this new English teacher has been brought there specifically to introduce courses in Middle English).

These faults on the part of both the faculty and the librarians result, of course, from the fact that they are human, and humans rarely come in perfect models. A little more humility and modesty might make the cooperation desired easier of accomplishment.

But, whatever the balance between the various responsibilities may be, ultimately, someone must have the power of decision. Someone must try to balance all the conflicting demands, someone has to see to it that all the parts of the collection get some attention; someone has to ensure that the books which fall between fields—or overlap fields—are bought by somebody. Someone must stretch that always inadequate budget to get at least minimal coverage of all subjects of interest.

It seems reasonable to assert that this responsibility is best vested in the librarian. He is in the best position for overseeing the growth of the whole collection. And one of his jobs will be to fight off the zealot who would make parts of the collection grow like a cancer at the cost of others. He will have to defend the interests of the quiet faculty members—and even of the indifferent ones—in order that their students may find the material they need.

But if the librarian is going to do this, he had better be fully aware of the curriculum, the collection, the faculty interests, and the student body. He cannot spend all of his time on housekeeping. He had better get out of that office and talk to the faculty; he had better watch the departments for the appearance of new courses and the hiring of new faculty; he had better know how courses are taught. And he ought to carry his power with wisdom and reasonableness. But the librarian, we believe, ought to bear the responsibility for the collection, and therefore must have the final authority in making decisions concerning it.

The Special Library

The special library has the most restricted purposes and homogeneous clientele of any of the types of libraries discussed thus far. It is created for very specific purposes—often to support the research or business activities of one particular company. It exists to serve the relatively small group of employees of that company in their work. The range of subjects may be very restricted; indeed, the library may concern itself with one narrow subject area. The budget is usually quite adequate, and special needs in terms of purchase are more readily supported by the parent company.

Selection is often difficult, however, because the regular book trade bibliography is usually not so significant. Emphasis is on such special materials as research reports, government documents, and the whole paraphernalia of research, which is hard to find out about and difficult to come by. The librarian must become thoroughly informed about the field and the persons or institutions who are doing work in that field in order to contact such sources of information directly, rather than depending on the standard book selection tools. There will be great pressure for the immediate acquisition of all important materials, and this, added to the scattered nature of the producers and the lack of general bibliographic aids, will make the selection process somewhat more hectic than usual.

It is advisable to have a library committee consisting of specialists who can advise on book purchases. The suggestions for specific purchase that come from the clientele should be given full consideration by the librarian.

The following excerpt from the standards for special libraries, taken from *Special Libraries*, December 1964, with the permission of Special Libraries Association, illustrates the variety of materials and libraries which must be encompassed under the general heading "special:"

III: Collection

The special library's collection consists of the information sources that are acquired, organized, and administered for use by or in behalf of the library's clientele.

Physically, the collection may include a variety of forms and types of materials, not all of which are appropriate to a particular special library; books, pamphlets, preprints, reprints, translations, dissertations and theses; periodicals, newspapers, press releases, indexing, abstracting, and other services, transactions, yearbooks, reports, directories of organizations; external and internal technical reports; research and laboratory notebooks, archival materials; patents, trademarks, specifications and standards; audiovisual materials (photographs, slides, pictures, motion pictures, filmstrips, tape and disc recordings); and special collections (maps, sheet music, manuscripts, catalogs, legislative materials, clippings, microforms).

THE SUBJECT COVERAGE OF THE SPECIAL LIBRARY'S COLLECTION IS INTENSIVE AND EXTENSIVE ENOUGH TO MEET THE CURRENT AND ANTICIPATED INFORMATION REQUIREMENTS OF THE LIBRARY'S CLIENTELE.

The library's collection includes all basic, frequently used, and potentially useful materials. The range of subjects covered is determined by the objectives of the organization; the depth of subject coverage in each field is governed by the nature of the organization's work. The special library administrator continually evaluates the scope and adequacy of the collection in the light of changes in emphasis or new developments in the organization's activities. Centralizing pertinent materials in the library, rather than scattering them in office collections, is important in effecting the basic goal of general accessibility of all sources of information. Occasional use of outside resources is necessary and desirable, but the criterion of immediate availability of materials demands major reliance upon the library's own resources. General reference works that supplement the library's special collections broaden the scope of the library's information services.

THE SIZE OF A SPECIAL LIBRARY COLLECTION DEPENDS UPON THE AMOUNT OF MATERIAL AVAILABLE THAT IS PERTINENT TO THE ORGANIZATION'S SPECIAL NEEDS.

The purpose and use of the special library's collection influence its size. Some libraries need large reference collections, multiple copies, and works that have historical value; others have highly selective collections, keep currently useful literature only, and retain only in microform older periodical sets and items of decreasing usefulness. Many libraries discard little used materials if they are available in the area. The rate and direction of growth of the library's collection should reflect the continuing requirements of the library's clientele.

ACQUISITION POLICIES OF A SPECIAL LIBRARY MUST BE ESTABLISHED WITHIN THE FRAMEWORK OF THE LIBRARY'S STATED OBJECTIVES.

The special library administrator is responsible for establishing specific acquisition policies pertaining to depth and extent of subject coverage, types of materials, gifts, and exchanges. He is constantly alert to new sources for procuring special materials and he systematically reviews all announcements and listings of published materials. An efficient acquisition program requires sound business practices and well-organized records.

Libraries in organizations that issue publications may set up a program for the exchange of publications with other organizations. Procurement of individual titles or volumes on an exchange basis may be accomplished through a central clearinghouse or through cooperative arrangements with individual libraries or institutions. Both solicited and unsolicited gifts that add strength to the collection are desirable, provided no restrictions concerning their use or disposition are imposed.

The special library administrator can anticipate information needs if he is kept informed about all activities and future plans of his organization. Participation in planning sessions and discussions with subject specialists in the organization are essential to a continuing acquisition policy.

Conclusion

Emphasis has been placed in this chapter on describing the differences which exist among the various types of libraries, for it is clear that the general principles of book selection will be interpreted differently as the function of the library changes. To say that librarians will select the best books does not say anthing about the way in which the interpretation of what is best will vary. It is obvious that the "best" book on nuclear energy will turn out to be different as one moves from the elementary school library through the public library to the special library of a company engaged in nuclear research. The principle remains the same, but the results of its application will vary widely. The standards for judging the individual title must depend directly upon the type of reader being served and on the kinds of service which the library feels it should give. It would be a useful task—but rather extensive and perhaps laborious—to take each of the statements of principle outlined in the checklist of book selection principles appended to the first chapter and to interpret its meaning for each of the various types of library. Even without undertaking such a project, it is perhaps clear enough that the general principles serve only as general prescriptions for practice, which must be related to the specific nature of the individual institution.

Bibliography

College and University Libraries

"Acquisition of Library Materials from Newly Developing Areas of the World." *Library Resources & Technical Services*, Winter 1963. p.7-46.

Association of College and Research Libraries. *ALA Standards for College Libraries.* Chicago, ALA, 1959.

———. *ALA Standards for Junior College Libraries.* Chicago, ALA, 1960.

Bach, Harry. "Acquisition Policy in the American Academic Library." *College & Research Libraries,* November 1957. p.441-51.

Bixler, Paul H. "Development of the Book Collection in the College Library." *College & Research Libraries,* October 1951. p. 355-59.

Byrd, Cecil K. "Subject Specialists in a University Library." *College & Research Libraries,* May 1966. p. 191-5.

Clapp, Verner W., and Jordan, Robert T. "Quantitative Criteria for the Adequacy of Academic Library Collections." *College & Research Libraries,* September 1965. p.371-80.

Danton, J. Periam. *Book Selection and Collections: A Comparison of German and American University Libraries.* NY, Columbia Univ. Press, 1963.

Davidson, Carter. "Book Selection in a Liberal Arts College." (In Wilson, Louis R., ed. *The Practice of Book Selection.* Chicago, Univ. of Chicago Press, 1940. p.242-53.

Lyle, Guy R. *The Administration of the College Library.* NY, Wilson, 1961.

Sheehan, Sister Helen. *The Small College Library.* Westminster, Md., Newman Press, 1963.

Stiffler, Stuart A. "A Philosophy of Book Selection for Smaller Academic Libraries." *College & Research Libraries,* May 1963. p.204-8.

Tsien, T. H., and Winger, H. W. *Area Studies and the Library.* Chicago, Univ. of Chicago Press, 1965.

Wilson, Louis R. *The University Library; Its Organization, Administration, and Functions.* Chicago, Univ. of Chicago Press, 1945.

School Libraries

Heaps, Willard A. *Book Selection for Secondary School Libraries.* N.Y., Wilson, 1942.

Logasa, Hannah. *Book Selection Handbook for Elementary and Secondary Schools.* Boston, Faxon, 1965.

Lowrie, Jean. *Elementary School Libraries.* New York, Scarecrow Press, 1961.

Wofford, Azile. *Book Selection for School Libraries.* New York, Wilson, 1962.

Special Libraries

A.L.A. Library Administration Division. *Standards for Library Services for the Blind and Visually Handicapped.* Chicago, ALA, 1967.

Ashworth, Wilfred, ed. *Handbook of Special Librarianship and Information Work.* 2d ed. London, Aslib, 1962. (Chapter 3)

Kruzas, Anthony T. *Business and Industrial Libraries in the United States, 1820—1940.* NY, Special Libraries Association, 1965.

Special Libraries Association. "Objectives and Standards for Special Libraries." *Special Libraries,* December 1964. p.671-80.

Strauss, Lucile J., et al. *Scientific and Technical Libraries; Their Organization and Administration.* NY, Interscience Publishers, 1964. (Chapters 5 and 6.)

Chapter III

Selection by Subjects

In Chapters I and II, it was pointed out that the interpretation given to the principles of selection is affected by the type of library applying them. When the librarian applies the general principles to the several subject fields, he discovers that interpretations of the principles are also necessary here. These adjustments and alterations do not mean that the basic principles are abandoned. It merely means that more specific judgments have to be made in the light of the sometimes considerable differences in the types of books issued on the various subjects. Let one example of extremes suffice to illustrate the problem: Are the same tests for truth to be applied to the novel describing a future utopia as are applied to a treatise on chemical reactions?

In this chapter, the general tests for fiction and non-fiction titles will be discussed, followed by a section devoted to some of the problems in the specific subject areas. The chapter will conclude with a discussion of the selection of translations and editions.

The Criteria for Evaluating Non-Fiction

The first question which may be raised in selecting a new non-fiction title is "Who is this author?" Does he have any qualifications which fit him for dealing with the subject—is he by education, occupation, or experience in a position to write anything of value? If he has written other books on the subject, the librarian can check to see how they were received by the knowledgeable.

After the authority of the author has been established, the scope of the book should be ascertained. Does it treat the whole subject—or part of it? Does it concern itself with the history of the topic—or some present aspect of it? Is its treatment (either of the whole subject or part of it) exhaustive or brief? Once its scope has been determined, it should be compared with titles already in the library to decide if it really makes a contribution to the collection in terms of the material it covers.

Next the selector should attempt to ascertain the manner in which the material is treated. Is there anything in the writing itself which recommends the book? Is the style clear and readable, or muddied and tortured? Does the author organize the material so that the reader can follow his thought easily, or is he disjointed and confusing? Does the text have vitality and interest, or is it characterized by tedium and monotony? If the text popularizes a technical subject, is it done with accuracy and care, or has it oversimplified so much that it is really misleading? Does the author attempt to summarize the facts only, or does he present the material in such a way as to support some thesis he is committed to? (This does not necessarily mean that he has done wrong: many books have an important contribution to make by advancing arguments for consideration in the social sciences, in science, in musical or literary criticism, etc. If the author has very strong convictions, however, he may manipulate the evidence to suit his ends. The librarian must look for evidence of bias in the treatment of the material, trying to decide whether the author is fair-minded or a strong partisan.)

The physical features of the book may also play a role in deciding whether or not the item makes a positive contribution to the collection. The typography should be reasonably clear and readable. Some printing jobs—and particularly with the new methods of reproduction—may reduce the usefulness of a book because of blurring, smearing, too light an impression, and general sloppy appearance. Most often, of course, a title will be available in only one edition. If the text is important, there is nothing the librarian can do except blink at the poor typography and sympathize with the future readers of that particular book.

The presence of important illustrations, maps, bibliographies, or significant appendix material may provide the library with materials not elsewhere available and may be reason enough for the purchase of a book whose text is only adequate, but whose special features are invaluable.

The date of the book may be very important—especially in certain of the subject fields. In literature, of course, one does not exclude *Tom Jones* from purchase because the text was written in the eighteenth century—but perhaps this is too painfully obvious an example. If the book is old, however (and a recent imprint date may conceal a text which actually dates back, substantially unchanged, for half a century), and the field is one which changes rapidly, the librarian would want to decide if an historical treatment were important to the library, or whether the library had not better pass the title by in favor of one including more modern scholarship.

An important consideration in selecting non-fiction involves the kind of reader for whom the book would be useful. Would it serve the needs of the general reader, the beginning student of the subject, the advanced scholar? It might happen that a really brilliant treatment of a subject by a sound authority would be exactly suited to a kind of reader which the library does not serve. The utility of its purchase by such a library is certainly highly dubious.

In general, the selector seeks to identify those titles which will have permanent value (remembering always that some titles will be important because they deal with a topic of current interest), while trying to eliminate those which are unimportant, trivial, or deliberately distorted. In the selection of non-fiction, a sound knowledge of the subject involved is the central requirement for adequate selection.

The Criteria For Evaluating Works of Literature

The problems involved in evaluating a work of creative imagination are quite different from those met with in evaluating books of fact. In this field, we are enmeshed in matters of taste, in matters of esthetic response, in matters of artistic discrimination—none of which are very susceptible of objective verification. One can ask about a book on physics, "Is it accurate? Is it up-to-date? Is it authoritative?" What does it mean to ask if a novel is "accurate"? Yet traditional statements of tests for fiction have asked the librarian to consider whether a given novel is "true to life," whether it "blurs the hard-won line between right and wrong," whether "the psychology of its characters' acts ring true." One can only ask, true to whose version of life? Blurs the line between right and wrong drawn by which of the many groups who define that line differently? The acts of the characters "ring true" according to which school of psychology? The whole subject of the evaluation of fiction will be discussed later in this chapter when the problems involved in the selection of literature are taken up. At this point, it will only be remarked that the traditional guides to the evaluation of fiction are less satisfying than those for non-fiction—and for reasonable cause.

There are, of course, certain less controversial areas of judgment: the plot and structure of a novel or a play, the effectiveness or woodenness of the dialogue, the clarity or obscurity of the style, the authenticity of setting and facts in historical novels or plays, the effectiveness with which dramatic interest is sustained. Even here, the standards of judgment are less objective and more often a matter of personal response to the imponderables of style and presentation than is true in non-fiction. It is in this field especially that the judgments of many informed readers are useful for adequate selection, in order to avoid the acceptance or rejection of a book on the basis of the esthetic response of one individual.

Problems in the Selection of Books in the Several Subjects

Religion

The field of religion—like those of politics, economics, and literature—represents an area in which people have strong convictions, a fact which complicates the selection of books, since the titles published sometimes reflect these profound attachments to particular points of view. Since the truths of religion are, in the minds of many people, of a kind which are not susceptible of objective demonstration, the judgment of books in the field runs into something like the problem of evaluating books in the field of literature. What criterion of truth—in the sense of physical reality—does one bring to a book of religious revelation? Since the librarian may himself have strong convictions on the subject, it may be very difficult for him to be impartial when confronted with a book which holds views on religion very different from his own—and hence very shocking. This general problem will color the whole process of selection and should be borne in mind as the following more specific problems are discussed.

One of the difficult problems in selecting books on religion arises out of the polemical book. No irony or sarcasm is intended in remarking that religion has bred many disputatious books, some of them quite violent. If the public library tries to carry out its purpose of presenting the various points of view on matters of controversy, it may find itself buying books which bitterly attack one or another of the organized churches. Such books do exist, and there may well be demand for such titles from some members of the community. In considering polemical books, it seems reasonable to demand that they contain no distortions or misrepresentations of fact, that there be no attacks made on the basis of emotional opposition alone, without substantiating evidence.

A second area which causes some difficulty is the unsolicited gift to the library, often periodical materials. Many of these periodicals are of a polemical nature, especially those issued by the more energetic proselytizing groups. Many are quite vocal in demanding that their gift be represented on the open magazine racks—they may even return regularly to make sure that their gift is there, not buried somewhere in the stacks of the library. The general rule would be that gifts meet all the requirements for selection as the library's own purchases. If the magazine does not meet the standards of objectivity, utility, and general interest, it could be rejected. However, the protagonists of violent religious literature are themselves liable to be rather violent in their attempts to spread their particular version of the truth, and there is no rule which will enable the librarian to handle this problem easily. The work of the diplomat may be needed in the attempt to show the zealous that the library does not consider their materials suitable for the public library's shelves.

If one asks whether the library collection should serve as a

sort of Sunday school library, i.e., one in which people can come
to prepare themselves for membership in a given church, the
answer seems fairly clear. Materials which are of an instructional nature, materials which are intended to catechise the aspiring
member of one particular church, are too specialized for the
general interest of the community. They are properly the province of the church concerned or of the religious bookstore.

Another category which is liable to be troublesome is the
popularization—of Bible stories, of lives of Christ or the saints—
and the religious "self-help" book. Some of these are characterized by lack of good taste, by sweeping and unfounded generalizations, by suppression of all details which do not support the
author's thesis. The style is often a nauseous blend of weepy
bathos and the most superficial sentimentality. It is precisely
this category of religious literature which is liable to be most in
demand, rather than the scholarly histories of religion, the
treatises on theology, or the collections of sermons. If the librarian operates on the theory that the library must supply whatever
its patrons demand, regardless of quality, he will find a good
part of his budget for religious literature being spent on books of
no real worth or permanent interest. The librarian who wishes
to build a collection of books which represent intrinsic worth
would find such a situation distressing and will be much less
friendly to the cheaper kind of popularization. The solution to
the problem—or the compromise which is arrived at—will go
back directly to the librarian's conception of the purposes of the
library.

Other areas in which decisions will have to be made include,
first, the amount of technical material which will be bought—
sermons, exegeses, manuals for theological study, doctrinal materials, etc. This question is no different in this field than in
other subjects: how much specialized material will the library
purchase for the worker in the field or for the scholar? It is a
long-standing admonition that libraries will buy at least some
books which will benefit the whole community only indirectly
through their use by doctors, lawyers, ministers, and other
professionals whose work is of importance to the community.

Secondly, the library will have to decide how much material it
will buy to represent the non-Christian religions, and what type
of material it should be. Some librarians have inclined to the

view that the sacred writings of all the major religions of the world ought to be in every library; others have felt that the demand for such materials would not justify their high cost to the ordinary collection. The size of the community, the interests of the library's users, and the amount available for purchase of materials in the area of religion are certainly all factors which will weigh in the decision made.

In the selection of editions of the Bible, the librarian must be aware of the various inclusions or exclusions of books which result from the acceptance or rejection of certain writings as canonical. The Bible is also available in a wide variety of formats, each with its own special advantages or usefulness. There are various kinds of books supplementary to the study of the Bible which the library will also have to review for purchase: concordances, atlases, interpreter's editions, dictionaries, etc.

Philosophy

Just naming some of the topics covered by the Dewey classification in the field of philosophy suggests a major problem: ontology, cosmology, epistemology, teleology, positivism, nominalism. The very words for the topics bring to mind the fact that technical philosophy is a very technical subject, indeed. The public library will have to decide just how far it wishes to go in presenting the authoritative—but very difficult—treatment of these specialized philosophical discussions. The average public library—omitting from consideration the stack collections of the large metropolitan libraries—will probably not find such materials of great value to its readers. Hence, these topics are more likely to be represented by popularizations, if at all, which brings the librarian face-to-face with the usual problems involved in selecting a popular treatment of a specialized subject. If the librarian is not trained in philosophy, he will have to have recourse to those book selection aids which will record for him the judgments of the informed.

A second issue to be decided is the extent to which individual philosophers will be represented by their own works. It may be found more useful to buy expositions of the philosopher, or to content oneself with having the various philosophers represented largely in histories of philosophy. In purchasing histories, the library will have to decide whether it will satisfy itself with a few general histories of Western and Eastern philosophy, or whether it will buy more in the way of histories covering shorter periods in greater detail.

Psychology

Pope may have remarked that the proper study of mankind is man, but the study of human psychology delves into many topics which were only recently considered taboo, and which still are highly offensive to many members of society. At least five areas raise problems in selection for the psychology section. The first is the old problem of the popularization for the general reader versus the technical work. Its solution involves the same considerations as to the purposes and the type of reader as is true in other fields.

The second problem area arises in the field of the mental health book. There are many "pseudo-scientific" books available, which often have great popularity, as they assure the harried citizen that they can teach him to live at peace with his nerves or can train him to think his way to success. The librarian will have to weigh the demand for the book against his own conception of the demand for quality and authority in any title.

A third problem comes from the books on the occult sciences: numerology, astrology, palmistry, spiritualism, fortune telling, crystal gazing. These subjects are given credence by many people, while their claims to authenticity are scornfully rejected by others. The library will have to ask itself how much of its money it is willing to divert to fields which are considered highly dubious by many, but defended zealously by their adherents. Refusing a request for the purchase of a book in this area presents a problem: how does the librarian tell a patron in any acceptable manner that he is asking for material which the library will not buy because the librarian believes that the field is charlatanry? No diplomatic librarian would make such a blunt reply, perhaps, but this field does illustrate the general problem which is faced less extremely in every field: someone has to make decisions as to the quality and reliability of materials, and these decisions will not always be agreed to by some of the library's users.

The fourth problem involves the "case study" type of material, in which the problems (particularly the sexual ones) of individuals are presented in what is often graphic detail. The case study is no longer restricted to the technical book intended for the use of psychiatrists or psychoanalysts: such titles have been published for the general public. With the spread among the general population of greater knowledge of psychology (not all of it very thorough or precise, to be sure), the more lurid details of personal development have lost some of their power to shock and dismay. But some people in every community, and many people in some communities, would be disgusted and revolted by case studies which their more sophisticated neighbors could take in stride. The librarian will have to decide the extent to which such books would be useful in his community for serious study of human problems. It is true that even some of our wilder modern novels have not approached the frankness of some of the sober works on human sexuality. Those sober works are intended to be read as such, however. Certainly there is considerable need for clear and reliable information on the problems of the human sex life, but the area does present possibilities for turmoil in the community.

One example of the power of such books to disturb the even tenor of the librarian's life may perhaps be permitted. A sixteen year old boy took a case study of sex problems out of a public library. After he had read it, he brought it to his mother with the horrified remark that it made him feel as if he had fallen into a pit of slime. The next morning the librarian received a telephone call from a friendly member of the board. "Hang on to your hat," he said, "the police are on the way over to get the names of all the people who have read book X." That conversation had hardly been concluded when the phone rang again. This time it was the mayor, who wanted the librarian to be in his office at 11:00 A.M. to explain why the library was distributing pornography. The mayor's call was followed by a call from the president of the library board, who notified the librarian that her presence was required at an emergency session of the board that afternoon. The next call was from the editor of the local newspaper—a good friend and supporter of the library—who wanted to know the real story concerning the alleged purveying of obscenities by the library.

The mother had been busy on the phone that morning, calling the police, the mayor, the members of the library board, the newspaper, and her minister, attacking the library almost hysterically. She was intensely disturbed because of the damage which she felt the library was doing to her son and other young people of the community.

The outcome of this particular case is not important in itself, nor is it cited to discourage librarians from buying books in this potentially controversial field. It is introduced only to indicate that the problem is not an academic one. Buying of such books—like the buying of any other—should be done on the basis of a clearly realized position which can be explained and defended.

A fifth problem area overlaps the case study somewhat: it is the area of abnormal psychology, ranging from the psychoses, through the neuroses, to the problems of social deviation (as, for example, homosexuality). Technical medical books on the problems of the abnormal mind do not appear to fall into the province of the ordinary collection intended for the "home reader." But this area is one in which greater understanding on the part of society seems desirable. The library may well wish to have some books intended for the general reader, which will help him understand the problems of the insane or the seriously neurotic. Books dealing with such deviations from normal behavior as homosexuality certainly do present a difficult decision for the librarian. The problem cannot be resolved by any general prescription: its solution depends once more on the kind of community the library serves and the usefulness which such books would have to the particular library's users. The general faith that knowledge is always better than ignorance might be invoked here, but it is probably true that some of the readers of such books—as one librarian has put it—will not read them for the light they may shed on their own problems, but rather for the titillation they may provide. It is truly a vexing issue. One can only hope that librarians will be neither neurotically prudish nor neurotically scatalogical.

The Social Sciences

The various social sciences also present areas of potential difficulty in selection. Law, political science, economics, social welfare, sociology, education: the simple listing of some of the subjects covered by the Dewey 300 class is enough to invoke the realization that selection here often involves considerable care. Many of the books in these fields may reflect strong convictions on the author's part. Economics, to take one example, is frequently presented with overtones which are not entirely scientific. Periodically people rush into print with commentary on the educational system or educational theories which is often more distinguished for its heat than its light. Books on the legal aspects of civil rights—racial problems or freedom of speech—are not always presented with the calm, judicial manner or scrupulous concern for facts which one might expect in matters of law. The whole field of political theory—democracy, communism, fascism, anarchism, etc.—presents opportunity for slanted or propagandistic books. The distant, cold eye of the scientific sociologist may distress those not accustomed to seeing the assumptions of their lives and their society put through the terrible mill of objective analysis. Unorthodox views of society, of mother, of love, of social structure can be encountered among the sociologists, as well as among the political theorists.

In the social sciences the librarian should sharpen his perceptions, looking for reliable, unbiased; factual accounts. He should try to decide whether a given book helps to clarify problems, or whether it confuses issues by presenting stereotyped, emotional, or deliberately distorted arguments. When conflicting social values are presented in books, the librarian will have to decide how to represent them in the library: shall he attempt to balance opposing views? Shall he consider some views so far outside the accepted pale that he will banish them from the library? He should inspect the author's qualifications carefully and be concerned with the up-to-dateness of the contents. He must expect to find instances of propaganda, dogmatism, polemics, partisanship, and personal bias—and perhaps he might only conclude that this really ought to be one of the livelier sections of his library collection, that its books ought to encourage discussion and excitement.

Science

In an age of science, it seems appropriate that the general collection of a public library should have on its shelves a good collection of books which explain to the lay reader the general nature of science and the scientific method, as well as the central aspects of the several sciences. The major problems involve the selection of sound popularizations of science for the general reader, and keeping the collection up-to-date, since science is characterized by continual change. The popularizations should be done with scholarship and accuracy, appeal of presentation, and must somehow succeed in presenting highly technical and complex matters in a manner which will not baffle the non-scientist. Such works are by no means easy to come by.

The majority of librarians come to their work without a background in science. Many of them have publicly expressed their feelings of insecurity in trying to select in an area in which they are not only untrained, but in which many of them feel alien and uncomfortable. They are forced to rely on the aid given them by the selection tools to an even greater extent than is true in many other subjects. When these aids are deficient most librarians would probably feel in no position to dispute or question. Perhaps in this field, more than in any other, the humanistically-trained librarian ought to call on informed specialists from the community for help in selecting books. This is a resource always available, but not always used. Relying on the scientific periodicals for authoritative reviews of current popularizations will ordinarily not be too happy a solution: their reviews often run very late, and they are not likely to devote space to the popular treatment of a specialized subject.

To summarize briefly: in the sciences, the public librarian seeks to identify books written with scholarship and accuracy by a person qualified by education and training to speak with authority on the subject; which contain either new material or replace outmoded books; which are presented in a style having some appeal to the reader; and which are timely in terms of the subject, or timeless in terms of treatment. After all, the average librarian is himself an "average library reader," i.e., well-educated, intelligent (we trust), and with a reading experience considerably broader than the average member of the community (who is not, it must be remembered, an "average library reader"). Many of the aspects of the popularization can be judged by the librarian. As a person without scientific specialization, but with a good general education, he can judge how successfully the popularization was able to make the subject clear to him. The matter of authority can also be estimated by using the ordinary searching procedures of the reference librarian. The accuracy of the facts presented may be the major area in which he feels he cannot judge, and here he can consult the reviewing media or ask a person trained in that field of science to aid him in evaluating the book. The problems of selection in the sciences may be exacting, but they are not insurmountable.

The Fine Arts

One of the impelling pragmatic reasons for careful and effective selection in the fine arts is the high cost of many of the books. A mistake in choosing in this field can be very expensive indeed. The prices of books of paintings reflect the high cost of good color reproduction. Unfortunately, it is also true that some highly priced books are by no means so well reproduced as others. The librarian will then need another skill—the ability to judge the quality of reproduction.

The cost of art materials has often caused the smaller library to pass them by even though the librarian may have felt that his small community would have appreciated them as much as the metropolis, and perhaps even more. Since the smaller community is not likely to have the museums and art galleries which are available to the city dweller, the only chance a citizen of the small town may have to see works of art easily would be in the form of the art book. Where the budget is very limited, librarians have sometimes been enabled to buy such expensive materials through the aid of a Friends of the Library group or a woman's club. This is, of course, something of an administrative problem, but it has a close relationship to selection policy. If the librarian finds sources for support, he must then be ready to select.

Whether or not the library can afford to embark on the purchase of expensively illustrated books of individual artists, it ought to represent in its collection at least the history of art in its various aspects. These histories may serve as selection aids for the librarian interested in purchasing either books of reproductions or reprints for circulation.

If the library circulates framed prints of famous paintings or even—mirabile dictu!—framed originals (by local artists usually), there will arise the problem of selecting the paintings for the circulating collection. Here one might wish to approach the circulating collection historically (representing the major painters of all periods, perhaps with examples of the various periods of each painter); from the point of view of family acceptability; or perhaps even from the interior decorator's view (which pictures have the largest assortment of neutral colors to fit every decor?).

In the selecting of circulating prints, the librarian will also have to decide at what level of quality he will draw the line. As in the case of books, there may be demands for the popular, prettified, wholesome type of dime store art. How "high" shall the standard be? Or—to put the converse—how "low" may we sink? Some patrons might be much more profoundly moved by a charming picture, slickly executed, of a boy and his dog, with the boy carrying the light burden of fishing rod, freckles, and carefree youth into a blue summer day, than by any Botticelli goddess on a half shell. What stand shall the library take?

The field of music also offers a number of areas for decision. Shall the library stock only books about music and musicians, or shall it also embark on the collecting of phonograph records and the printed music itself? In the field of books, shall the library carry only general works, or technical works also on harmony, counterpoint, composition, orchestration, conducting, etc.? Shall it concern itself with books on the classical composers or composers of serious contemporary music, or shall it also buy works on popular music? Shall it restrict its purchase of phonorecords to the classics—or include the popular contemporary crooner? How will the librarian evaluate the comparative excellence of the various recorded versions of a given work? Shall the librarian select a few titles from all the major composers, plus many of the more popular items by lesser composers, or should he attempt a fuller representation of all the works of only the really major composers? These questions are all raised, not to be answered ex cathedra, but to call attention to areas in which decisions will have to be made. Aids to selection of materials in the fine arts will be found in the bibliography at the end of this chapter. Further discussion of the problems involved in selecting recordings will also be found in the chapter devoted to the selection of non-book materials.

Literature

The field of literature presents a number of very knotty problems for the consideration of the librarian. The first general question involves the level of quality. Shall the library attempt to select only great literature? or good literature? or popular literature? The problem of judging the quality of a work of literature is not as simple as might be desired. What makes a novel good? Or, to make the problem more difficult, what makes it great? It is obvious enough that the style, the structure, the characterization, the problems presented all play a part, but it is very difficult to get at the elusive quality which makes a novel lasting and important, which distinguishes the work of a master craftsman from the work of a master creator. If one simply lists some of the novels which are generally agreed to possess great distinction (*Pride and Prejudice, Moby Dick, The Scarlet Letter, War and Peace, Crime and Punishment, Tom Jones*—to name only a few), he can recognize that they represent greater diversity than uniformity. The simplest definition of a great work of art is probably that it is one which has appealed to many people over a long period of time. Let us assume, then, that in the selection of a novel just off the press we are not going to be able to decide with any degree of certainty that we are faced with a great novel. Only time will determine that fact.

Let us settle then for trying to decide a lesser question: is this a good novel? As far as the present authors can tell at this moment in time, a reasonably secure answer to that question can only be based on ascertaining the judgment of a group of readers who are informed, well-read, and esthetically sensitive. If a large group of intelligent and perceptive critics rush into print with high praise, one can conclude that the title has something to offer the reader. Unfortunately, the history of

criticism will reveal that works which later achieved fame were
not always well received at their first appearance, and some
works which were later to fall into the discard were extrava-
gantly praised on their first publication. There does not appear
to be any crystal ball which will enable one to foresee such
results, and the librarian is left with the conclusion that, uncer-
tain as it is, there is no present mechanism which can supplant
the judgment of the informed reader.

A special problem is found in the best-selling novels. A study
of best-sellers over a period of several generations will reveal
that a great many of the titles have faded into obscurity. Some
librarians have been loath to buy novels which would become
obsolete after a year or two, while others have decided that they
will buy every best-seller and duplicate freely. They feel that
great popular interest in a title is in itself sufficient grounds for
purchase, particularly since it is so difficult to get agreement as
to whether or not a novel is "really" good.

This problem of the best-seller is part of the larger problem of
the light, recreational type of novel versus the classic or standard novel. How much money should the librarian spend on
westerns, mysteries, and science fiction? How many light romances are justified? How much—to generalize the question—
of the popular should be acquired as compared with the cultural? The answer to these questions—as was pointed out in
Chapter I—will depend on the view the librarian takes of the
purposes of his library. If he is convinced that it has an important, educational purpose, that it should attempt to stock serious
materials for the sober student of life and society, he may well
reject light, ephemeral, popular fiction. Some librarians have
tried to make an economic compromise by buying the services
of those companies which specialize in supplying rental collection types of novels. Some libraries do not charge rental, but pay
the cost themselves. They feel that by not processing the titles,
they provide a constantly revolving collection of light fiction
without heavy expense and without adding those ephemeral
novels to the permanent collection. Other libraries rigidly restrict the number of fiction titles which will be purchased in any
given year.

A very practical problem involved in this area of the popular
title is the number of copies to purchase. Here the librarian

must function like a bookseller and attempt to predict the "market" for a given title. When a large library buys 800 copies of a title for its main and branch libraries, it is investing a considerable sum in the library's guess that this title will be in heavy demand. A librarian needs a sound knowledge of the reading interests of his public in order to make successful estimates of the number of copies needed.

A problem area which has been discussed earlier in this book involves the modern naturalistic novel, which has placed heavy emphasis on the less pleasant aspects of human life and which often concerns itself with sex almost to the exclusion of any other aspect of human life. Some recent writers have begun to react unfavorably to the novel which resembles the psychiatrist's case book more than it resembles a piece of creative fiction. These critics do not object to the presentation of ugly or distorted human beings per se, but they suggest that the writer must do more than describe psychological problem cases, that he has the obligation to use this material for literary ends. Librarians have diverged in their treatment of these novels, and the same titles have been bought in some libraries while they were being scornfully rejected by others.

In the field of drama, the library will have to decide whether it feels that anthologies of plays are sufficient to satisfy the demand for this type of literature, or whether the library will buy separate plays. It may also be faced with the decision as to whether it should buy multiple copies of plays for the use of play-reading groups. The number and range of plays by the standard and classic playwrights will have to be decided, as will the extent to which the library will buy copies of current Broadway successes.

Poetry represents a field of literature long held in the highest regard and not read extensively in our day. Again the library will have to weigh the relative values of presenting poetry largely in anthologies, in the separate collected works of authors, or in individual volumes of poetry. In the field of contemporary verse, the library will have to decide how far beyond the very major writers it wants to go, and to what degree it will invest in the works of the more obscurantist of contemporary authors. It may also decide to set some standard of quality, which would rule out the newspaper versifier.

The library may also feel some concern for representing important foreign literature, either in the native langue or in translation. The great classics of the major European countries will probably represent no major problem, but how far should the library go in buying foreign authors who are not widely known in this country, yet who may be very significant on the contemporary scene in their native land?

The best insurance the library can have to assure selection of literature of good quality is to have a staff which is itself well-read, which has developed a sense of discrimination based on knowledge of the best that has been written, which is familiar enough with the reviewers of literature to know which represent informed and able judgments. In this area of taste, however, one cannot expect to find precise and rigid standards. This difficulty does not mean, of course, that it is desirable for the librarian to respond by shrugging his shoulders and abandoning any attempt to discriminate.

History

In selecting works on history, authority and accuracy are prime requisites. In addition, clarity of presentation and an effective style should be sought. The best historical writing has often been of distinguished literary quality. The tradition of fine writing in history is so well established that it seems reasonable to ask that new titles meet this requirement.

One of the problems in historical writing is bias on the part of the author, which colors his interpretation of the facts. This is especially true in studies of the very recent past, as in such topics as the New Deal and World War II. But even on past issues—the Civil War, Andrew Jackson's administration, Napoleon—one can find startlingly partisan histories, especially startling when one considers that they were written very long after the events.

The distribution of the collection by historical periods will call for decisions on the selector's part. How much of ancient or medieval history should be bought? Should we be satisfied with a general history of the Italian Renaissance, or will the library buy volumes on limited aspects of the various Italian states of the period? Will the library buy heavily in the area of the

American Civil War, in which there is being issued a constantly increasing amount of studies, which are narrower and narrower in scope? How far will the library go in purchasing in the subject matter of World War II, on which an almost incredible quantity of contemporary material has appeared? At what point can the multiple contemporary works on important historical events be replaced by broader treatments?

The library will also have to decide on the proportion of scholarly to popular treatments of history. Will it insist on books which make new contributions based on examination of the source material, or will it prefer books based on secondary sources, but perhaps more popular in treatment?

Conclusion

Answers to the problems of selection in the various subject fields are arrived at by taking into consideration the purposes of the library, the type and size of library, and important local factors in determining how the general principles will be applied. Librarians solve these problems in various ways. The authors of this work have their own personal convictions as to what the only true, eternal, and justifiable solutions are. But, alas, librarians whose judgments they respect do not agree with them in every case. On the other hand, librarians whose judgments they also respect do agree with them on some of these issues. Where does this state of affairs leave the librarian? With, we hope, the realization that the selection of books is not a mechanical process to be done unconsciously by fixed rule and by rote, and that the only person who can decide any of these problems for a given library is the librarian employed in that library. Only he has enough knowledge of all the factors which go into decisions to make sound judgments.

Editions

The question of selection of editions has attracted the attention of librarians for some time. It is recognized that the physical appearance of a book will have its effect on the prospective reader, either attracting or repelling him. The qualifications of a "good" edition, however, include more than mere physical makeup. The addition or omission of special introductions, notes, and illustrations should be observed. Changes in the text are a part of revised editions and are especially important in text-books and scientific or technical material. In a reprint, the text remains the same even though the physical make-up may be drastically changed. This is especially true of the unabridged paperback editions that are put out by the same publishers as the hard cover editions. Both abridged and enlarged editions should be evaluated for possible library purchase. A good source for definitions of terms relating to editions is the *Terminology Report* of the Joint Committee of the Subscription Books Committee and Reference Books Section.

A knowledge of book production and an appreciation of book design and typography will assist the librarian in the selection of editions. A correctly proportioned page is pleasing to the eye and easier to read. Sufficient margins are necessary to achieve this effect and also to facilitate rebinding. Acceptable margins are usually wider at the outside edges and the bottom than the inside and the top. Colorful bindings add to the attractive appearance of books on the shelves. Size can be an important factor because neither very large nor very small books are convenient for shelving or circulating. The esthetic appreciation that arises from examining a truly beautiful edition is one of the great satisfactions of working with books. The inclusion of some fine editions adds considerably to the collection. But for the average circulating book, durable and sound book manufacture should be combined with "the beautiful." Since popular fiction will be read in any edition that is available, some libraries purchase paperbacks as added copies and discard them when they are worn out or the demand abates. A certain number of expendable copies should be supplied for titles already approved for inclusion and in great demand.

The librarian should develop the ability to compare editions quickly in relation to these factors and also in relation to the library's book budget. The selection of an appropriate edition also raises the old question of "Best for whom?" For the general reader? the scholar? the researcher? In selecting editions, it is necessary to go much farther than merely selecting the latest one. Just as in general book selection, knowledge of the library clientele is important. The ordinary reader, who has just seen a

Shakespearian play on television, would probably be more interested in an attractive, illustrated edition than in an elaborately footnoted edition intended primarily for the student or scholar.

Ideally, the librarian should examine actual copies of the various editions and then make the decision as to which to purchase for a particular book collection and for a specific use. Unfortunately, except in metropolitan libraries, selection from first hand inspection cannot usually be done, and it is necessary to rely upon various printed aids. There are notes on editions in the *Standard Catalog* series. The *Reader's Adviser and Bookman's Manual* lists various editions and frequently adds annotations. Selected bibliographies in books on special subjects indicate editions. Current aids should not be forgotten. The *Booklist* contains lists of editions with good descriptive notes. It also gives indication of any title changes which tend to occur frequently when a book is published both in an English and an American edition. *Publishers' Weekly* notes the latest editions published. The weekly book reviewing periodicals, *New York Times Book Review*, and *Saturday Review*, also give information about the latest editions as they appear.

Translations

The selection of translations of foreign books into English can present a variety of problems. The qualifications of the translator, the types of material to be translated, and the potential readers of translations are all matters which the librarian must take into consideration. It has been remarked that "Life, liberty, and the pursuit of happiness" translated into Russian and then back into English reads "Freedom permits lustful living," which is a far cry from the original meaning. The primary responsibility of the translator, then, may be said to be to interpret the meaning of the original, rather than to translate literally. It is generally agreed that the translator should be faithful to the original in that he attempts to produce the same emotional reactions. The ideas and the style of the original work should also be maintained. The carrying over of style and mood from one language to another requires great skill.

To this quality of complete bilingual ability, one must add the capacity to write fluently in the language into which the book is being translated. Sympathy for the material being translated and some knowledge of the literary and historical background are distinct assets. Familiarity with the locale, the manners and customs of the people, as well as with the literary history of the author and his work, give the translator added advantages. These qualities are part of the background of the translator who aims to recreate a book in another language in such a way that it will affect the reader in the same way as the original.

The type of material also has a bearing on the way it should be translated. It may range from the simple and factual to the literature of the scholar. There are intermediate types, intended for that large amorphous audience, the general reader, which composes the largest group of readers of the public library. The general reader is frequently not aware—or, if he is, is not concerned with the fact—that he is reading a translation; he is primarily concerned with the subject matter. The aim of the translator would then be to reproduce this material from another language in as readable a form as possible.

Translation of literature for the scholar is another matter. Here the style is just as important as the content, if not more so. Translations of scientific or technical material must presuppose a good knowledge of terms on the part of the translator, as well as close adherence to the original. UNESCO has prepared a report on scientific and technical translating and related problems which should aid in selection in these areas.

Who are the readers that the librarian should keep in mind when selecting translations? First, there is the reader who is interested in the literature of a given country, but who never intends to learn the language. If the spirit of the original is retained, a free translation would be satisfactory. The student who is learning a language frequently adds to his knowledge by reading the literature of that country in translation. In this case, a careful and reasonably literal translation in good English is best because it will help him to understand the grammar and correct use of idiom. The scholar, on the other hand, may want different translations of the classics for comparison and study. If it is a Greek classic, he will want the translation to be close to the original with frequent use of characteristic idioms.

The names of the translators are frequently given on the title page, and the day of the hack translation is almost over. The hastily produced, stupidly literal translation of a popular foreign book, issued in an unattractive, cheap edition, is now a thing of the past. It is unfortunate that more credit is not given to the translator, for a satisfactory translation requires meticulous work combined with ability and considerable scholarly and linguistic background.

To judge a translation adequately, the critic must also be fluent in both languages. Lacking this ability, the librarian will have to depend on the reviewing media and the book selection aids for evaluation of translations.

Bibliography

Asheim, Lester. *The Humanities and the Library.* Chicago, ALA, 1957.

Copeland, Alice T. "Philosophy Journals as Current Book Selection Guides." *College & Research Libraries,* November 1966. p.455-60.

Haines, Helen. *Living with Books.* 2d ed. NY, Columbia Univ. Press, 1950 (Chapters 12-22.)

Haselden, Clyde. "The Social Attitudes of Librarians and the Selection Of Books on Social Issues." *Library Quarterly,* vol. XX, 1950. p.127-35.

McElroy, Elizabeth W. "Subject Variety in Adult Reading." *Library Quarterly,* vol. XXXVIII, 1968. p.154-67; 261-69.

Milgrom, Harry. "Science Books—Thirty-three Keys to Evaluation." *Library Journal,* February 15, 1962. p.821-22.

Moon, Eric. "Problem Fiction." *Library Journal,* February 1, 1962. p.484-96.

New, P. G. "The Public Provision of Light Literature." *Library Association Record,* April 1955. p.149-53.

Reader's Adviser and Bookman's Manual. NY, Bowker (latest edition).

Teitelbaum, Priscilla. "Building a Science Collection." *Choice,* January 1966. p.753-55.

Tripp, Susan. "Non-Western Religion: Acquisitive Themes." *Choice,* November 1967. p.947-51.

Vainstein, Rose. "Science and Technology, Their Impact on

Public Library Resources and Services." *Library Journal*, July
1961. p.2417-24.

Editions and Series

Baer, Eleanora A. *Titles in Series; a Handbook for Librarians
and Students.* Vol. I, 1954; Vol. II, 1957; Vol. III, 1960. New
York, Scarecrow Press, 1954-60. [Suppl., 1967]
Carlson, Pearl G. *The Choice of Editions.* Chicago, ALA, 1942.
Joint Committee of the Subscription Books Committee, A.L.A.,
and the Reference Books Section, American Textbook Pub-
lishers' Institute. "Terminology Report." *Subscription
Books Bulletin* 24:33-39, April 1953.
Orton, Robert H. *Catalog of Reprints in Series.* New York,
Wilson, 1956. (With Supplement)

Translations

Bower, Reuben A., ed. *On Translation.* Cambridge, Mass., Har-
vard University Press, 1959. (Harvard Studies in Comparative
Literature, v. 23)
*Index Translationum: International Bibliography of Transla-
tions.* 1949- Paris, UNESCO.
(Previously published by the league of Nations. International
Institute of Intellectual Cooperation, 1932-1940.)
Savory, Theodore. *The Art of Translation.* London, Jonathan
Cape, 1957.

Chapter IV

Selection of Non-book Materials

Libraries have always collected some types of non-book materials, such as pamphlets, maps, periodicals, and clippings. Recently there has been growing emphasis on such materials as films, musical and spoken recordings, microfilms, and microcards. The enlarged acquisition of such materials has brought with it an increased concern with problems of selecting the material, sources of information about and methods of acquisition of the various types, and problems of handling the non-book forms once they are acquired. This field is so extensive that full treatment of the problem in all its aspects would require a separate volume. In the present context, only the briefest introduction can be attempted.

The selection of non-book materials is, of course, based ultimately on the same principles as the selection of books: one seeks the best material available in terms of authority, accuracy, effectiveness of presentation, usefulness to the community, etc. As with books, selection will be affected by the type of library, its size, the community in which it functions, and the librarian's conception of the purposes of the institution. The library will try to have selection done by people who are informed about the subject matter presented in the non-book form, and it will employ sources of reviewing for evaluation of each item, just as it would for a book.

Some of the selection tools would be familiar enough companions, encountered in selecting books, but some tools would be new to the book selector, since there are sources specifically concerned with given non-book forms.

It is true that in addition to the general principles which one would apply in selecting non-book materials, there would be special matters to be taken into consideration in selecting the various forms, especially technical matters involved in the production of films or records or microfilm. One would be interested in the quality of the recording in a musical performance, in the lighting and cutting of a movie; but these are also like the judgments of the quality of the printing and binding job in a book. To judge these special materials adequately, a librarian needs additional skills (which, of course, is also true as the librarian moves from judging books in one subject field to evaluating those in another subject field). Lacking a knowledge of film sound tracks, of orchestral balance, of all the myriad technical matters involved in films and records, the librarian again can turn to the judgments of those who have such knowledge recorded in reviewing and selection media, just as he does in selecting in a subject field in which he feels he needs assistance because of his own lack of knowledge.

The major problems involved in the non-book field are really not selection problems, but administrative ones. Many librarians have boggled at the tasks involved in checking films for damage, splicing broken film, keeping motion picture projectors in order. The problems involved in cataloging, storing, and preserving recordings in decent condition have weakened the resolve of some librarians to be modern and progressive in their acquisition of the other media. The difficulties involved in handling such materials, once acquired, may be related to selection in that they may lead the hesitant to avoid the problem altogether by not selecting films or records.

Films

Problems arise in the selection of some of the non-book materials because they add facets not found in books. A pamphlet, after all, is only an abbreviated book. One can judge the effectiveness of the organization and style, one can evaluate the facts presented, one can compare it with other written materials

with some ease. But a film, on the other hand, presents its ideas
with some additional factors which influence the effect of the
presentation. Words spoken in the film are susceptible of shad-
ing by the very tone of voice, the inflection of certain words, the
facial expressions of the speaker. The film may be accompanied
by background music, which can be employed to heighten the
emotional impact of some scene or idea. There is, therefore, an
emotional meaning built into films which is not found in books,
and this emotional meaning may be as important as the content.
To some extent, of course, the manner of presentation in a book
functions in the same way, but most Americans are conditioned
to think of movies as a source of pleasure, and they may not
react as critically to the presentation of a film as they would to
the same biased presentation in a book.

Thus the selector must consider the manner of presentation,
which involves a wide variety of different factors. He must also
consider, of course, the technical aspects of the film's production: lighting, quality of photography and sound, transitions
between scenes, quality of the narration, etc. Since a film often
involves the expenditure of a considerable sum of money, no
library will want to purchase a film without first viewing it.

The sources of information about films, their producers, and
their printed evaluations do not present so neat a pattern as the
sources of information about books and their publishers. Most
libraries are probably interested in the 16 mm educational film,
rather than the film produced for commercial entertainment. It
must be admitted that, although there are some very excellent
educational films, there are many which have little to recommend them, being fairly uninspired, sometimes downright distorted (especially those produced for free distribution by organizations interested in promoting their own interests), or at best
merely passable. The annotation in the producer's or distributor's catalog may not be a fair summary of the film, so that the
librarian had better make sure to have the film viewed before
purchase.

The field of reviewing media presents a plethora of riches.
There are many magazines devoted to the motion picture
world, and, although all are not concerned with educational
motion pictures, there are enough of those to present a wide

spread. *Educational Screen and Audio-Visual Guide* has been published since 1922. It is a monthly which carries reviews of educational films. *Film World and A-V World* is another monthly with film reviews. *Business Screen* is particularly concerned with those films of use to business and industry. The Department of Audio-Visual Instruction of the National Educational Association issues two journals carrying reviews of films—*AV Communication Review* (bi-monthly) and *Audiovisual Instruction* (monthly, September-June). Librarians who select films should be familiar with the publications of the Educational Film Library Association (EFLA), including their film evaluation cards.

Librarians should keep in mind the film services offered by universities, state libraries, and some other libraries in providing films for use. Even the library which cannot afford to embark on the purchase of a film collection can borrow films or can join a film circuit in its state. In addition, the catalogs of such organizations as a university or state library can be an added source of suggestion for purchase. In Michigan, for example, the University of Michigan and Michigan State University issue a joint catalog of their combined film holdings, which can offer many useful titles to the interested librarian for consideration for his own collection. Individual libraries also issue catalogs of their films, which have met the selection standards of the library concerned, and may thus furnish other librarians with valuable guidance. The New York Public and Enoch Pratt are among the institutions which have excellent lists.

A selected list of titles recommended for purchase has been issued in several editions by the Audio-Visual Committee of the American Library Association. The 1962 edition contains about 400 films. Only those films which met high standards of excellence are admitted to the list. There is a descriptive annotation for each film, and such data as price, distributor, running time, whether in black or white, etc., are given. The subject index allows an approach to titles on desired topics.

A very large list, which is not so much a selection tool as a full bibliography, is the Library of Congress catalog's *Motion Pictures and Filmstrips*. The subject index will allow one to pick up titles on a desired topic which can then be checked out against the reviewing media.

In summary: the librarian interested in films will keep up with the field by reading the reviews in current periodicals, by getting on the mailing list of distributors and producers, by seeing as many educational films as he can, in order to develop a sense of discrimination, and by viewing all films before purchase or use.

Recordings

The library which has elected to add phonorecords to its collection faces a bewildering array of riches in great variety—variety of types of material recorded, of types of recording and reproducing systems, of performances of a given work (especially in the so-called "standard repertory" of the classics), of sources of information concerning the myriad of choices available. The bibliographical network for all non-book materials does not exhibit the same degree of organization as that for books. Perhaps this only means that selection is less routine—and hence more interesting?—than book selection.

The materials available on sound recordings encompass a wide scope. Predominant in terms of bulk is music, of course, ranging from the whole pre-Bach universe to the latest atonal effort of our contemporaries. In addition to the standard composers, modern records allow one to hear the music of very minor figures, some of whose music has not been performed in hundreds of years, but which can now be heard on records.

In deciding to build a record collection, one must first decide how far the standard composers—and the standard works by each of them—will dominate the collection of musical works. One can see the general principles entering into consideration as the question of "completeness" is raised. How delightful to have *all* the works of Beethoven in the collection. Opera, symphony, concerti, chamber works, songs—a full representation of the great man! And—consider the joy—a glorious collection which would have, not only each work, but each work in every performance ever recorded! For most libraries, such a collection would be burdensomely expensive, to say nothing of being somewhat overbalanced in Beethoven's direction (though some of us would hardly find this objectionable!) To buy all of Beethoven, one would have to forego buying other composers.

The selection of a good, basic representation of the standard classical repertory demands, naturally, some acquaintance with composers and the history of music.

In addition to the collecting of the standard classics, the library may wish to consider adding non-western music, for educational purposes at least. (Of course, the more conservative in musical taste might prefer to put some modern western composers along with oriental music, for some of the newer electronic music is not just atonal—to some it appears "so far out it's just plain gone!") In addition to less usual-sounding music, the library may elect to broaden its collection of western and non-western classics by adding light classical works, folk music, jazz, Broadway musicals, and perhaps even downright popular singers and orchestras.

In addition to this vast array of musical material, the library can also add non-musical recordings. There are anthologies of recorded poetry: some read by well-known actors and including the works of one or more poets, some read by the poet himself and being restricted to his own works. Plays have been recorded in considerable quantity. The library might elect to attempt a collection of all Shakespeare's plays on records, to be checked out along with the text. Instructional materials (as, for example, foreign language courses) seem a reasonable choice for a library which stresses its educational role.

To the variety of materials available one must add the variety of forms in which recording is done. A library may still have a formidable collection of the old 78 r.p.m. recordings. (One hopes that some of the great performances available only on the old 78's will have been put on tape by a library owning them before the records were worn out.) Currently, 33 and 1/3 r.p.m. is the vogue—on discs, that is, for one must put tape recordings alongside the disc. Both 33 and 1/3 and tape recordings are available in monophonic or stereophonic versions (not all re-cordings are available in both forms, and the number of mono-phonic versions seems to be decreasing). The different systems require different machines—or machines with a double stylus in the case of discs—and although this is not a book selection problem nor a record selection problem, it raises the whole new area of machinery selection problems. Which type of record player is best for library installations? How highly fi do we want our library hi-fi equipment to be? What about tweeters and woofers—and all the other arcane components of such equipment? Can one install tape players and trust patrons to thread the tape? What about cartridge types?

Variety is introduced at another level by the recording of a given work by different artists or groups. The library may desire, not merely to have a recording of the Beethoven Fifth Symphony, but to have the best performance of it, so those who are being introduced to it will hear it at its most stunning. Many of the most famous works are available in at least a dozen versions—and the selector may even have the joy of choosing from as many as thirty versions. Conversely, of course, a less familiar, less popular, more remote work may be available in only one performance, and that not a stellar one, perhaps also recorded with less than standard technical excellence. The library may want this particular work as an example of a period or a type, and it might be forced to buy this product, just as it sometimes has to buy a book in less than perfect physical shape if no other edition is available.

As with books, selectors will be interested in reading reviews of new recordings. Such reviews appear in *Library Journal*, in general magazines like *Saturday Review, Harpers,* and *Atlantic,* and in a whole host of magazines devoted to records, such as *American Record Guide, High Fidelity, HiFi Stereo Review,* and *The Gramaphone.* Kurtz Myers prepares a quarterly "Index of Record Reviews" which appears in the Music Library Association's *Notes.* He indexes about 2,500 reviews per issue.

The *PTLA-BIP* of the record business is the monthly Schwann catalog, which lists records available from a wide variety of producers, including all types of material, musical and non-musical. The Library of Congress Catalog's *Music and Phonorecords* is a full record of recorded material, while such works as Arthur Cohn's *The Collector's 20th-Century Music* (Lippincott, 1961) serve as little Winchells to help guide the selector. The catalogs of individual companies are also useful in furnishing a full listing of their production.

Microforms

With the microform (whatever its shape or size), the principles of book selection apply very directly, since the bulk of the microform material is simply a direct copy of a printed original. Many of the decisions relating to the purchase of microforms involve administrative rather than selection problems. One may decide to buy microfilmed newspapers when his stacks are filled to the ceilings—the microfilm will solve the administrative problem of lack of space.

Microforms have greatly enlarged the scope of materials from which the library can select, however, and this has widened the choices open to the selector. Many libraries which never could have hoped to build up a collection of early printed English books in original editions can now subscribe to University Microfilm's project for producing the items in Pollard and Redgrave's *Short Title Catalogue*. Even if a library does not subscribe to the whole series, it can now indulge the professor of English who longs for copies of the Caxton editions of Chaucer and of Mallory's *Morte d'Arthur*. With the advent of Xerox Copyflo, the scholar no longer has to put up with reading microfilm—he can hold a respectable-looking book in his happy hands, blown up from the microfilm. It must certainly be tempting to purchase copies of items (at 3 and 1/2 to 6 cents per page—say $7.00 to $12.00 for a 200 page book) which in the original could not be bought at any price, since they are simply not available, or, if available, could cost a fortune. A whole universe of books is now added to the current trade and ordinary o.p. market. The principles of selection, however, remain the same.

The major problem in the selection of microformed materials consists in discovering what exists in microform. In addition to the great scholarly projects and the work of commercial firms, many libraries are busily engaged in microfilming materials, a fact known only to them. Microcard issues an annual *Guide to Microforms in Print* (the first edition appeared in 1961). It attempts to list all microforms (microfilm, microcard, microtext, microlex, Readex Microprint, etc.) available from commercial publishers, and those of non-commercial organizations which issue lists or catalogs on a regular basis. Another type of approach to the riches of the microform world is the Philadelphia Bibliographical Center and Union Library Catalogue's *Union List of Microfilms; a Basic List of Holdings in the United States and Canada.* Other special lists have been issued by various groups. Readex Microprint has published such highly specialized research materials as the complete texts of all Atomic Energy Commission reports and non-A.E.C. papers and reports abstracted in *Nuclear Science Abstracts* (basic set to 1956, $7,-000); the Early American Imprints series, 1639-1800, giving the text of every book, pamphlet, and broadside printed in the United States from 1639 to 1800 ($8,000); the microprint edition of more than 5,000 English and American plays (1500-1830; $1,250); and the *Sessional Papers* of the British House of Commons, 1801-1900, $9,000). The prices of these materials suggest that they are not likely to be avidly sought after by the smaller public libraries—or smaller college and university libraries either, for that matter. Other kinds of projects are suggested by such catalogs as the LC Union Catalog Division's *Newspapers on Microfilm;* the American Historical Association's Committee on War Documents' *Index of Microfilmed Records of the German Foreign Ministry and the Reich's Chancellory Covering the Weimar Period;* the American Studies Association Committee on Microfilm Bibliography's *Bibliography of American Culture,* etc. Given the administrative decision to "go microfilm!", the selector has a massive—and rapidly-expanding—treasury of expensive materials open for his selection.

Periodicals

Libraries buy periodicals to cover the most current events or the most recent developments in subject fields (which will not get into book form for some time), to provide reference materials, and for general reading. The type of library involved will strongly affect the original selection of titles and the choice of those for binding and retention. A very small library may buy only a few general magazines and bind only the *Reader's Digest.* The large university may buy and preserve tens of thousands of titles, most of which would be dignified with the title "journal," rather than be referred to inelegantly as mere "magazines." Part of the choice of titles is based on the indexes one can afford. If one purchases *Readers' Guide*, it seems eminently desirable to try to buy as many of the magazines indexed in it as one can afford, to get the maximum use out of both the indexes and the magazines. In the area of coverage of current events, the library should strive to represent a variety of points-of-view, as it does in book selection. Since commitment to subscribe represents a potential continuing annual charge, as well as possible annual binding costs and a constantly expanding storage space, periodicals should be selected carefully, and only after they have demonstrated that they make a solid contribution to the collection. Selecting a periodical for binding reflects the judgment that it will have continuing reference use.

Various selected lists have been assembled in the past to guide selection. Farber's *Classified List of Periodicals for the College Library* (4th ed., 1957), Martin's *Magazines for School Libraries* (1950), ALA's *Periodicals for Small and Medium-Sized Libraries* (1948), Brown's *Scientific Serials* (1956) represent selection for various types of libraries. (Brown's was not originally intended as a selection tool, but a study of the use of scientific periodicals.) Ulrich's *Periodicals Directory* lists approximately 20,000 periodicals by subjects, including world-wide coverage.

Pamphlets

The pamphlet collection can form an important adjunct to the book collection by providing up-to-date material. The problems of selecting are complicated by the almost incredible number of producers of pamphlet material, much of it intended for free distribution. The producers are often engaged in distributing the pamphlets to present some point of view which is connected with their business, and the librarian will want to insure that the materials are factual and unbiased. Obtaining the material involves writing to many different sources, and this in itself can be a very time-consuming task. In addition, the usefulness of a pamphlet file can be much reduced unless there is a program of continuous weeding, to eliminate those materials which have become out-dated. There are a number of guides to this voluminous material, which are of real service to the librarian in guiding him through the veritable flood of materials. Among the major ones are the *Vertical File Index* and the guides (to free materials, curriculum materials, etc.) òf the Educators' Progress Service. But hundreds of organizations issue lists of free and inexpensive materials available on almost every subject imaginable.

General Bibliography

American Association of School Librarians. *Standards for Media Programs.* Chicago, ALA, 1968.

American Library Association. Public Libraries Division. *Minimum Standards for Public Library Systems.* Chicago, ALA, 1966.

Brown, James W., and Norbert, Kenneth D. *Administering Educational Media.* NY, McGraw-Hill, 1965.

Brown, James W., and Thornton, James, eds. *New Media in Higher Education.* Washington, National Education Association, 1963.

Collison, Robert L. *The Treatment of Special Materials in Libraries.* London, Aslib, 1955.

Goldstein, Harold, ed. *Illinois Libraries,* February, 1966. (Audiovisual issue)

Horn, Andrew H., ed. *Library Trends,* October 1955 ("Special Materials and Services,")

Kujoth, Jean S. *Readings in Nonbook Librarianship.* Metuchen, N.J., Scarecrow Press, 1968.

Lohrer, Alice. *The School Library Materials Center.* Champaign, Ill.; Illini Union Bookstore, 1964.

Lyle, Guy R. *Administration of the College Library.* 3d ed. NY, Wilson, 1961. p.268-319.

Mason, Donald. *Primer of Non-Book Materials in Libraries.* London, Association of Assistant Librarians, 1958.

National Education Association of the United States. Department of Audio-Visual Instruction. *Quantitative Standards for Audiovisual Personnel, Equipment, and Materials.* Washington, the Association, 1965.

Rufsvold, Margaret. *Audio-Visual School Library Service; A Handbook for Librarians.* Chicago, ALA, 1949.

Rufsvold, Margaret. *Guide to Newer Educational Media*. 2d ed. Chicago, ALA, 1967.

Wheeler, Joseph L. & Goldhor, Herbert. *Practical Administration of Public Libraries*. NY, Harper & Row, 1962. p.399-407.

Wittich, Walter A. *Audiovisual Materials; Their Nature and Use*. 4th ed. NY, Harper & Row, 1967.

Curriculum Materials

Aubrey, Ruth. *Selected Free Materials for Classroom Teachers*. Palo Alto, Cal., Fearon, 1965.

Dever, Esther. *Sources of Free and Inexpensive Educational Materials*. 2d ed. Grafton, W.Va., 1964.

Educators' Guide to Free Science Materials. Randolph, Wis., Educators Progress Service (annual)

Educators' Guide to Free Social Studies Materials. Randolph, Wis., Educators Progress Service (annual)

Elementary Teachers' Guide to Free Curriculum Materials. Randolph, Wis., Educators Progress Service (annual)

George Peabody College for Teachers. Division of Surveys and Field Services. *Free and Inexpensive Materials*. (Latest edition)

Pepe, Thomas J. *Free and Inexpensive Educational Aids*. 3d rev.ed., NY, Dover, 1967.

Films and Filmstrips

General

Commiskey, Margaret. *Film Utilization*. (ASD Guide to the Literature of Libraries, no.6). Chicago, ALA, 1960.

Educational Film Library Association. *Film Evaluation: Why and How?* NY, 1963.

Lindgren, Ernest. *The Art of the Film*. 2d ed. NY, Macmillan, 1963.

Jones, Emily S. *Manual on Film Evaluation*. NY, EFLA, 1967.

Reviews and Evaluations

Educational Film Library Association. [EFLA cards]
Educational Film Library Association. *Film Evaluation Guide,*
   1954-64. (Cumulation of EFLA cards)
Educational Screen and Audio-Visual Guide
Film News
Film Review Digest
Film World
Landers Film Reviews
Solomon, Albert E. *Teacher Evaluations of New Classroom*
   Films, 1964-65. Albany, N.Y., 1965.

Bibliography

American Library Association. Audio-Visual Committee. *Films*
   for Libraries. Chicago, ALA, 1962
The British National Film Catalogue. 1963-
Educators' Guide to Free Films. 1941-
Educators' Guide to Free Film Strips. 1949-
Films for Children: A Selected List. New York Library Associa-
   tion, 1966.
Films for Young Adults: A Selected List. New York Library
   Association, 1966.
Indiana University. Audio-Visual Center. *Educational Motion*
   Pictures. Catalog.
Iowa. University. Division of Extension and University Services.
   Catalog of Audio-Visual Aids for Educational Use.
Michigan. University. Audio-Visual Education Center and In-
   structional Media Center, Michigan State University. *Educa-*
   tional Film Catalog. [See also their joint Educational Film
   Index]
U.S. Library of Congress. *Films and Filmstrips.*

Microforms

Diaz, James, ed. *Subject Guide to Microforms in Print, 1966-67.*
   Washington, Microcard Editions, 1967.
Guide to Microforms in Print. 1961-

National Register of Microform Masters. 1965-
[See also the catalogs of individual companies; e.g., Microprint, Readex, University Microfilms, etc.]

Pamphlets

Alexander, Raphael, ed. *Business Pamphlets and Information
Sources*. NY, Exceptional Books, 1967.
American Library Association. Small Libraries Project. *The Ver-
tical File*. [Suppl. C to Pamphlet no. 9]
Educators' Progress Service. [Their guides to free materials
contain listings of pamphlets]
Ireland, Norma. *The Pamphlet File in School, College, and
Public Libraries*. Boston, Faxon, 1954.
Public Affairs Information Service. *Bulletin*. NY, 1915-
Vertical File Index. NY, Wilson.

Periodicals

Ayer and Sons. *Directory of Newspapers and Periodicals*. Phil.,
1880-
Brown, Charles. *Scientific Serials*. Chicago, ACRL, 1956.
Cundiff, Ruby E. *101 Magazines for Schools, Grades 1-12*. 4th
ed. Nashville, Tennessee Book Co., 1964.
Dobler, Lavinia G. *The Dobler World Directory of Youth Perio-
dicals*. NY, 1966.
Faxon, F. W. *Librarian's Guide to Periodicals*. Boston [annual]
Irregular Serials and Annuals. NY, Bowker, 1967-
The International Guide to Literary and Art Periodicals. Lon-
don, 1960-
Madison, Wis. Board of Education. Dept. of Curriculum De-
velopment. *Magazines for Elementary Grades*. Madison, 1965.
Martin, Laura. *Magazines for School Libraries*. Rev.ed. NY,
Wilson, 1950.
Muller, Robert H., ed. *From Radical Left to Extreme Right*. Ann
Arbor, Campus Publishers, 1967.
New Serial Titles. 1951-
Osborn, Andrew. *Serial Publications*. Chicago, ALA, 1955.
Southern Assoc. of Colleges and Secondary Schools. Commission
on Colleges and Universities. *The Classified List of Reference*

Books and Periodicals for College Libraries. 3d ed. Atlanta, 1955.
Standard Periodical Directory. 1964/65-
Ulrich's International Periodicals Directory. NY, 1932- . (And annual supplement, 1967-)
Willing's European Press Guide. London, 1966/67-
World List of Social Science Periodicals. 3d ed. UNESCO, 1967.

Recordings

General

Hanna, Edna Frances. "First Steps Toward a Record Collection." In *Illinois Libraries*, Feb. 1962. p.134-49)
International Assoc. of Music Librarians. *Phonograph Record Libraries; Their Organisation and Practise.* Hamden, Conn., Archon Books, 1963.
March, Ivan. *Running a Record Library.* Blackpool, Eng., Long Playing Records Library, 1965.
Pearson, Mary D. *Recordings in the Public Library.* Chicago, ALA, 1963.

Reviews and Evaluations

Children's Record Reviews.
Index of Record Reviews (in Music Library Association's *Notes*)
Such magazines as *American Record Guide; Atlantic Monthly; The Gramaphone; Gramophone Record Review; HiFi/Stereo Review; High Fidelity; Library Journal; Nation; New Republic; Saturday Review.* Newspapers like *New York Times.*)

Bibliography

Educators' Guide to Free Tapes, Scripts, and Transcriptions. 1955-
New York Library Association. Children's and Young Adult Services Division. *Recordings for Children; a Selected List.* 2d ed. 1964.
Schwann Long Playing Record Catalog.
U.S. Library of Congress. *Music and Phonorecords.*

Chapter V

The Selector and His Tools

If a standard for evaluating the book selector were to be constructed, what qualities could be outlined as a measure against which the individual selector could judge his own fitness for the task? This list of qualities, to be sure, might not be found completely in any one individual, or the individual might find that he possessed all of them, but in varying degrees. The list of characteristics that follows does not permit the inference that the failure to have all of them means failure in selection. They are listed to provide a picture of what the ideal selector might be like.

A Profile of the Ideal Selector

First, the selector would have full and detailed information about all the titles being currently issued. He would have read every current book in every subject field for which he is responsible, since it is obvious that in order to select the best titles from a group of books, the librarian must know each book in the group. He would, therefore, have developed some system for covering the field of current publishing. He would, in addition, have full knowledge of each writer's previous works and their worth, he would know the authors of each subject and their relationship to one another and to the total subject. He would have a clear picture of the development of the literature of each field and could fit current titles into this pattern. He would know all about all publishers; their specialities, strengths, and weaknesses, their past triumphs or transgressions. He would know what to expect from any book bearing a particular publisher's imprint.

His own subject knowledge would be vast and constantly increasing. He would have extensive education in each field for which he was responsible for selection, so that he could competently judge the accuracy, reliability, and authority of any given book.

In addition, he would be intimately familiar with the people his library served. He would know the level of education and reading sophistication of each and could decide accurately which books would be of interest to and of suitable difficulty for each reader. His information about the reading interests of the whole community would be detailed and exact. He could estimate the reading difficulty of books accurately and match them to the reading skills of his users. He would be familiar with the problems of the community, with current affairs and with the needs of the citizenry. There would be no group in the community whose activities were unknown to him, and his eyes would continually be watching for books which would serve and support those activities.

In his selection of materials, he would maintain perfect impartiality and freedom from bias. He would select materials on the basis of their worth and not on the basis of any extraneous matters. He would be able to understand and appreciate all the variety of attitudes held by the various groups and individuals in his community, and would represent them all in his selection. He would not hesitate to buy books reflecting unpopular or unorthodox ideas, and he would be careful to buy titles representing the various positions on controversial subjects.

He would, of course, know what his own library had on every subject, and in his selection he would be able to answer accurately the question as to what any given book had to add to the information already in the library. He would—in short—be intelligent, educated, informed, courageous, honest, and impartial.

Some Pragmatic Considerations

These, then, are the qualities possessed by our paragon. It is obvious that we are describing a superhuman creature. There are certain realities of life which militate against the production of such a theoretically desirable personage. In the first place, it would be rarely, if ever, in our complex world that we would find a person whose specialized subject knowledge is universal.

Furthermore, if he makes the attempt to keep up with all current publishing, he will find the task beyond any single individual's abilities and time. In the United States alone, the annual publishing output of trade titles has passed the twenty thousand mark—to say nothing of the production of the other English-speaking countries. Covering the field at first hand is simply impossible. Any one individual can do no more than take a sampling. If we add to this reading the millions of books published in the past, it becomes even more painfully obvious that no single individual can hope to read more than a tiny part of the universe of books.

But, granting that the librarian cannot read everything, and granting that he cannot have intimate knowledge of every subject, he can work constantly to improve his acquaintance with books. The first person to receive the benefits of adult education which a library affords ought to be the librarian himself. Librarians would do well to take Corinne Bacon's advice to know books through a constant perusal of them. It is impossible to pass by her pungent remark without quoting: "Someone has said that the librarian who reads is lost. The librarian who doesn't read isn't worth finding."

Our paragon would also select books from a position of absolute impartiality and freedom from bias. All agree that book selection should be objective. But—to return to the problem raised in the preceding chapter—is this humanly possible? Take, as an example, a potential librarian who learned to read at an early age, and who enjoyed having books read to him as a child; who has been exposed to the most appropriate books at each age and reading level; who loved the children's classics and the best contemporary children's literature. In college, he majored in English literature and read widely in various literatures. It is only natural that he should have built up certain reading preferences along with his special knowledge of the best literature. Will he be able to sympathize with the taste of the reader of mystery or western stories? Will he not have developed a rather exalted literary standard by which he will judge books?

Assume that he comes from a family which is financially

secure, his whole political environment has been that of ultra-conservatism; he genuinely reveres the doctrines of laissez-faire, of personal independence, of sturdy self-reliance. He mistrusts welfare governments, he dislikes change in the political or social apparatus. How will he be able to look impartially on the writings of liberal economists, whom he sincerely believes to be tools of Incarnate Evil?

His theoretical personal characteristics could be outlined in greater detail, but this much should suffice to point out that every librarian is a human being with his full set of pre-conceptions, of blind spots, of passionate adherence to a philosophy of some sort. Is it really possible to set these personal convictions aside to judge a book's value to one's users objectively?

It is not advocated that the librarian abandon his personal opinions and point of view. But he can attempt to imitate our paragon and recall that, when he selects books, he is selecting for others. When he sits down to select let him remember that he is now functioning—not as a private person selecting his personal reading—but as a professional selector, choosing what others will find of interest and value, however dull or valueless he himself might find it in his present state of enlightenment.

This kind of problem is by no means restricted to libraries, and it may be well to remind ourselves that it is the same difficulty which any human institution faces. Every human organization must devise some system which can be operated successfully by people who are competent and even gifted, but not perfect. If the library cannot be staffed by book selectors who are all perfect, is there no system we can devise to accomplish satisfactory book selection?

Aids to Effective Selection

If it is impossible for the individual librarian to cover the whole field of current publishing, it is possible to fall back upon the helpful principle of division of labor. In a large library, various members of the staff can be assigned to follow particular aspects of the publishing output. In the small library, the librarian will have to rely upon the various book selection aids, which represent a coverage of current publishing by many people, reporting their pooled judgment of the best being published. If it is impossible for each librarian to be a specialist in every subject, it is possible to divide the labor once again, and let those on the staff who are specialists in a subject be responsible for selection in that subject. If there are subject areas in which the library does not have a person with training, the book selection aids can be called upon for help, since their lists in the various subjects will represent the judgment of people who are informed in those fields. If it is difficult for the individual librarian to suppress his own convictions in selecting, the use of committees, whose members will represent a variety of attitudes, will serve as a useful protection against personal bias, since the other members can serve as a counterbalance if one selector goes too far afield.

There are many book selection aids which can assist the average librarian to do a satisfactory job. They vary in the speed with which they cover current publishing, in the type of book listed, in the kind and amount of information given for each title, in the type of library for which they are intended, in format, frequency, and usefulness. The librarian must know the various aids and their special characteristics. Even when he can examine approval copies of new books or see the books in galley proofs in advance of publication, the librarian will want to read the reviews.

Advance notices may be seen in the advertising pages and forecast lists of *Publishers' Weekly,* and *Forthcoming Books,* or in the announcements of individual publishers. After the bare bibliographic bones—author, title, publisher, date, and price—have been noted, the title should be checked in *The Virginia Kirkus' Service, Inc.,* which carries informal and informative reviews approximately six weeks before publication date. In the "New Books Appraised" section of *Library Journal* are found signed reviews written by librarians, useful because the evaluation is made in terms of type of collection or type of library. Many of the reviews appear in advance of publication.

About the time of publication, the title appears in the "Weekly Record" of *Publishers' Weekly,* if the publisher has sent in a copy of the book in advance of publication date. At about the same time, reviews appear in the weekly book review sections of such newspapers as the *New York Times* and those carrying *The*

Book World (*Chicago Tribune* and *Washington Post*). Local newspapers which publish book reviews should be read regularly also, as these reviews will be reflected in library requests.

Weekly periodicals frequently carry lively and critical reviews. *Time, New Yorker, Newsweek,* and the *Saturday Review* feature one or more reviews and give brief and pertinent annotations about other books.

All of the reviewing media mentioned above present timely reviews either before publication or near the date of publication.

The librarians of Fiske's California study were asked which reviewing media they used, and the results rank them as follows (from heaviest used to less used): *Kirkus, Library Journal, Saturday Review, New York Times, Publishers' Weekly, ALA Booklist,* and *New York Herald Tribune.* Thus the California librarians use most the two titles which carry the most reviews.

Let us now turn our attention to reviews which appear after publication, but which can still be used as aids to the selection of current books.

The American Library Association's guide to current books is the *Booklist and Subscription Books Bulletin.* The *Book Review Digest,* published by the Wilson Company, lists new books after a substantial number of reviews have appeared. General periodicals, notably *Atlantic* and *Harpers,* have excellent book review sections, but are inclined to review books after publication date. The scholarly journals also contain reviews, although they generally appear long after the book is published.

There are also aids for the selection of basic collections, which can be used for retrospective buying to fill in gaps and strengthen the library in the various subject fields. The American Library Association and the H. W. Wison Co. have been responsible for the development of basic book selection aids for various types of libraries. That pioneer librarian, Melvil Dewey, envisioned an *A.L.A. Catalog* as early as 1877, the year after the organization of the A.L.A. Its historical background has been traced by Russell E. Bidlack in his article "The Coming Catalogue; or, Melvil Dewey's Flying Machine." The catalog was originally published as a government document by the Bureau of Education and bears the imprint date of 1893, although it did not make its appearance in final form until 1894. Its full title was *Catalog of the "A.L.A." Library; 5,000 Volumes for a Popular Library Selected by the American Library Association and Shown at the World's Columbian Exposition.* The books listed were displayed at the exposition at Chicago, and the preparation of the catalog was under the direction of Mary S. Cutler, Vice-Director of the Albany Library School.

This was the forerunner of the *A.L.A. Catalog; 8,000 Volumes for a Popular Library, with Notes (1904),* which was prepared by the A.L.A. in cooperation with the New York State Library and the Library of Congress for the St. Louis World's Fair. The *ALA Catalog, 1926; an Annotated Basic List of 10,000 Books,* was followed by periodic polyennial supplements. Aimed at informing the librarian of the smaller public library, this annotated basic list was selected cooperatively by some four hundred librarians and was limited in its inclusion to a selection of standard and popular titles available at the time.

Growing up beside the later supplements of the *ALA Catalog* was the *Standard Catalog* series of the H. W. Wilson Company. The *Standard Catalog for Public Libraries* was published at first in eight separate sections which were brought together into a single, non-fiction volume in 1934. As in the case of the *ALA Catalog,* the selection of titles was a cooperative venture, with a number of librarians taking part. About one-fourth of the titles were starred for first purchase by small public libraries or those with limited book funds. The *Fiction Catalog* was first published in 1908, and is kept up-to-date by new editions and by supplements. Its purpose is to serve as a buying list of the best fiction for library use. Mention must also be made of the *Standard Catalog for High School Libraries* and the *Children's Catalog.*

There are several aids to the selection of books for junior college and liberal arts college libraries. The most recent college lists are *Books for College Libraries* (A.L.A., 1967) which includes a selected list of books published before 1964, and A.L.A's current reviewing medium, *Choice.* Two older basic lists are (1) *Catalog of the Lamont Library* (1953), which was intended to support the particular needs of the Harvard undergraduate program, and (2) the *Shelf List of the University of Michigan's Undergraduate Library* (1958-62). For junior colleges, Frank J. Bertalan's *Junior College Library Collection* (1968) is a useful aid.

A librarian charged with building a collection for a new college library will have need of retrospective tools, as well as guides to current publishing. Checking the *Lamont Library Catalog* and the *University of Michigan Undergraduate Shelf-list* as well as *Books for College Libraries* for a given subject would provide a broader review of past titles than using any one of them alone. All three were developed with somewhat different aims, and thus complement each other. An excellent older list, Charles B. Shaw's *List of Books for College Libraries* (1931, and its 1931-38 continuation, 1940) may be used profitably for retrospective buying; in retrospective acquisition, care must be exercised to avoid selection of obsolete materials.

An annotated list of the book selection aids appears at the end of this chapter.

Summary

Most librarians must depend upon the various selection aids for their information about new titles. It is important, therefore, to consider whether there are any weaknesses in this system for aiding librarians in their choice of titles. Various studies have revealed that most of the reviews of books tend to be favorable, which might cast some doubt upon their objectivity. This tendency to praise is accounted for in part by the fact that only those books considered worthwhile are chosen for reviewing, and omission constitutes a negative review. It is certainly true that many books are never reviewed, and the librarian depending upon the general reviewing media would never become aware of their existence. Furthermore, if the conscientious librarian wants to read a number of reviews, in order to form a more sound judgment of a book, he may well be disappointed. Except for the very popular titles—particularly in non-fiction— only a bare minimum of reviews are likely to appear, and some titles may not be reviewed at all. It is also well to recall that the reviewer for the general periodical or newspaper does not have the particular needs of a given library in mind when he writes his review—indeed, it is highly unlikely that he is thinking of library problems. These are real limitations upon the usefulness of the reviewing media, and yet the system appears to work reasonably well. It seems safe to say that the really significant titles of any given year receive full attention, and that the librarian will not be seriously misled by the reviews, in spite of their limitations. He may develop various techniques for compensating for the weaknesses of the reviewing system: as one wit put it, if one can find only favorable reviews, he can start judging a book on the basis of the degree of enthusiasm expressed by the reviewer. A consistent reading of the various media over a period of time will reveal their individual characteristics and enable the librarian to make these adjustments.

In this chapter, the librarian who selects books has been urged to have a personal knowledge of books, to continue developing his knowledge of subject fields (a task which he ought to consider a lifetime part of the librarian's job), to know the general reading interests of people and the special interests of his own community. He ought to have the courage to implement the principles of book selection with honesty and impartiality, avoiding arrogance on the one hand and an unprofessional subservience on the other. It is to be hoped that he will make balanced, sane, and informed judgments. When he feels that his own knowledge is weak, or where he suspects that his own bias is creeping into selection, let him have recourse to that composite judgment of many librarians and critics which is embodied in the various book selection aids.

Book Reviewing And Annotations

Facility in reviewing books should be a part of every librarian's background, for books are the librarian's business, and he should be eager and willing to talk to groups or individuals about books. The ability to talk about and write about books is an important adjunct to successful librarianship. The art of annotation and of book reviewing should be acquired by anyone who has a lively interest in books and who wishes to share that interest with others.

There are some skills to be acquired which will facilitate the preparation of reviews and annotations. Reading with reasonable speed and comprehension, ability to exercise a balanced and informed judgment, and to summarize for the use of others will play a part in the process. As long ago as 1885, William E. Foster of the Providence (R.I.) Library observed that the librarian had to develop the ability to skim the book, to get at the kernel of it, and to place it in the literature of its subject.

First of all, the evaluator—in reviewing a book for library selection purposes—should obtain an overall impression of the book by examining the information on the book jacket, the table of contents, and the preface. Aside from the publisher's blurb, the book jacket usually gives some information about the author which can be supplemented from other sources, as well as listing some of the other books which the author has written. It may also furnish a summary of the book. The table of contents gives the plan of the book, and the preface indicates what the author is trying to do.

By reading a few chapters—a hundred pages or so—and scanning the rest of the book, it is possible to determine its style, scope, content, form, structure, and the manner of treatment of the subject. The librarian's purpose, then, is to get the gist of the book. In order to do this, he must cultivate the ability to glean its main points swiftly, comprehensively, and accurately, always keeping in mind its potential library use. He should attempt to place the book in the class to which it belongs and then compare it with other books on the same subject in an attempt to determine whether it is a necessary or valuable addition to the collection. At this point, a recommendation for purchase or rejection of the book should be made. This usually takes the form of a written annotation or book note giving reasons for the decision.

Annotations

An annotation or book note is a brief, compact characterization of the book, either descriptive or critical. There are two types of annotations—the librarian's note and the reader's note. The librarian's note is intended to help librarians decide whether the book should be added to the collection and to point out the groups of people to whom it will appeal. The reader's note, however, assumes that the book is already in the library and that there is a potential reading public for it. It is written to attract readers.

There are a few points which both types of book notes have in common. They should both be discriminating and impartial, based on definite knowledge of the book. The scope of the book, information about the author, and an explanation of the title—if it is not self-explanatory—should appear in both types. If the material has appeared serially or has been used in lectures, this fact should also be indicated.

The divergence comes in the kinds of information included. In the librarian's note, both favorable and unfavorable criticism has its place. Special points of interest to the librarian are the appeal to certain groups of readers and the possible influence of the book. The note should include a comparison with other books of the same type. In non-fiction, the matter of arrangement is often of importance: Are there appendices which may be useful and important? Is there an index? In the case of fiction, it is inadvisable to give the plot, but important to give some idea of the place of the book in literature.

The reader's note should appeal to the reader for whom the book is intended. The writer of the reader's note must be able to discern the essential part of the book and disregard the immaterial, while at the same time distinguishing both intellectually and sympathetically the kinds of readers to whom the book will appeal. When the writer of the note describes the book, he should recreate the spirit and atmosphere in such a way that the people who would like such a book are attracted to it, and, conversely, those who would not enjoy such a book are not.

After the note is written, it should be reread, to make sure that words have not been wasted and that the material is suitably phrased. Since an annotation is frequently limited to from fifty to one hundred words, every word must count. Ability to eliminate non-essential words and phrases and still reflect the spirit of the book is an accomplishment which comes with practice.

Although the language and style of the reader's note should fit the character of the book, this may be carried too far. For example, in writing a note about a book that is poetic in style, be sure that a clear idea of its content is given, that the writer has not been carried away into the realms of the precious. An annotation describing *Wisdom and Destiny,* by Maurice Maeterlinck, might read: "An individual philosophy of life which is rare, delicate, and fragile, beautiful as a floating mist." Such a note may sound charming, but might be found a bit too flowery for many readers. The following annotation, which is somewhat more prosaic, still conveys information concerning the poetic quality of the book: "A philosophy of life essentially happy in its conception, centering in the thought that destiny cannot utterly destroy the wise. Somewhat mystical and elusive, but full of poetic beauty." The reader's note is usually brief, consisting of not more than one or two sentences.

Examples of librarians' notes may be found in the basic book selection aids, such as the *Standard Catalog,* the current issues of *Library Journal,* and the *Booklist.*

Use of Annotations

The librarian's note is an aid to the librarian in deciding whether or not a certain book will be added to the collection and to what types of readers it will appeal. It is frequently clipped to printed reviews and kept on file. If unfavorable, it is convenient to refer to in explaining to a patron why the book has not been bought. The reader's note should be used to inform readers, either as brief notes in newspapers or in book lists prepared for distribution by the library. In some libraries, the notes are placed in the catalogs or in the books themselves.

Oral Book Reviewing

The oral book review is used in the evaluation of a book for library selection purposes and also as a means of interesting prospective readers. Ability to talk about books is an essential part of the librarian's professional equipment. It is important to organize the review to achieve a clear and effective result. Notes can be used as a guide in the presentation but it is generally inadvisable to read the review unless one is a very skilled reader. It is wise to talk to the person farthest back in the room and to watch his face to see if he hears you.

Timing the review before it is given and keeping within the

time limit is a basic rule. Do not talk too quickly, or much of the presentation will be lost; good planning will enable you to speak at a reasonable pace. Try to avoid mannerisms which may distract from what is being said, such as fiddling with one's glasses, mumbling into the notes, figeting, "oh'ing" and "ah'ing" before each sentence. A few sessions with a tape recorder will reveal much about one's speech habits. It is usually advisable to repeat the author and title several times during the talk to fix it in the minds of the audience, and to have a copy of the book on display. The best results can be obtained by being sincerely interested in the book and presenting the review with honest enthusiasm.

Uses of Oral Book Reviews

Some of the larger public libraries have book selection meetings, usually held at regular intervals, in which oral book reviewing is a part of the selection process. The point of view of the librarian's book review is the same as the librarian's book note: the review is critical and evaluates the book for possible inclusion in the library. The points to be covered in such a review include the following: (1) information about the author; (2) date of publication; (3) what the author is trying to do in this book, what he has actually done, and how he has done it; (4) comparison with other books of the same type or in the same subject field; (5) reviews and criticisms of the book; (6) type of library for which the book is suited; (7) type of borrower to which it will appeal.

When oral book reviews for public consumption are planned, the librarian should adjust the type of treatment to the intended audience, remembering that the backgrounds and interests of various groups differ, and that what might be a successful review for one group would not be satisfactory for another. The aim of a review for the general public is to try to interest those who hear it in reading a certain book, or group of books. The preference in public library reviewing is to talk about groups of books, thus differentiating the library-oriented review from the "women's club" review, which has been characterized as an attempt to substitute hearing about the book for reading it. The primary purpose of any library book review is to draw attention to books, not to substitute the review for a more substantial first-hand knowledge of the book.

The technique for doing this involves piqueing the curiosity, arousing the interest, catching the attention of the group and making them feel that a book is worth reading because of content, type, or timeliness. If the reviewer becomes sufficiently involved in the book himself, he can usually interest the reader in it.

Book reviews are given by librarians to community groups of all kinds and also over the radio and television. It is well to remember that reviewing is time-consuming and should not be undertaken unless time for preparation is provided. Radio is a particularly good medium for book reviewing. Radio reviews may be given by a single person reviewing several books, or by several people, with one acting as a moderator. A formal script or an ad lib program can be used. Usually an informal atmosphere is more easily created by using notes and talking from them in the same way as is done before a live audience.

Both radio and television programs improve with professional direction, which is frequently provided by the station. Station time for educational programs is generally provided free of charge. Many of the larger libraries cooperate with the radio and television stations in their communities to produce effective book reviewing programs. Such programs should be linked with the library's name as a means of promoting more and better reading.

Book Selection Aids

American Book Publishing Record. New York, Bowker, 1960- The monthly cumulation of the listings in *Publishers' Weekly.* Arranged by subject according to Dewey Decimal Classification; with annotations. [See also the discussion under current American bibliography in Chapter IX.] The five year cumulation of the 109,221 books published in 1960-64 (4v.) is excellent for retrospective buying.

ALA Catalog, 1926; an Annotated Basic List of 10,000 Books. Chicago, ALA, 1926. Supplements: 1926-31; 1932-36; 1937-41; 1942-49.

Projected by Melvil Dewey as a primary guide to book selection by librarians for librarians, it is aimed at informing the librarian who purchases books for the small public library. The titles on this basic list were selected cooperatively by a number of librarians. Inclusion was limited to selection of standard and popular literature available during the time of compilation. It is arranged by Decimal Classification, with the following information given for each entry: complete name of author (with dates), title, publisher, place of publication, pagination, price, date, LC card number, illustrations, maps, bibliography are given in separate lists. Author, title, and subject index. The annotations are drawn largely from the *Booklist*.

A Basic Collection for Elementary Grades. 7th ed. Chicago, ALA, 1960.
A Basic Collection for Junior High Schools. 3d ed. Chicago, ALA, 1960.
A Basic Book Collection for High Schools. 7th ed. Chicago, ALA, 1963.
Useful lists for selecting books for new libraries and for evaluating older collections. Arranged by Dewey Classification. The collection for elementary grades was compiled by Miriam Snow Mathers, assisted by consultants from A.L.A., N.E.A., A.C.E.I., N.C.T.E., and others. The junior high list was edited by Margaret Spengler, with the assistance of counsultants from A.L.A. and related educational associations. The high school collection was edited by Eileen Noonan.

Bertalan, Frank J. *Junior College Library Collection*. 1st ed. Newark, N.J., The Bro-Dart Foundation, 1968.
A selected list of more than 19,000 books for junior and community colleges. Its purpose is to assist in the selection of titles, in all subject areas, that should be provided by new institutions and by established schools that are expanding their facilities. The scope reflects the curriculum trends in junior and community colleges and continuous updating is planned. This list is arranged by L.C. classification and it gives full bibliographic information. The classified section is arranged by author. Mr. Bertalan, the general editor, is Director of the School of Library Science, University of Oklahoma. He was assisted by ten associate editors. Eighty-eight junior colleges participated in selection of the titles.

Best Books for Children. New York, Bowker, 1961-

An annual list, chosen from books reviewed in the *School Library Journal.* Classified by age and subject, with author and title index.

Book Review Digest. New York, Wilson, 1905-

Its purpose is to aid in the evaluation of books by gathering excerpts from reviews. Each book is entered under author, with full bibliographic data, followed by a brief descriptive note and the excerpts, which are limited to three for fiction and four for non-fiction. Other reviews will be cited bibliographically. Formerly, favorable reviews were indicated by plus signs and unfavorable ones by minus signs, but this system was dropped on vote of the subscribers (March 1963). A list of periodicals from which reviews are taken is given, and the student of book selection should study this list carefully as a clue to the types of books which will be reviewed by *Book Review Digest.* It is published monthly except July, with cumulations.

Book Review Index. Detroit, Gale Research, 1965-

This monthly list, with quarterly cumulations, is an alphabetical list arranged by author of the book reviewed citing reviews in periodicals. Unlike the *Book Review Digest* it provides no descriptive notes or excerpts from reviews but only the citation to the review (periodical, reviewer, volume, date and page). It does provide, however, greater speed, diversity of sources, and number of citations than other indexes to book reviews. Highly recommended by *Booklist* and *Choice.*

Book World.

A combination of the *New York Herald Tribune Book Week* (after the demise of that newspaper in 1967) and *Books Today.* About 12-15 books are reviewed each week. The reviews are signed and reviewers are knowledgeable in the subject field. In 1968, it was appearing weekly in the *Chicago Tribune* and the *Washington Post.*

Books Abroad, an International Literary Quarterly. Norman, Oklahoma, University of Oklahoma, 1927-

Each issue contains several short studies of foreign literature and foreign writers, chiefly European, followed by brief reviews, classed in subject groups, of from 250 to 300 current publications in many foreign countries, contributed by reviewers from American universities. The reviews are thorough, yet compact, usually descriptive and limited to the humanities.

Books for College Libraries. Prepared under the direction of Melvin J. Voigt and Joseph H. Treyz. Chicago, ALA 1967.

Intended as a successor to Charles B. Shaw's *Books for College Libraries,* this work lists 53,410 titles, carefully selected to support basic undergraduate studies. The titles are restricted to those published before 1964. It is arranged by the Library of Congress classification, with author and title indexes. Each entry includes author, title, edition, pagination, and L.C. card numbers. One may consider *Choice* (q.v.) as its current continuation.

Booklist and Subscription Books Bulletin. Chicago, ALA, 1905-

Subscription Books Bulletin merged into the *Booklist* in September, 1956. Each current issue contains reviews of one hundred to one hundred twenty-five books recommended for library purchase. This selection is representative of the best judgment of library subject specialists, who are familiar with the new books in their respective fields. Full bibliographic information and excellent annotations are included. Titles are arranged according to Decimal Classification. Detailed reviews of one or two reference books, reviews of books for children and young people, as well as adult fiction and non-fiction, films, and recent European books are included, as are lists of books selected for the small public library and lists of free and inexpensive materials and government publications. ALA has also issued collections of reference book reviews: *Subscription Books Bulletin Reviews, 1956-60* (1961); *1960-62* (1963); *1962-1964* (1964); *1964-1966* (1967).

British Book News, A Guide to Book Selection. London, British Council, 1940-

A monthly guide to British books and periodicals. It is divided into three parts: (1) a general article dealing with some aspect of

the library, literary, or artistic world; (2) extensive and evaluative reviews of recommended books on all subjects, annotated,
with full bibliographic information; (3) a selected list of forthcoming books, not annotated.

Choice. A.L.A., Association of College and Research Libraries. March, 1964-
Financed by two grants by the Council of Library Resources,
this monthly (with combined July-August issue) evaluates current books of a scholarly or academic nature. Reviews of about
500 titles each month are provided in order to give a continuing
evaluation of new books. These are prepared by the editor and a
large roster of subject specialists. Originally intended to assist
the selection of books for college libraries, it is useful in many
types of libraries: public, junior college, secondary school, special and foreign libraries.

There are several special features; i.e., the "Opening Day
Collection" which began in July 1965, and several subject-centered
bibliographic articles. There are plans to include a supplement
of recommended titles dating from January 1964 since *Books for
College Libraries* includes only materials published through
December 1963.

The publication of a monthly review service on cards was
announced to begin March 1968. Its purpose is to facilitate the
use of these book reviews in the acquisition systems of many
academic and public libraries.

Forthcoming Books, 1966- New York, Bowker.
Published bi-monthly, this simple listing by author and title of
American trade books supercedes the *Publishers Weekly Inter-
im Index* and the indexes to the seasonal announcement issues.
It lists books planned for publication in the next five months.
Each issue overlaps and updates the preceding issue.

Subject Guide to Forthcoming Books.
The same five month forecast is classified under two hundred
subject headings.

Hackett, Alice Payne. *Seventy Years of Best Sellers:
1895-1965.* New York, Bowker, 1967.
Lists the facts and figures about best sellers in the United

States, with comments on the interpretations of the statistics. "Must" reading for those concerned with the problems of best-selling current fiction or interested in the relationship between popular success and continued life in books.

Harvard University. Library. Lamont Library. *Catalog of the Lamont Library, Harvard College*. Prepared by Philip J. McNiff and Members of the Library Staff. Cambridge, Harvard University Press, 1953.

Arranged according to the library's modification of Dewey. Information about each title includes short title entry, brief author entry, publisher, and date. Over 39,000 titles listed. Periodicals, mimeographed and ephemeral titles omitted.

Hoffman, Hester R. *Reader's Adviser and Bookman's Manual; a Guide to the Best in Print in Literature, Biographies, Dictionaries, Encyclopedias, Bibles, Classics ...* 10th ed. Revised and enlarged. N.Y., Bowker, 1964.

Lists the "best books of all times under thirty-four major catagories." An excellent annotated list of over 3,000 books, with considerable information about authors, editions, translators and price. In the case of reprints, the original publisher and date of the first edition is given.

The eleventh edition is to be in two volumes (V. I, announced for November, 1968 and V. II for 1969). The editor is Winifred F. Courtney. It aims to be "the most authoritative, self-contained library of current, selective book information ever published."

An Index to Book Reviews in the Humanities. v.1- 1960- Published by Phillip Thomson, 836 Georgia St., Williamston, Michigan, 48895.

Originally a quarterly review, it has been published annually since 1963. The list of periodicals indexed has grown from some 400 to over 700, including periodicals of both a popular and scholarly nature. It is arranged alphabetically by author of the title reviewed. The term "humanities" is broadly interpreted.

Library Journal. New York, Bowker, 1876-
Published twice a month except July and August (then monthly). The "New Books Appraised" section contains reviews writ-

ten by librarians, giving practical evaluation of current titles. The reviews are arranged by broad subject areas. Many of the reviews appear prior to the date of publication of the book. These reviews are also available on 3 x 5 cards. "Junior Books Appraised" is published as part of the *School Library Journal*, which is bound with *LJ* as *LJ*'s section on children's and young people's libraries.

New Technical Books. New York, New York Public Library, 1915-

With the January 1963 issue, the format, arrangement, and contents of this publication were changed. Entries are arranged by broad Dewey classes and are numbered consecutively throughout the year. Annotations are intended to be descriptive. Emphasis will be on American works pertaining to the pure and applied physical sciences and related disciplines, including those works suitable for use from college level to research.

New York Review of Books. 1963-

Heralded as a "review of depth, personality and bite, one that would treat books and their ideas with the seriousness they deserve," this book reviewing periodical is published twice a month. Reviewers have changed from time to time, and the tone of the reviews varies as the years go by. It does, however, make provocative reading. Each issue contains about fifteen reviews and one or more full length articles.

New York Times Book Review. 1896-

Published weekly as part of the Sunday edition. (Daily editions also carry reviews of books, not by the *Book Review* staff.) Informative reviews, often written by authorities in the subject field, often written by staff members. Fiction reviews are numerous and complete. This is a standard selection tool for many librarians, and those using it should make shift to read some of the criticism levelled at the *Times* in the early 1960's. These will not lead one to abandon using the *Book Review*—or other newspaper reviews—but it may lead one to a more judicious use of these sources.

Perkins, Ralph. *Book Selection Media: A Descriptive Guide to 170 Aids for Selecting Library Materials.* Champaign, Ill.,

National Council of Teachers of English. 1967 revision.
Provides pertinent data on 170 book selection aids for general
collections and for special age and interest groups. The titles are
arranged alphabetically, and special features are described
briefly on a single page. Numerous useful indexes are included.

Princeton University Library. Julian Street Library. *The Julian Street Library: A Preliminary List of Titles.* Compiled by
Warren B. Kuhl. N.Y., Bowker, 1966.
The catalog of a new undergraduate dormitory library at
Princeton. Not the catalog of an undergraduate instructional
library in the sense of the Lamont Collection at Harvard. As
explained in the Foreword, it is intended to include "those
books most frequently in demand by students for broad supplementary reading and other books in all fields which might open
new intellectual avenues for the students." L.C. cards are reproduced, in classed arrangement, for its 8,400 titles. There are
author-subject and title-price indexes.

Public Affairs Information Service Bulletin. New York, 1915-
A weekly publication with four cumulations within the year,
followed by a permanent annual volume. It is an index to
economic, social, and political affairs selected from periodicals,
papers, books, government documents, and typewritten and
mimeographed materials. There are brief annotations, which
enable the librarian to employ it as a selection tool.

Publishers' Weekly. New York, Bowker, 1872-
This standard American book trade journal carries "The
Weekly Record", a list of new publications of the week. The
books are arranged alphabetically by author, with brief descriptive annotations for many. "Forecasts" is a section of annotated
titles announced for publication information. Special issues include Spring, Summer, and Fall announcement numbers (again,
books to come) as well as a children's book number, etc.

Saturday Review. New York, 1924-
Formerly primarily a literary periodical, it has been expanded
to include articles of general information and interest, with some
consequent reduction in the amount of book information given.
The book reviews continue to be good, however, and make a

good supplement to the *N. Y. Times* and other general reviewing media. It also includes reviews of music, records, tape,
and films.

Shaw, Charles B. *A List of Books for College Libraries*. Chicago, ALA, 1931.
Shaw, Charles B. *A List of Books for College Libraries,
1931-38*. Chicago, ALA, 1940.
The first list, containing approximately 14,000 titles, was
prepared to establish a basis for determining the quality of the
collection of four year, liberal arts college libraries. The selection of titles was based on the recommendations of some 200
college teachers, librarians, and other advisors. The titles are
arranged by major subject fields, subdivided by types of materials—reference books, general works, and periodicals. The supplement contains 3,600 titles published between 1931 and 1938.
Titles known to be out-of-print were omitted. Now useful, of
course, only for retrospective buying.

Technical Book Review Index. New York, Special Libraries
Assoc., 1935-
Its primary purpose is to identify reviews in current scientific, technical, and trade journals. Brief quotations from reviews
are given, along with bibliographic citation of the review. A
complement to the *Book Review Digest's* coverage of more
general magazines. Published monthly (except July and August), it treats about 120 books in each issue.

Times Literary Supplement. London, 1902-
A weekly supplement to the *Times*, including reviews of books
in English and foreign languages, as well as historical and
literary articles. Spring and Autumn supplements discuss in
some detail the literary activities in the book trade of the world.

University of Michigan. Undergraduate Library. *Shelf List*.
A catalog of more than 86,000 books and periodicals, representing a collection built to serve the needs of undergraduate
students at the University. It is available in three forms: on
microfilm, in bound volumes, and as trimmed and punched
cards on card stock. Supplements to the original list have been

issued. The catalog is available from University Microfilms, Ann Arbor (which is not part of the University of Michigan, but a private corporation). Compare this item with the Lamont Catalog.

Wilson standard catalog series.

Children's Catalog. 1st- ed., 1909-
The 11th edition of this work appeared in 1966, containing 4,274 titles, selected for their usefulness in school libraries and public library work with children. The books are arranged in classified order, using the latest abridged Dewey. An author, title, subject, and analytic index follows the classified order. The books are also listed by grade level, and a directory of publishers is appended. The catalog is supplemented annually between editions. The 1962 annual supplement added 363 selected books. The consultants for this publication are nominated by the American Association of School Librarians and the Children's Services Division of A.L.A. Entry gives full bibliographical data, including subject headings and aids to cataloging, with an evaluative annotation quoted from reviews. A system of starring and double-starring is employed to emphasize especially recommended books.

Fiction Catalog. 1st- ed., 1908-
A guide to adult fiction found most useful in public libraries, it is published periodically, with annual supplements. The 7th edition, containing over 4,000 titles, was published in 1960, while the 8th is planned for 1970. It is arranged alphabetically by author, with full bibliographic information and annotation. The second part is a subject and title index, followed by a directory of publishers and distributors. It is intended for use by medium-sized and small public libraries.

Junior High School Library Catalog. 1st- ed., 1965-
Planned for quinquennial publication, with annual supplements between editions. Books are selected by a board of consultants nominated by the American Association of School Librarians. Titles included are intended for grades seven through nine. Part I is a classified list with full bibliographic information and a descriptive or critical annotation. Part II is an author,

title, subject index, with analytical entries for stories and plays in collections. Part III is a directory of publishers and distributors.

Senior High School Library Catalog. 1st- ed., 1926-
Formerly the *Standard Catalog for High School Libraries.* The 9th edition was published in 1967, with five annual supplements planned before the next edition. Emphasizes material for students in the 10th through 12th grades. The first part is a classified catalog, arranged according to the Dewey Decimal Classification, with an annotation for each title. The second part is an author, subject, and analytical index, while the third part is a directory of publishers and distributors. After April 1968, it will be available with a Catholic Supplement.

Standard Catalog for Public Libraries. 1st- ed., 1934-
Periodic editions, with annual supplements between. The 5th edition is scheduled for publication in the summer of 1969. Includes only non-fiction. Titles are chosen by a board of consultants nominated by the Public Library Association and the Association of College and Research Libraries. Part 1 is a classified list (by Dewey), with brief annotations. Part 2 is an author, title, and subject index, with analytical entries for parts of books. Part 3 is a directory of publishers and distributors.

Virginia Kirkus' Service Inc. *Bulletin.* 1933-
Issued twice a month, this bulletin makes available to booksellers, librarians, and interested individuals informal and informative reviews of books, including children's books. It is particularly strong in reviews of fiction. Although not all publishers are represented, reviews are given about six weeks before date of publication, a feature which librarians have found very useful, as they can order and receive books by the time they are published and reviews for them appear in the general reviewing media, leading to a demand by patrons for the books. The Service is widely used by public librarians as a primary selection tool, although the reviews are not presented from the library point of view alone.

Selected Supplementary Aids

Books for Children

A.L.A. Children's Services Division. *Notable Children's Books,* 1940-54. Chicago, ALA, 1966.

A.L.A. Children's Services Division. *Selecting Materials for Children and Young Adults.* Chicago, ALA, 1968. (A bibliography of 125 guides to printed and audiovisual materials, with brief annotations.)

Arbuthnot, May Hill; Clark, Mary M., and Long, Harriet G. *Children's Books too Good to Miss.* 4th rev. ed. Cleveland, Ohio, Western Reserve University, 1966. (Annotated; arranged by age level)

Baker, Augusta. *Books About Negro Life for Children.* Rev. ed., New York Public Library, 1967. (Briefly annotated; arranged under broad subject headings, some age grouping)

Best Books for Children. NY, Bowker [annual] (Arranged by subject within grade level. All titles listed have been recommended by standard aids.)

Booklist and Subscription Books Bulletin. Books for Children, 1960-65. Chicago, ALA, 1966. (Compilation of over 3,000 reviews from the Booklist, arranged in modified Dewey classification.) Note suceeding annual compilation: 1965-66; 1966-67.

Eakin, Mary K., ed. *Good Books for Children; A Selection of Outstanding Children's Books Published 1960-65.* 3d ed. Chicago, Univ. of Chicago, 1967. (Almost 1,400 titles; emphasis on books for grades 4-9; reviews originally appeared in the Bulletin of the Center for Children's Books, are both descriptive and critical.)

Horn Book Magazine. Boston, 1924- Six times per year. (Reviews all types of children's books.)

Strang, Ruth M., Phelps, Ethylyn, and Withrow, Dorothy. *Gateways to Readable Books: An Annotated, Graded List of Books in Many Fields for Adolescents Who Find Reading Difficult.* 4th ed. NY, Wilson, 1966. (1st ed. 1944; second 1958. About three-fourths of the titles are new to the 3d ed.)

U.S. Library of Congress. Children's Book Section. *Children's Books,* 1966. A List of 200 Books for Preschool Through Junior

High School Age. Compiled by Virginia Haviland. Washington, Government Printing Office, 1967. (An annotated list, giving grade level)

Walker, Elinor, ed. *Doors to More Mature Reading: Detailed Notes on Adult Books for Use with Young People.* Chicago, ALA, 1964. (Annotated list; about 150 adult books)

School Library Aids

California Association of School Librarians. *Book List for Elementary School Libraries.* Edited by Margaret H. Miller. Santa Ana, Cal., Professional Library Service, 1966. (Over 5,000 entries, classified by Dewey; with author and title indexes. Gives recommended grade levels.)

Children's Books for Schools and Libraries. NY, Bowker, 1968. (A list of some 18,000 books in print, author and title arrangement. Shows which source recommended each title.)

Eakin, Mary K. *Subject Index to Books for Primary Grades.* 3d ed. Chicago, ALA, 1967. (More than 900 curriculum related books, published 1950 to 1965, arranged by subject.)

Elementary School Library Collection, Phases 1-2-3. 2d ed. Mary V. Gaver, General Editor. Newark, N.J., Bro-Dart Foundation, 1966. (Intended as a guide to building a balanced collection; about 5,590 titles listed. Reproduces the catalog cards for titles; in classed arrangement. Author, title, and subject indexes.)

Paperbound Book Guide for High School Libraries. NY, Bowker, [annual] (Selected titles—more than 4,000—of interest to junior and senior high school students. Grouped under broad subjects.)

School Library Journal: The Journal of Library Work with Children and Young People. NY, Bowker, 1954- (Available as separate publication, but also issued as a special section of *Library Journal* under title Chidren's And Young People's Libraries. See reviews)

Science Books: A Quarterly Review. Washington, American Association for the Advancement of Science, 1965- (Reviews books in pure and applied sciences for students—elementary, secondary, and junior college.)

Paperback Selection

Kliatt Paperback Book Guide: Selected Annotated List of Current Paperback Books. West Newton, Mass., Feb. 1967- quarterly.

Paper Book Review. NY, Book Report Service, 1960-

Paperback Trade News; Journal of the Paperback Industry. Jersey City, N.J., 1962-

Bibliography

Craig, Florence S. "Talking About Books." *Library Journal,* October 1, 1953. p.1601-08.

Drewry, John E. *Book Reviewing.* Boston, The Writer, 1954.

Hollander, John. "Some Animadversions on Current Reviewing." *Daedalus,* Winter 1963. p.145-55.

McDonald, Dwight. "The New York Times, Alas." *Esquire.* Part 1. April 1963, p.55+; Part 2, May 1963, p. 104+.

Peyre, Henri. "What's Wrong with American Book Reviewing." *Daedalus,* Winter 1963. p.128-44.

Regnery, Henry. "Bias in Book Reviewing and Book Selection" *ALA Bulletin,* January 1966. p.57-62.

Reviews in Library Book Selection. Leroy C. Merritt, Martha T. Boaz, and Kenneth S. Tisdel. Detroit, Wayne State Univ. Press, 1958.

Chapter VI

Surveying and Weeding Collections;
Surveying the Community

Every librarian would like to be able to answer the question: "How good is my collection?" Books are selected by different librarians over a period of time. Librarians may vary in their conceptions of the purposes of the library and their interpretation and application of the general principles of selection. Most librarians are interested in discovering some objective, qualitative measure of the value of their book collections, but that is a difficult task. It is easy to compare the size of two collections, but much more difficult to decide which of two collections is the better. It is usually assumed that a collection of four million volumes is better than one of four thousand volumes. The chances seem better that a very large collection will have more material in any given subject field. Even in such a case, there is no assurance that five hundred carefully selected titles in a field like anthropology is poorer than five thousand titles, representing random gathering of titles. But, if there are two collections of a million volumes each, how is one to tell which is the better collection?

To decide how good any library collection is we must have information about three important factors: (1) what kinds of books are in the collection and how valuable each is in its relation to other books in its subject which are not in the library; (2) the kind of community served, in order to decide whether the books in the collection are actually appropriate to that clientele, regardless of how valuable the books may be in terms of an abstract evaluation of their worth; (3) the purposes which

133

that collection is supposed to accomplish, given that particular community of readers.

There are various methods which can be used to get some judgment of the worth of a book collection. If there is a fairly regular stream of requests for titles which the library does not have, the librarian might conclude that there is a lack of correlation between the books being purchased and the interests of the community. Of course, if readers are requesting cheap novels of sub-literary standards, and the librarian does not conceive of the library as a source of such materials, he might conclude that no change in selection practice is warranted. But if he discovers that substantial and worthwhile materials were being requested, but had not been purchased by the library, he might well want to look into the book selection practices. Conversely, if the librarian observes large numbers of titles on the shelves which are never used, he again might want to look into the selection practices. In both cases, it would appear—at first glance, anyway —that the collection was not adequate for serving that community.

The librarian may be moved by such observations to take more formal steps toward evaluating his collection. He might decide to bring in an outside librarian—or group of librarians—to make a survey of the collection and give their personal estimates—based on their own knowledge of books. This method assumes, of course, that there are certain titles which belong in any collection, and that a reading of the shelf list can give a fair and reliable over-all impression of the collection. The results of such a check would have to be considered in terms of the special local requirements of that library. Perhaps it is most useful for identifying a really inadequate collection. A library without any encyclopedias or dictionaries, with only the most popular and most maudlin fiction, with no books in a dozen of the sciences— such glaring gaps could be pointed out. For a larger collection, and for one which is reasonably adequate, this method would seem too imprecise.

In the past, at least, there were some librarians who felt that the evaluation of a collection could be reduced to very quantitative measures. Mathematical formulas could be produced which would measure the demands of readers and compare them with book provision. Certainly there is something appealing to the twentieth century mind in this vision of being able to reduce a

large and unwieldly assortment of discrete items to a simple
and understandable formula. The system breaks down because
of what appears to be an untenable assumption: it attempts to
reduce judgments of quality to quantitative terms. There does
not appear to be any really fine mathematical tool for making
this conversion. The evaluation of a novel, for example, involves
esthetic discriminations, involves—if it may be put this way—
emotional responses to an artistic creation. To reduce this esthetic experience to algebraic terms, to compare one such experience with another and reach numerical conclusions seems to
be most difficult. At some future time it may be possible to
convert esthetic responses into such terms as the level of adren-
alin in the blood, the rate of activity of the pituitary, the
electrical patterns of the brain waves, and then to compare these
data as a person reads first book A and then book B. At the
moment, human technology and our knowledge of the human
physiology and emotions are not sufficiently developed for
mathematical expression of quality.

The most widely used system of evaluating a collection is that
which compares a library's holdings with one or more lists of
selected titles. Such lists as the *Standard Catalog for Public
Libraries*, the *ALA Catalog* and its supplements, the catalog of
the Lamont Library, *Books for College Libraries*, the various
lists of best books, have been commonly used as guides to
checking the effectiveness of past selection policies. (Discussion
of the lists will be found in Chapter V, in the section devoted to
book selection aids.) The assumption is made that such lists,
which represent the composite judgment of many librarians, will
pick up the most important titles in the several subject fields.
What the librarian accomplishes by checking his holdings against
such a list is to come up with a figure representing the
percentage of the titles on that list which he holds. He will not,
of course, be told by this figure what percentage of the titles he
ought to have on his shelves. He may discover—to his comfort—
that he has a large part of the titles on the list. Sometimes,
however, this result could be predicted in advance. If the
librarian uses the *Standard Catalog for Public Libraries* as his
buying guide, and then later evaluates the collection against the
Standard Catalog, a high correlation would seem inevitable.

The checklist method has been criticized because any checklist, it is asserted, represents a very arbitrary selection of titles. All the titles on the list will not be of equal value, some titles may be omitted which are better than the titles on the list. The smaller the list, the more arbitrary the selection is liable to be. A list of the five best books in chemistry in the past fifty years, selected by one individual, might well fail to satisfy others. A list of five hundred titles in chemistry, selected by three dozen experts in the field, with general agreement on the most valuable, would reduce the arbitrary character of selection considerably.

The checklist will, of course, say nothing about those titles which it does not list. The books which a library has, but which are not on the standard list being used for checking, may be as good as those on the list. But if the librarian finds groups of unlisted books, he may well want to make a further check on those titles to assure himself that they really are equivalent. The checklist will also fail to do a complete job in that it does not single out automatically those stocks of old and superseded books which the library may have gathered. The checklist method is useful only for estimating the strength of a collection, to the degree that the collection approximates the list.

Another criticism of the checklist is that, although its titles may be very authoritative, readable, and worthwhile, the list bears no necessary relationship to the particular community served by a given library. This is certainly a justifiable criticism, and it should emphasize the fact that this method must be used intelligently and not blindly. The degree of divergency will depend on the kind of list used: to check the holdings of a branch library serving a factory labor community against the catalog of the Lamont Library, intended for the use of Harvard undergraduates, would make the disparity between the list and the community great indeed. But a general list, like the *Standard Catalog for Public Libraries*, would almost certainly reflect many of the reading interests of the ordinary community. No doubt, it would not fit every community exactly, but this method makes no claim to absolute exactitude.

The comparison of a library's holdings against a list is costly and time-consuming. It is probably most practical to think in terms of surveying some part of the library collection, with the checking being limited to those areas about which doubt has arisen. Even here, the librarian must remember that the checking is the beginning only. It will furnish a rough guide, indicating that a certain percentage of a given group of titles (which have been judged to be reliable, important, or of interest to the general reader) is not available to his patrons. He might then look more closely at the titles which he has, to see if those not on the list are adequate substitutes. This would involve examining reviews of the books. He might also import—from the community or from some other library—experts in that subject field to evaluate those titles which he holds and to make recommendations for purchase.

The list of titles in the guide, not held by the library, will furnish a group for consideration. Some may be ordered immediately; some may be put on a want-list for later purchase. The librarian will have to decide whether it is more important to fill in the gaps, or buy newer books, which may be in greater demand.

The gaps in the collection may also lead to closer consideration of book selection practices and may raise fundamental questions concerning the purposes of the library. If the library has failed to buy a substantial number of titles which were judged by the compilers of the standard list to be important, the librarian might well wish to ask himself if the library has been placing too much stress on mere popularity of titles.

The results of a survey of the collection furnish the librarian with facts upon which he can base decisions, they do not furnish him with an automatic machinery for righting all the wrongs of his collection. The results must be weighed in light of the purposes of the library, the clientele served, the book funds, and the nature of the gaps revealed. As is true in the original selection of materials, so in the evaluation of collections, there is no substitute for intelligent and informed judgment.

Weeding the Collection

In all libraries which do not pretend to become permanent depositories of all that has been published, weeding the collection becomes as important a part of the maintenance of the library as the initial selection. Its importance has been underscored with great frequency in library literature, and impressive lip service has been paid to the process. The standards for various types of libraries include recommendations for weeding. It is not practiced as often as it is preached, as has also been pointed out repeatedly. There seem to be a number of reasons why this state of affairs obtains.

First, librarians are liable to point out the cost involved in weeding. It takes time from some regular job to decide which books must go; it costs money to withdraw the records; it takes time to arrange for the disposal of the books withdrawn. Some librarians have concluded that since it is so costly, it is best passed by in silence.

There have been other reasons for avoidance of the task of weeding. Librarians often take a very exalted view of the book, agreeing heartily with Milton in his view that a book is the life's-blood of a master spirit, and there is a hesitancy to think of any book as "dead." Discarding a book approaches too closely to burning of books, to vandalism, to wanton destruction of something which is almost holy. Furthermore, there is always the chance that the librarian may make a mistake, may weed out a book which will be wanted the next day by some reader. How can one tell whether a book, which may not have been heavily used in the past, may not suddenly become very important? Certainly there is no sure way of learning about future demands.

Perhaps the most immediate, practical reason for omitting weeding is simply lack of time. Beset by a dozen projects which are under way, plagued by lack of sufficient staff, busy and rushed and harried by the day-to-day demands of keeping the institution running, many librarians put off the task until some happier day, when they will have enough time. Eventually, of course, they may be forced to do a rush job of weeding, when they find that there is just not enough space left in the library to cram in more books. Then they may fling themselves into the task, discarding furiously, and perhaps without sufficient reflection. They then discover their mistakes, and weeding takes on an even less appetizing appearance.

Weeding should be a regular, continuing, and steady process. There are many arrangements which could accomplish this end. It might be desirable to allot a week of the year as the time for considering some part of the collection, with the librarian or librarians responsible for that part of the collection studying that group of books for those titles which have outlived their usefulness. It might be possible for the selectors to consider a new title in relation to the possibility of discarding one already on the shelves. If the new title really supersedes the older, the material might be withdrawn upon receipt of the newer books. In some libraries, inventory time is used to identify titles for consideration for discard.

There are certain categories of books which are the most obvious candidates for weeding. First, there are the duplicates of titles, purchased when the book was in heavier demand, but which are no longer needed. Ten or fify or one hundred copies might be reduced to two or three. Superseded editions of books might well be eliminated, if the library is not attempting a historical collection of all the editions of a given title. Books that show the signs of wear, which have become dirty, shabby, or just plain worn out, might be replaced if still significant, or placed in deposit collections. This might be the time to get rid of the mistakes in selection—books which were judged to be of interest and use to a community, but which have turned out to be shelf-sitters. Books which have become obsolete, in contents, style, or theme, should be eliminated by the library which aims at building a vital, useful collection. It is not always difficult to discover books which are now out-of-date. A medium-sized public library which discovers that the only work it has on the economic and political conditions of the Middle East was published in 1900, might justifiably conclude that this book would not give its readers up-to-date information.

Let this distinction, however, be recalled again: there is a difference between the research collection and the ordinary working collection of the public library. In the large public libraries, there may be extensive research collections; in the smaller, there may be special collections which are gathered for their historical importance, as, for example, collections on local history. One ought not to bring the principle of up-to-dateness to bear when looking hard and long at the local history collection. It is unhappily true that some basic collections have been hit hard by a librarian too intent on getting rid of everything which had not circulated in the past three years, or which had been published over ten years ago. To seize one of these injunctions and apply it blindly is as futile as the seizing and blind application of a principle of book selection. Weeding of the individual title is not done in the grand isolation of the book vis-a-vis some weeding principle. There are a number of factors which must figure in the decision: relation of the book to other books in that subject; money available for more satisfactory titles (if this is all one can afford, it may be better to act on the principle that something is better than nothing at all); consideration of the degree to which the library wants to represent older material; possible usefulness of this particular title to some special group or individual in the community: the list could be extended at length. Weeding, like the original selecting, requires judgment; weeding in a particular library requires judgment based on factors which could be known only to the librarian of that particular library. The general injunctions for weeding, like the general injunctions for selecting, must be interpreted and adapted by type of library and type of material, and they will certainly be adapted by the type of librarian doing the job.

This warning has been given at length as a prelude to a list of some suggestions for weeding. It is hoped that no one will seize upon these suggestions as an infallible formula. It is imperative that the librarian recognize them as suggestions and not laws.

Religion and Philosophy: retain systems of philosophy, but discard historical and explanatory texts when superseded, older theology, old commentaries on the Bible, sectarian literature, sermons, and books on the conduct of life, popular self-help psychology, and other guides to living which are old or no longer popular. Be sure to take into account the use made of such materials, which will vary greatly from community to community.

Social Sciences: requires frequent revision, because much of the material will deal with problems of temporary interest, which can be replaced later by historical coverage of these topics. Economics needs careful watching for dates. Superseded almanacs and yearbooks should be discarded.

Language: discard old grammars, ordinary school dictionaries (rarely discard the larger dictionaries). Weed the rest of the collection on the basis of use.

Pure Science: discard books with obsolete information or theories; all general works which have been superseded, unless they are classics in their field; all ordinary textbooks can usually be discarded after ten years. Botany and natural history should be inspected carefully before discarding.

Applied Science: try to keep this section up-to-date by discarding older material. Five to ten years will date much material in fields such as medicine, inventions, radio, television, gardening, business, etc.

Arts, Music, Hobbies, Etc.: discard in the fine arts sparingly. Keep collections of music, engravings, finely illustrated books.

Literature: Keep literary history, unless it is superseded by a better title; keep collected works unless definitely superseded; discard poets and dramatists no longer regarded in literary histories and no longer read; discard the works of minor novelists whose works have not been re-issued and who are no longer of interest to readers.

History: Discard inaccurate or unfair interpretations, much contemporary writing which is now recorded in basic histories (as World War II materials), historical works which are only summaries and are not authoritative, and works of travel over ten years old, unless distinguished by the style or the importance of the author. Keep histories which have become literary classics.

Biography: keep collected biography, but individual lives of persons whose importance is no longer great may be discarded after several decades.

Generally, the following classes should be inspected carefully as potential areas for much weeding: privately printed verse, memoirs, and essays; subjects not currently popular; unused or unneeded volumes of sets; publications of municipalities; multiple editions of books; incomplete runs of periodicals, or periodicals without indexes.

The Community Survey

In the past several years, there has been renewed interest in the problems, procedures, and uses of the community survey for library purposes. The Library-Community Project of the American Library Association, supported by the Fund for Adult Education of the Ford Foundation, carried on a program of community studies in several towns. The idea of studying the community is not new, of course. Librarians have long been admonished to know the community, and Joseph L. Wheeler, in his *The Library and the Community* (published by the American Library Association in 1924), gave an excellent summary statement on the community survey. The addition of specific aids by the Library-Community Project may encourage more librarians to undertake what has been so widely praised but so infrequently practiced.

The importance of knowing the community is, of course, undisputed. The library's selection of books, its special services, its whole operation, is aimed at providing that specific community with what it needs and wants. It is clear that the librarian must know something about his users to function effectively. But just what kind of information he must have, and to what degree of statistical sophistication it must be developed are matters which are not quite as clear. An alert and intelligent librarian can learn a great deal about the library's users simply by using his eyes and ears in his daily stint at the public desk. A careful perusal of the local newspapers and a reasonable amount of contact with the community through service club membership, PTA, church groups, etc., will broaden his knowledge of and understanding of the town and its people. Over a period of time, by using intelligently his opportunities for learning, the librarian can become highly informed. What need would there be for such a librarian to do the more formal survey?

Part of the answer lies in the choice of the adjective "formal". The survey will provide a systematic view of the community; it will enable the librarian to rearrange what he already knows in a larger framework while adding data gathered especially for the survey. The librarian may identify new groups, spot areas of the community not well served, or pick out groups in the community which are not making use of the library. In the very act of organizing the topics which the survey will try to cover, the librarian may discover aspects of the town's life which had not occurred to him before.

Most libraries do not have sufficient staff to undertake such a highly formalized survey, and even if they did, most librarians are not trained for this work. There are two answers to this dilemma: (1) most library studies do not have to be as rigorously formalized as a scientific experiment. The large majority of libraries operate in areas of relatively small populations: one can learn much about them without elaborate statistical instruments. Even the larger libraries may not be interested in a full-scale sociological study. (2) The second answer presupposes that the library is interested in a fairly formal study. This answer reminds the librarians that if they are not trained as social analysts, there are those who are, whose services can be called upon by the library in advising in the planning stages, and again, in aiding in the interpretation of data. Part of the library's ordinary reference material ought to include information on such specialists. Failure to find this information in the library would in itself be the first dividend received in making the survey—it would reveal an area of weakness. State universities, state agencies, local organizations, the state and national library organizations: there are a host of sources of expert advice and consultation.

After planning the survey, perhaps with the aid of outside experts, the actual gathering of the data need not be confined to the library staff. There is much to be said for having a community survey carried on by the members of the community. If the library can enlist the aid of citizens, it will reduce the burden on its staff and involve some members of the community in a library activity, thus spreading an awareness of the library's existence where it may not have been strongly realized before. This also promotes an educational end by having the citizen-participants learning something about their own community. When the survey results are completed, they will form a useful part of the library's own resources.

To recapitulate: in general, a library's survey of the communi-

ty need not be an elaborate statistical enterprise. It seems
advisable to involve members of the community as active workers, while experts in social analysis may be invited in to aid in
the planning stages and in the final evaluation of data. Much of
the data one wants to assemble will already be found in the
library or in the heads of the librarians—all that will need to be
done in those areas is to identify and organize it.

What are the sources of information and what should one look
for in them? There are first the census reports, which will give
general summary information about the population. The figures
in themselves are not so significant. It is when one starts
comparing the community's population with other communities'
that the figures begin to take on meaning. To discover that a
town has a population with a median age of 42.7 years does not
tell much. To compare this figure with a national median age of
30.2 tells a great deal. To say that 33.6 per cent of the families in
a community had incomes over $5,000 takes on added signifi-
cance if the national average is 20 per cent. Comparing with the
averages for the state or for other cities of comparable size will
help characterize the community. One can look for changes over
the years. Has the population increased or decreased? (and what
were the national and state populations doing at the same time?)
Has the level of education risen? How does it compare with
state and national levels? The census figures, then, should be
checked for highs and lows, for variations from state and national norms, and for evidence of change.

A second source consists of reports and studies of that community which have already been made. Do these reports single out
any special problems? Do they attempt any explanations of the
reasons why the community is what it is? Do they attempt to
predict the future conditions of the community? The reports
may be enlarged upon by a study of histories of the community
or locality, which may reveal the patterns of cultural change, the
development of traditions, the history of institutions and their
activities.

The organizational structure of the community should be
studied. The various educational groups and agencies may have
reports which will indicate their purpose, membership, and
activities. The same type of information should be gathered for
the several service or social clubs. Knowing what groups are

operating in a community and knowing what people constitute their membership can tell a great deal about a community. The survey might also study the newspapers, radio, television, and sources of books—bookstores, newstands, etc.—to discover what kind of informational materials are available to the community and how the community makes use of these resources. Members of the community may also be interviewed to ascertain how they view their city and how closely the facts about the community agree with the image held by the citizens.

When all these data are gathered and analyzed, the librarian has to decide which of the facts are significant for the library, and what it can do to meet the problems revealed. All the facts piled up in the report of the survey do not equal a decision as to what the library should do. But the facts may indicate what groups make up the community and what those groups are doing, which activities the library might be able to support with appropriate materials; they may reveal certain areas of the city or elements of its population which are not now being served effectively; they may reveal reading interests which could be used as a guide to book selection; they may reveal data useful in planning new buildings or guiding the selection of staff for the various branches.

Bibliography

Surveying and Weeding Collections

Ash, Lee H. Yale's *Selective Book Retirement Program*. Hamden, Conn., Archon Books, 1963.

Erickson, E. Walfred. "College and University Library Surveys, 1938-52." Chicago, ALA, 1961. (ACRL Monograph No.25). Chapter VIII, p. 70-75.

Fussler, Herman H., and Simon, Julian L. *Patterns in the Use of Books in Large Research Libraries*. Chicago, University of Chicago Library, 1961. (See material on weeding for storage.)

Line, Maurice B. *Library Surveys: An Introduction to their Use, Planning, Procedure, and Presentation*. Archon Books, 1967.

Tauber, Maurice F., and Stephens, Irene, eds. *Library Surveys*. NY, Columbia University Press, 1967.

Wisconsin Free Library Commission. *Weeding the Library: Suggestions for Small Libraries.* Madison, Wisconsin, 1949.

Surveying the Community

A.L.A. Library-Community Project Headquarters Staff. *Studying the Community: a Basis for Planning Adult Education Services.* Chicago, ALA, 1960.

Carnovsky, Leon and Martin, Lowell, eds. *The Library and the Community.* Chicago, University of Chicago Press, 1944.

Sanders, Irwin T. *Preparing a Community Profile; the Methodology of a Social Reconnaissance.* Lexington, University of Kentucky, Bureau of Community Service, 1952.

Warren, Roland. *Studying Your Community.* New York, Russell Sage Foundation, 1955.

Wheeler, Joseph L. *The Library and the Community.* Chicago, ALA, 1929.

Chapter VII

Censorship and Book Selection

A Fundamental Problem

The basic cause of attempts at censorship of library collections derives from the very nature of our society. Democratic societies are characterized by constant tension between the freedom of the individual and the demands of organized living. It is clear that in a free society, no matter how much liberty to differ men may have, there must be some areas of general agreement or community life could not continue. We have agreed to accept many limitations of our God-given right to liberty: we patiently apply for drivers' licenses; we submit to limitations on the number of deer we may shoot or the number of fish we may catch; we accept the prescribed times allotted to the hunting and fishing seasons; we allow the government to withhold our income tax in advance; and we accept a great many similar restrictions. However much we may be irked by one or another of these curbs on our actions, we are quite passive in accepting most of them.

American society has always believed that in the area of intellectual life, as opposed to the series of actions which make up our social life, such restrictions are abominable. The concept of thought control is abhorrent to us. We shrink from the idea of subliminal advertising to sell us a product. We submit to the curtailment of our actions but rebel at the curtailment of thought. Here at least we will be free!

Libraries represent the embodiment in books of human thought which we respect so highly. Our feeling for the sacredness of living thought adheres to these artifacts which preserve

147

the record of past thought. The burning of a book strikes the lover of freedom with something like the same horror as the burning of its author. Attacks on library collections for their inclusion of one title or another seem attacks on the human intellect itself. And ˙certainly, as a general principle of life, librarians ought to stand strongly for the freedom of communication, for the freedom of intellectual activity, for the freedom of thought which their institutions represent. They ought to resist all attempts to limit the use of libraries in the search for wisdom, knowledge, peace of mind, or entertainment.

However, there is a difference between freedom of thought and freedom of expression. Society may be willing to allow us to think what we please, but it does not allow us complete freedom to communicate whatever we think. The moment thought moves out of the mind in written or spoken form it becomes action and encounters licenses and rules, seasons and withholding taxes. The law restrains us from uttering libels and slanders, from false reports of crimes and fires; it limits and restricts the products of our fertile imaginations from finding unlimited propagation.

Books are thoughts put into concrete form. Society has laid restrictions on the freedom of the book to communicate, just as it has restricted the individual's freedom to communicate. The problem which confronts society eternally with regard to books is simply this: at what point does a book-contained communication become dangerous and thus subject to suppression?

This question implies that there is someone who can decide when that point has been reached and that there are measures which can be applied; that there is a calculus of sedition, a yardstick of moral disintegrativeness. Unfortunately for the easy application of this necessary social regulation, democratic societies are not homogeneous. The very nature of the principles underlying freedom gives rise to a certain degree of dissimilarity among the citizens. Even in mass-production, robotized cultures, the assembly line worker is not a carbon copy of all his fellows; he is an individual. He may be less various in some of his attitudes than another type of worker might be (the researcher in pure mathematics, perhaps, building unthought-of geometries), but he still retains the stamp of individual humanity.

The existence of this variety leads to complications in attempting to protect the people from evil. Attitudes toward what is evil are not uniform. The old admonition that one man's meat is another man's poison certainly applies in this area of attitudes. To attempt to determine the median attitude or to attempt to measure the sum of total attitudes in a large population and then strike an average attitude appears to be quite difficult and not a little silly. The would-be censor has to fall back on guesses as to what the community feels, or he relies on his own shocked attitudes and extrapolates from them. "What dismays me," he is forced to say, "must necessarily dismay thee."

If the censor is delicate and tender of mind, he may restrict long before the danger point for his readers is reached. And, in any case, there will be different points of danger for different readers in his community. He may hit on the solution of shutting off all books which might offend the most sensitive or the least mature mind. The basic fact which must be faced is that all the people do not conceive of evil in the same way, and that even among those who do, the thresholds of titillation or sedition vary. This is the inevitable conundrum for the censor in a free society, for the free society does not require such uniformity of attitudes as the censor must have for the operation of his rules.

There is another variation which arises. The line marking off the socially permissible from the socially dangerous is not fixed, it shifts from time to time and from place to place within the same period. What shocked or horrified the reader of 1910 may seem innocuous today. What shocks or horrifies the reader in the rural hamlet today may leave his big-city contemporary unshaken.

This shifting in what is considered permissible is amply demonstrated in the efforts of the courts to find some stable definition of obscenity. For some 90 years, the United States Supreme Court followed the doctrine set down by British Chief Justice Cockburn in *Regina v. Hicklin* (1868). Judge Cockburn defined obscenity as follows: ". . . whether the tendency of the matter charged is to deprave and corrupt those whose minds are open to such immoral influences, and into whose hands a publication of this sort may fall." The Lord Chief Justice maintained that even if the purpose of the work were honest and laudable, it did not matter: what is obscene (by his test) is obscene—and there's an end to it!

In 1933, however, enough time had marched on past great

Victoria's heyday so that the Cockburn definition could be refined. In the case of the *United States v. Ulysses*, District Judge John M. Woolsey found that theretofore infamous novel not pornographic, if frank. He noted that the legal definition of obscenity is "that which tends to stir the sex impulses or to lead to sexually impure and lustful thoughts." But, he pointed out, the law is concerned only with the normal person, and thus the court must attempt to assess the effect of a particular book upon a person of average sexual instincts. Judge Woolsey borrowed a French phrase to describe this hypothetical normal man which the court would use as a test—*"l'homme moyen sensuel."* His decision was upheld by Circuit Judge Augustus N. Hand. (Both decisions make excellent reading. They are reproduced in Robert Downs' *First Freedom*).

Thus the doctrine that all reading must be safe for the weakest, most susceptible mind was set aside. In 1957, the Supreme Court gave its endorsement to the view that the stable adult mind must be the governing factor when it struck down the state of Michigan's censorship law in *Butler v. Michigan.* Justice Felix Frankfurter remarked: "[Michigan] insists that, by thus quarantining the general reading public against books not too rugged for grown men and women *in order to shield juvenile innocence* [italics added] it is exercising its power to promote the general welfare. Surely this is to burn the house to roast the pig ... [This reduces] the adult population of Michigan to reading only what is fit for children."

The Court had second thoughts in 1968, at least to a limited extent, when it sustained a New York law which makes it a punishable offense to sell certain types of materials to young people, even though their sale to adults would be legal. This decision followed a decade of court decisions which seemed to be widening the area of permissible publications.

On January 1, 1968, President Johnson named 18 members to a Commission on Obscenity and Pornography, which had been authorized by Public Law 90-100. The Commission is to conduct a thorough study of the effect of obscenity and pornography upon the public and of the relationship of pornography to anti-social behavior. It is to analyze the laws pertaining to the control of obscenity and pornography; to recommend definitions of obscenity and pornography; to investigate the methods employed in the distribution of obscene and pornographic materials as well as the nature and volume of the traffic; and to recommend actions to control that traffic without in any way interfering with constitutional rights. Frederick H. Wagman, Director of the University of Michigan Library, was the only librarian appointed to the Commission. To carry out its work, the Commission is empowered to "make contracts with universities, research institutions, foundations, laboratories, hospitals, and other competent public or private agencies to conduct research." The final report is due January 31, 1970; after that date, perhaps Congress will pass definitive legislation, perhaps ending the uncertainties and confusion in this matter.

At the state level, the uncertainties have been even greater, and have certainly not been as permissive. Many state laws are more restrictive than the Supreme Court and not all those laws have been challenged and brought before the high tribunal. The Supreme Court seems to judge obscenity by the effect of a book taken as a whole (not merely basing judgment upon passages taken in isolation) upon a mature, intelligent, and fairly sophisticated adult. Even when the book seems pretty far out on the scale, the Court has refused to condemn it if it had any redeeming social significance or artistic merit. But state courts—and certainly many local magistrates and police forces—have been less ready to depart from Cockburn's century-old definition. Thus the same old variations in judgment, feeling, and opinion arise to create continuing difficulties at the local level.

The fact that these difficulties are real and do exist does not mean that censors will abandon their efforts. They might say—to cite the classic case, which is so often advanced in this argument—that we all know it is dangerous to cry "Fire!" in a crowded building. Similarly, we know it is dangerous to issue a book which cries its own version of "Fire!" for all to hear. It may be that panic does not ensue every time someone falsely raises the alarm in a theater. Does it then follow that laws against such an action are unnecessary or undesirable? A wicked or seditious book may not lead to social upheaval in every case, but does it therefore follow that no attempt should be made to protect society against evil and sedition?

Such a question is legitimate and is very difficult to answer. For the problem is not simple, however much we might wish it were. No matter how strong our conviction in the ideal of a free press, there is a realization in every one of us that there is a line beyond which we do not believe it is right for a publisher to go. There are books which each of us would find too disgusting, too vile, to countenance (although some of us might be far out along the scale before we rebelled). Somewhere there is a book which even the most trusting of us might consider so devilishly clever in its treason as to constitute a threat to the security of the State.

The central weakness of all demands for censorship can be put simply: the censor is sure that *he* can recognize evil—but that the people cannot. The desire for censorship arises from a simple lack of faith in the powers of judgment and discrimination of others. Other people must be protected from evil, we say, but what we are really saying is that they are not bright enough, not good enough, not trustworthy enough to protect themselves. They cannot see what we see so clearly; so we must not allow them to look upon the book whose evil is so obvious to us.

In any other area, such an attitude would be characterized as the most blatant arrogance. And for a member of a democratic society, in which the sovereign power resides with the people, such a lack of faith in the people's judgment is strange indeed. If the people cannot be trusted to read and react intelligently to books, what can they be trusted with? If the censor is honest, he must perforce reply that, of course, they cannot really be trusted at all; they must be shepherded and guided along the right ways. This is by no means a new idea in the world, but it is truly, fundamentally, and completely anti-democratic. If we are to be truly free to choose what we wish, we must be allowed the luxurious freedom of choosing wrongly. To take the view of democracy that the people are free to believe whatever they choose, so long as what they believe is right, is to confess oneself no believer in freedom.

The people do not need to be protected from evil by any self-appointed or official vigilante group, because most people will not be utterly corrupted by any reading experience. Even the most normal and balanced person has his moments and his areas of undesirable desires, but this fact does not warp his whole personality. To say that because a person occasionally enjoys a book that is not all it should be, is only to say that we are all human. But to say that such occasional reading demonstrates complete rottenness and unreliability of the mind is too extreme a statement. The reader must make moral choices for himself, and, while we believe that in the long run he will be a responsible and stable citizen, we cannot deny to him his basic human right to make his own mistakes. Broadening one's horizons is not only a matter of going always onward and upward—it includes also the experience of sinking downward and backward. These regressions are a normal part of life, and the human right to err, to slip, to sin, to stumble—and to recover oneself—must be insisted upon.

A special problem arises, of course, in dealing with minds which are not wholly normal, which are particularly weak or susceptible, which are inclined to corruption. But who is qualified to pick out these minds? It must be assumed that an adult is responsible for carrying the burden of his own adulthood. The psychiatric or psycho-analytic treatment of the non-normal mind must be left to those qualified to deal with it. The library is not a mental hospital, and society cannot tolerate that its activities should be limited by the restrictions necessary in a hospital ward in order to give treatment to the few who are unbalanced. To restrict all sound and intelligent adults to the reading safe for the near-insane is as unsound a procedure as to restrict all sound and intelligent adults to the reading safe for children.

A Contemporary Problem

In addition to this general problem, arising out of the very nature of democracy, there is a further current problem caused by a change in the understanding—by some people, at least—of the meaning of democracy. There has been a tendency in mid-twentieth century America toward a more restricted view of democratic life, which might be described as a belief in the freedom to conform. We all recognize that the public library is a social institution whose characteristics have been determined by the nature of the society in which it developed. What we sometimes forget is the additional truism that society is not static and that as society alters the institutions which it supports also change.

Perhaps the simplest definition of democracy which one

could make would be that it is a system in which every man is equal before the law. He cannot be arrested without due process, he cannot be condemned without a trial, his house cannot be invaded without a warrant, his speech cannot be limited except by the libel and slander laws, his religion remains a matter for his private conscience. By a simple extension of that idea of equality, one moves out of the realm of democracy into something which is really quite different, and which has been ponderously described as conformatarian equalitarianism. In its most extreme form, this point of view holds that man is not only equal before the law, but that he is intellectually, socially, spiritually, esthetically, and morally equal to all other men. Equal, in a democratic society, means entitled to the same treatment; in an equalitarian society, equal means alike.

The argument behind this system of thought is simple. Nature is a uniform mechanism; her laws are everywhere and at all times the same; the minds of men are part of that natural machinery; they too—everywhere and in all ages, like all natural things—have been alike. Why do all men not think alike, if this is true? Because of a faulty system of social training and education. If one could only reform this faulty system, all men would think alike.

The development of mass-production economies has added impetus to the belief that all men are fundamentally alike. We eat the same prepared cereals, hear the same broadcasts, enjoy the same sports, drive the same kinds of cars, wear the same kind of clothing, talk about the same scandals, value the same goods, are buried in the same way. Exterior appearance and the daily life of society seem to argue that all men are alike.

If this point of view continues to extend itself unchecked, the public library as we have known it will not be able to survive. One of the unique features of the library collection was the fact that the reader could find books there of every complexion, that he could· find ideas aired there which would not be disseminated through the agencies of mass communication. This function makes the library most suspect in the eyes of the equalitarian, for this diversity is dangerously subversive of their conception. Censorship becomes much more understandable if one accepts this view. It is the aim of the equalitarian to discourage controversy and discussion in order to preserve essential community uniformity. To talk of presenting trustworthy information on all sides of a subject, to think of furnishing people with evidence which can broaden their understanding of a problem, to try to present contemporary issues in their full complexity violates their cardinal principle—that all issues are really very simple.

Book selection in the equalitarian framework becomes a very simple matter: one selects those things which are general enough and harmless enough to be handed out to the least intelligent, the least capable, the least discriminating. There is always the possibility that if one chose books in any other manner one of the less capable might stumble on a book which would disorganize his simplified thinking, and so the book collection must be directed at the lowest level of comprehension.

In the struggle between equalitarianism and democracy, librarians may feel few and weak. They may feel that the library as an institution makes no great impact upon the community. Let the less optimistic librarians never underestimate the power of a book, let them reflect on the fact that one of the first acts of the tyrant is to destroy books, those dangerous purveyors of freedom.

The public library was conceived as a democratic institution—that is, one to which individuals with widely-differing capabilities and ambitions could come for a variety of books on every subject. To attempt to make it an equalitarian institution is folly, for it cannot survive under such a system. It could make its peace with such a master only at the price of surrendering all those attributes which have made it what it is.

Public librarians must decide whether they will set their institution's force—whatever it may be—against the tide of equalitarianism, or whether they will permit their libraries to serve the forces of robotization. They must decide whether they will work to preserve individual thought, or help to obliterate all independent thinking. They must decide whether they will help to carry the gospel of individual freedom or sink back inactive.

The public library is a social institution whose nature is determined by the society which supports it. There is nothing in this commonplace which dictates that the library must play a passive role in society. As a social institution, it has the potentiality—and librarians have the moral responsibility—to use the force of the institution to help preserve free access to reliable and unbiased information.

Some Pragmatic Considerations

In discussing the principles of book selection, a distinction was made between the ideal library and the actual library in any given community. Thus far in this chapter, discussion has consisted of prescriptions for the ideal attitude toward censorship. It is easy to give assent to these principles as long as the discussion remains general. What happens to this easy assent when the discussion begins to involve an actual library, trying to function in a real community?

It has been enunciated as one of the guiding principles of selection that a librarian should know his community and select for its needs. Let us suppose that a librarian has selected a book which he judged the community wanted, or needed, and that he is then faced with vehement, angry, impassioned criticism for having chosen such a book. Does not the very existence of this principle justify him in removing the book post haste? After all, if he is supposed to select for his particular community, it is implied that he is not to select books which are of no interest to that community. Is it not obvious that he has even less right to select a book to which the community is opposed?

The librarian does indeed select for his community. But if this means the whole community (whether conceived of as the community of actual library users, or the community of non-users as well, who are all potential users), then one can ask, is it the whole community which objects to a given book? Does such objection not usually start, at least, with some individual or group? Is the librarian justified in removing a book to which only part of the community objects? Even if a majority of the users object to a book, do not the minority have a right to find it in the library?

One could, of course, raise the legal question as to who has the ultimate responsibility for book selection. An objecting individual or group could be told that the library board has legal responsibility for selecting, that the job is one to be done by those trained in this area, that the board will not surrender its prerogatives, that it will insist upon buying what it considers good. This may all be true enough, if the current law so states, but it may not be the best way of meeting the situation. Will financial support be forthcoming if the library acts in an autocratic and high-handed manner, no matter how legally correct its stand may be? Such a position might well engender greater hostility toward the library than the presence of the controversial book itself.

Once the issue has been joined the problem moves out of the realm of book selection into that of library administration, but the fear of such a situation can be intimately connected with book selection. A librarian may attempt to avoid any such turn of events simply by not purchasing a potentially controversial book, even though it might be of interest to part of the community. This might be called, not book selection, but book evasion. That such a procedure is sometimes followed has been demonstrated in *Book Selection and Censorship* by Marjorie Fiske. A sampling of librarians in California revealed that although the librarians interviewed believed that the controversial nature of the book should not enter into selection, about one-fifth actually omitted such books. In other cases restricted circulation of these books was substituted for refusal to purchase. She found that professionally trained librarians with professional association affiliations were less restrictive, although the longer such a librarian had worked in a community, the more cautious he became in the selection of controversial materials. Without studies of other states, it is not possible to generalize her findings. It seems reasonable to assume, however, that avoidance of controversy would be found to some degree in other places.

Another problem is the danger of censorship by the librarian because of the librarian's own personal disapproval of a given book. How can the librarian himself maintain impartiality when he has his own strong convictions and sees them violated by a book? Will the librarian who disapproved of a political demagogue buy books defending him? If a novel outrages the librarian's personal standards of morality and decency—assuming, for the sake of argument, that those standards were more rigid than those of his readers—would there not be a temptation to pass it over in silence? If the librarian is firmly

convinced that America stands in dire peril of Communist subversion, would he not be very loath to represent the Communist
point of view in his collection?

When the discussion moves from the general principles to a
specific book in a particular library in a real town inhabited by
actual people, the problem gets harder and harder to solve
easily and comfortably.

Once again, it can only be concluded that there are no
general prescriptions whĭch will enable us to achieve desired
results without judgment. But the problems raised here suggest
(and this moves once more into the realm of administration) that
one of the constant activities of the library must be that of
explaining its role in a democracy. The library has the responsibility for making clear to the community that it represents the
democratic ideal of tolerance, that it has the duty to be many-
sided, to give service to all of the citizens, and not just those of
one particular shade of opinion. That this task will not always be
easy, that on occasions it may be impossible, that sometimes it
may not be worldly wise, is beyond doubt.

There is at least the comfort that the proponents of censorship
remain convinced that books are important enough to be concerned about. They firmly believe that books make a difference,
that they can lead to actions in the real world, and that the work
done in this world by the librarians is important enough to
demand watching.

Realizing that the librarian cannot evade the responsibility for
making decisions in this difficult matter, one begins to see
clearly that the personal characteristics of the librarian acting as
selector are very important in determining how he will react to
the problems of censorship. The personality, convictions, honesty, and courage of the librarian will influence the course of
action taken when groups or individuals outside the library
attempt to control its holdings, just as these characteristics will
also figure in the librarian's own attempt to select impartially. It
is essential that we look closely at the librarian-selector, on
whom we have laid so heavy a charge. What kinds of librarians
must we have to insure the satisfactory performance of this
difficult task?

Bibliography

A.L.A. *Bill of Rights.* [See Appendix A]

A.L.A. Intellectual Freedom Committee. *Freedom of Book Selection.* Chicago, ALA, 1954.

A.L.A. Intellectual Freedom Committee. *Freedom of Communication.* Chicago, ALA, 1954.

A.L.A. "How Libraries and Schools Can Resist Censorship." *ALA Bulletin,* March 1962. p.228-9.

A.L.A. *Intellectual Freedom Committee. Newsletter.* v.1- 1952-

A.L.A. Intellectual Freedom Committee. *Supporting the Library Bill of Rights.* ALA, 1965.

Asheim, Lester. "Not Censorship, But Selection." [See Appendix A]

Asheim, Lester. "Problems of Censorship in Book Selection." *Bay State Librarian,* January 1962.

Blakey, G. Robert. "Obscenity and the Supreme Court." *America,* August 13; 1966. p.152-6.

Daniels, Walter. *The Censorship of Books.* NY, Wilson, 1954. (Reference Shelf, v.26, no.5)

Danton, J. Periam, ed. *The Climate of Book Selection; Social Influences on School and Public Libraries.* Papers Presented at a Symposium Held at the University of California July 10-12, 1958. Berkeley, Univ. of Cal. School of Librarianship, 1959.

Downs, Robert B. *The First Freedom; Liberty and Justice in the World of Books and Reading.* Chicago, ALA, 1960.

Ernst, Morris L. To the Pure; *A Study of Obscenity and the Censor.* NY, Viking, 1928.

Fiske, Marjorie. *Book Selection and Censorship; a Study of School and Public Libraries in California.* Berkeley, Univ. of California Press, 1959. [Reprinted 1968]

Frank, John P., and Hogan, Robert F. *Obscenity, the Law, and the English Teacher.* National Council of Teachers of English, 1966.

Freedom to Read Kit. Bureau of Independent Publishers & Distributors, 1966.

Haight, Anne L. *Banned Books.* 2d ed. NY, Bowker, 1955.

Kerr, Walter. *Criticism and Censorship.* Milwaukee, Bruce, 1954.

Kilpatrick, James J. *The Smut Peddlers.* Doubleday, 1960.
  1960.
McClellan, Grant S., ed. *Censorship in the United States.* NY,
  Wilson, 1967.
McCormick, John. *Versions of Censorship; An Anthology.* Doub-
  bleday, 1962. (Anchor Books A297)
McKeon, Richard P. *The Freedom to Read; Perspective and
  Program.* NY, Bowker, 1957.
Molz, Kathleen. "The Public Custody of the High Pornography."
  American Scholar, Winter 1966/67. p.93-103.
Nelson, Jack, and Roberts, Gene, Jr. *The Censors and the
  Schools.* NY, Little, Brown, 1963.
Pilpel, Harriet F. "But Can You Do That? *Publishers' Weekly,*
  July 29, 1968. p.36-37.
Rembar, Charles. The End of Obscenity; *The Trials of Lady
  Chatterley, Tropic of Cancer, and Fanny Hill.* NY, Random
  House, 1968.
Westchester Conference of the American Library Association
  and the American Publishers Council. *The Freedom to Read.*
  [See Appendix A]

Chapter VIII

The Publishing Trade

The publishing trade is closely connected with library book selection in that it sets the limits within which the library book selector must work. Libraries cannot select books which are not published, and thus the willingness—or lack of it—on the part of publishers to risk producing a book will determine what the libraries find available to choose from. If the publishers do not feel a responsibility to produce quality materials, the libraries will not be able to select quality materials. If the publishers find that the nature of their market limits the types of books they can produce, libraries may find that a full representation of subjects and a wide range of treatments of subjects will not be made. It is not the purpose of this chapter to discuss in great detail the history and nature of the book trade, but to restrict the discussion to those aspects of the trade which have an impact on the books available for library purchase.

The Structure of the Industry

The publishing trade is not one of the giant industries of the United States. Since 1958, total sales have exceeded $1 billion per year, reaching $2 billion in 1966. To put this figure in its proper perspective vis-a-vis our larger industries, one must remember that the *net profit* of one of our truly large corporations exceeded $2.5 billion in that year. One spokesman for the book industry remarked that people spend more for dog food than for textbooks and more for caskets than for trade books.

The trade was characterized in the past—and is still largely so today—by a larger number of relatively small producers. The total number of American publishers has been estimated variously. There are certainly more than 1,000 trade publishers, but, if one includes publishing agencies outside the book trade, the number would certainly reach several thousand. If one thinks of governmental units at all levels of government as publishers, then the count would soar impressively. Of the trade publishers, only 25 produced more than 100 titles in 1955; by 1962, the number was increased to 66, and by 1967 the total had reached 94—almost a 50% increase since 1942. In 1955, only 313 publishers issued over five titles that year; by 1967, 618 were issuing at least 5 titles. By way of contrast, one might invoke the automobile industry, which has substantially only three major producers, and, indeed, perhaps it is just to say two major producers. Over the years, however, this industry of book publishing, with its many, independent, and small producers, has been turning out more and more books.

One of the striking features of the book trade in the late 1950's was the beginning of a series of mergers, which is altering the former structure of the trade somewhat. In the past, librarians were admonished to become familiar with individual publishing firms, to learn their characteristics, to estimate their reliability— and firms had, by and large, individual and stable personalities. It is becoming increasingly difficult to make very definite statements about individual firms, because firms are merging, being bought out, buying out other firms in turn, and generally swirling around at a giddy pace which leaves the onlooker somewhat confused. When mergers reach the hundred mark— and push on beyond—it becomes difficult to remember just who has merged with whom. Many of the mergers are of recent enough vintage so that it is difficult to estimate what the impact will be on the character of the old firms. The reason for this development can be found in the growing disparity between the inefficiencies of the small, independent companies and the steadily rising costs of a mass production economy. As costs have risen steadily, publishers have been forced to seek the economies implicit in large scale operations. There has been a tendency for the general trade publisher to ally himself with a textbook publisher—anyone familiar with the statistics of the burgeoning school population can see the reasonableness of such a move.

In the 1960's, the mergers continued (between 1962 and 1967, for example, some 124 publishers were involved in some kind of merger). A second interesting development was the invasion of publishing by non-publishing corporations which bought up established firms. Xerox bought Bowker as well as University Microfilms; Columbia Broadcasting System bought Holt, Rinehart, and Winston, itself a product of mergers; Radio Corporation of America bought Random House; *Time* cast abroad to buy Editions Laffont (France), while it also bought the American firm, Silver-Burdett, and then joined with General Electric to turn Silver-Burdette into General Learning.

That last name, "General Learning," gives some clue as to the nature of the attraction of publishing firms to outside organizations. The level of education has been rising steadily, and every study of reading has shown that the amount of reading done rises as level of education rises. The book market is bound to increase if an ever-increasing percentage of a constantly-increasing population goes on to college. In addition, the federal programs of aid to schools, college, university, and public libraries for the purchase of materials have certainly made publishing more attractive as a source of earnings. In fiscal 1967 and 1968, the money appropriated for purchase of materials under the Elementary and Secondary Education Act, the Library Services and Construction Act, the Higher Education Act, and the Medical Library Assistance Act amounted to more than 295 million dollars.

Still another development in publishing is the great expansion of the reprint business, reflecting the growth in the number of new colleges and junior colleges; the evolution of teachers' colleges to universities (with a concomitant need to build up collections, including retrospective materials in order to support the expanded curricula); the development of new programs at universities (such as the area study programs) which also demand the purchase of retrospective materials; the development of new methods of reproducing books, especially since the end of World War II. The number of firms engaged in reprinting has increased, as has the number of titles reprinted—whether in traditional type settings, facsimile, or reproduced from microfilm.

One of the complaints librarians have made about publishers in the past is the speed with which they let their books go out of print. For many titles, if the library did not purchase copies within a year, or even six months, after publication, it would discover that the book was out of print and not easily obtainable—if at all. When the long-awaited *Books for College Libraries* was published, some librarians were unhappy because they calculated that some 40% of the titles listed were out of print, and thus not much help for the college trying to develop an "instant collection." But the need for such retrospective materials, coupled with the injection of federal money and increases in libraries' book budgets, has led to the reprinting of many out-of-print titles. Indeed, reproduction from microfilm has enabled at least one firm to offer reprint editions of a single copy. Selection and acquisition librarians must now add to their necessary bibliographies those lists which attempt to keep track of "reprints-in-print." (Some bibliographies of reprints are included in the bibliography at the end of this chapter.)

Another important change has been the enormous growth of the paperback industry. Larger and larger quantities of copies are sold, with prices moving up as "quality" paperbacks appear. In the early 1960's, paperbacks reached a rate of sale of 1 million copies a day. Standard publishers moved into the publishing of paperbacks, drawing on their backlists, publishing classics in the public domain, and sometimes issuing original editions of new works. The paperback market came of age when it developed its own in-print list (Bowker's *Paperbound Books in Print*). Paperbound books are now not only distributed through the old magazine stand channels (as they had been for decades in the cheaper versions), but appear in bookstores, in direct competition with their hard cover cousins. Librarians have been mixed in their reaction to the paperback blessing, but the past decade has seen steadily growing use of the paperback in libraries of all kinds.

Another important development in publishing has been the burgeoning of the book clubs, which has turned out to be a marvelously successful way of distributing books, rather than through the high cost book store route. It is essentially a mail order procedure, and its ease has tapped a very large audience, who will buy a book by mail, but who may never have patronized a book store. The clubs have expanded from the big, general reader type (Book-of-the-Month Club, Literary Guild, etc.) to smaller and more specialized clubs (history, mysteries, etc.), which appeal to a narrower audience.

Problems of the Industry

What are the problems of this industry which may affect the kind of books which libraries will find on sale? Various spokesmen for the trade have all fairly well agreed that the dominant factor is the rise in the break-even point, i.e., the number of copies at which the publisher recovers his investment and begins to show a profit. Postwar costs have soared for the publisher as for others, with the result that publishers are finding it more and more important to discover books which will sell large numbers of copies. Even more unfortunate, several spokesmen for the industry have asserted that—particularly because of the high cost of distribution—a publisher may suffer a small loss on each trade copy of a book sold. He must rely on the sale of subsidiary rights (to movies, TV, book clubs, paperback reprint publishers) to realize a profit. There is, as a result, an understandable tendency for the publisher to search for some books, at least, which will achieve the kind of popularity which will create a demand for the title in Hollywood. The book which can appeal to such a wide audience as is represented by the movies, TV, and the book clubs, must have some of the characteristics of the product of the mass media—that is, it must be enjoyable to millions and must not be offensive to any large group. It may tend to take on some of the colorlessness or lack of originality in presenting new or different ideas too often characteristic of the product of the mass media.

This trend could have unfortunate effects in the long run. The publisher used to be able to put out a book if he thought he could find an audience of a few thousand readers. He would not have to stake his whole investment on any departure from any expected pattern in his publishing. He could attempt to reach many different audiences with many different kinds of books,

any one of which would not have to appeal to his total audience.
Printed books were one of the few places where unpopular or
unorthodox or untried ideas could get an airing; such a luxury
cannot often be indulged in by the mass media.

One way of meeting these rising costs, as was remarked
earlier, is to form larger firms, pooling resources and elimina-
ting duplicating and inefficient facilities. This reduction of the
cost would help to meet the problem of rising break-even points.
In addition, book publishing firms have "gone public," that is,
they have begun to sell stock on the open market in an effort to
raise larger amounts of capital. Raising capital by stock sales,
rather than borrowing, reduces interest charges, but this is of
course offset to some degree by the need to issue dividends if
the stock is to continue to sell. A general publisher who has
consolidated shipping and billing operations by merging with
another firm (or two, or three), who has raised capital by sale of
stock, and who has been wise enough to merge with a textbook
firm with a good solid line of elementary and secondary
textbooks may well find himself in the position of being able to
publish some of the worth-while books he wants to publish, for
which he knows there will not be a large market. In this way he
becomes less dependent on the need for the patronage of the
mass media markets—movies, television, the book clubs. It is
possible, of course, that the pressure of producing presentable
returns on the stockholders' investment may lead him to seek
fewer and fewer titles, all as mass-media-like as possible. Only
time will decide whether the optimists or pessimists among the
commentators on the recent changes in publishing are right.

A very common way of meeting rising costs in any business is
to raise prices. The book publishing industry is no different from
others in this regard. There has been a steady rise in prices since
the 1940's, as a check of the annual figures compiled by *Publishers' Weekly* will demonstrate. This particular solution has hit
libraries especially hard, because in the last 20 years, library
salaries have had to be increased to attract staff, at a time when
library budgets have not risen as fast as library needs. A larger
and larger part of total budgets has had to go to salaries. Many
libraries now spend less than 15 per cent of their budget on
books, periodicals, and binding. While the amount available for

books has been shrinking, the cost of the individual book has been rising, producing an intensified effect. One solution to this doubling effect would be to shift larger amounts of money to the purchase of more inexpensive paperback books, but this particular solution, as was remarked earlier, has not seemed a happy one to many librarians.

When one considers the special interests of libraries in the publishers' product, the question immediately arises as to how much influence library demands might have on the publishing trade. If libraries represent a large part of the publishers' business, the need of libraries would undoubtedly be given serious consideration. If, on the other hand, the bulk of sales go to other types of consumers, it is clear that their needs or desires must be given primary consideration. The 1957 total dollar receipts of publishers have been estimated at $919.7 million, while library budgets for book purchase in that year (including all types of libraries and all types of books) were estimated at $90 million, or approximately 9.7 per cent of the total publishers' receipts. In 1965, total dollar receipts of publishers had risen to $988 million, while library budgets had risen to $167 million—or about 10 per cent of publishers' receipts. If these figures really mean what they appear to, library business would not seem to be a major factor in the publishing trade.

This over-all figure is somewhat misleading, however. Mr. Daniel Melcher, Vice-President of R. R. Bowker Co. and publisher of *Library Journal* has presented a more detailed breakdown of the library market by type of book in *Publishers' Weekly*, March 2, 1959. His total figures are close to the estimates cited in the preceding paragraph. He gives the total sales by publishers in 1957 as $799,000,000, with the libraries' total purchases as $75,000,000, or approximately 9.4 per cent, a slightly lower figure than the 9.7 per cent cited above.

However, Mr. Melcher estimates that libraries' purchases represented 27 per cent of adult trade sales (unfortunately, this figure was not broken down by fiction and non-fiction categories), 50 per cent of juveniles costing over $1.00, 53 per cent of university press books, 44 per cent of business, technical, and scientific books (as well as 22 per cent of the mail order sales of these types), and 27 per cent of law and medical books. On the

other hand, libraries purchased only 3.5 per cent of gross sales of
subscription books, 2 per cent of book club titles, 2 per cent of
paperbound titles, 9 per cent of juveniles under $1.00, and 0.4
per cent of textbooks. Thus, the general figure must be interpreted in terms of the type of book, for these percentages
indicate clearly that the library market bulks large in certain
categories. Although the over-all percentage of total gross sales
to libraries is low, university presses, publishers of business,
technical, scientific, law, and high-priced juveniles depend very
heavily on the library market. On the basis of his counts and
estimates, Mr. Melcher feels that the library market is of real
importance to book publishers. The authors have seen no comparable analysis for more recent years, but they feel that there
would not have been any significant reduction in the importance attributed to library purchasing. If anything, the addition
of federal funds would have increased the importance of the
library market.

In talking about the publishing trade in this chapter, especially in regard to the production of books which appeal to large
audiences versus those which have a more limited appeal, the
authors have been thinking largely of the "trade" book. They
suspect that when public library book selectors talk about the
publishing trade they more or less automatically also think in
terms of the kind of book that the former Knopf firm used to
publish, or the former Harper Brothers. But this type of book,
which figures so largely in public library book selection, represents less than 10 per cent of the sales of books produced by
the trade publishers. The bulk of trade publishing is made up of
textbooks (which lead the list), encyclopedias, paperbacks, juveniles ... works which are not quite the "hard cover adult
trade item." Some writers do not use the term "trade publishing" to include the textbook, encyclopedia, and paperback publishers, but the present authors feel that they belong to the same
publishing world as general publishers, and they would consider
publishers like federal, state, local, and international governmental bodies as being "outside" the trade, along with such
publishers as societies and institutions.

There is one type of publisher which began as a producer of
works really "outside the trade," but many of whose present
publications aim at trade sales. The university presses began as

organizations dedicated to publishing those books which make a contribution to knowledge, even though they cannot have a wide audience, and even though they have to be published at a loss. Such a program requires subsidization, either by the parent educational institution, the author, or some foundation. This original aim has not been hewn to in all university presses, however. Some have had the fortune to issue a book which turned out to be a heavy seller. Having once experienced the financial joys of best-sellerdom, there appears to have been a temptation to look for other best sellers, rather than to adhere to the original purpose of the press. One hopes that press directors and their institutions will continue to make their contribution to serious scholarship, especially in light of the growing difficulty a trade publisher has in supporting unlikely ventures.

In summarizing the present state of the publishing trade, one would need to recall the various types of publishers, fitting each into his particular niche. The federal government in all its many branches publishes vast quantities of material, including books, pamphlets, periodicals, reports, research papers, and a wide variety of processed materials. The state governments, the counties, the townships, the municipalities, school districts, metropolitan authorities, sewage disposal districts, etc., etc.—there are a host of local governmental agencies that publish. Societies, fraternal organizations, business associations, committees, corporations—there are thousands of publishers of material never intended for sale in the book trade. Although the bulk of much of this publishing will not be of interest to the average public library, some of it will be of considerable importance to specialists who may have recourse to the large metropolitan public library's central collection, or to a university, or to a special library. For the purposes of library selection, all these extra-trade publishers must also be kept in mind, since selection is not limited to the choosing of general books for the general reader, but includes also the selection of highly specialized materials for the specialist or scholar. In the chapter on bibliography which follows, an attempt will be made to distinguish among the bibliographies, to point out which are substantially lists of trade books only, which run to more specialized materials, and which combine both.

Bibliography

Publishing

Escarpit, Robert. *The Book Revolution.* NY, UNESCO, 1967.

Grannis, Chandler B. *What Happens in Book Publishing.* 2d. ed. NY, Columbia Univ. Press, 1967.

Gross, Gerald, ed. *Publishers and Publishing.* NY, Grosset & Dunlap, 1962.

Jovanovich, William. *Now, Barabbas.* NY, Harper & Row, 1963.

Jovanovich, William. *The Structure of Publishing.* NY, American Book Publishers Council [n.d.]

Madison, Charles B. *Book Publishing in America.* NY, McGraw-Hill, 1966.

Melinat, Carl H., ed. *Librarianship and Publishing.* (Frontiers of Librarianship no.4). Syracuse, N.Y., School of Library Science, Syracuse University, 1963.

Miller, William. *The Book Industry.* NY, Columbia University Press, 1949.

Publishers' Weekly. "Annual Statistical Summary." (3d week in January).

Smith, Datus C. *A Guide to Book Publishing.* NY, Bowker, 1967.

Smith, Roger H., ed. *The American Reading Public; A Symposium.* NY, Bowker, 1964.

Directories

American Book Trade Directory. NY, Bowker [latest ed.]

Literary Market Place. NY, Bowker [annual]

Publishers' International Directory. 3d ed. Verlag Dokumentation, 1967. [distributed by Bowker]

Reprints

Guide to Reprints, 1968. Washington, Microcard Editions [annual]

Orton, Robert. *Catalog of Reprints in Series.* 1967 Suppl. Metuchen, N.J., Scarecrow, 1967.

Reichmann, Felix. "Bibliographical Control of Reprints." *Library Resources and Technical Services.* Fall 1967. p. 415-35.

Williams, Sam R., comp. *Reprints in Print—Serials; 1966.* Oceana, 1967.

Chapter IX

National and Trade Bibliography

Introduction

An ideal national bibliography would attempt to record all materials published in a given country, whether available through the regular book trade or not, whether copyrighted or not, and regardless of format. It would include books, pamphlets, films, printed music, phono-records, government publications, theses, newspapers, periodicals, prints and engravings, microforms—and any other form. This happy ideal would enter each item under author, under title, and under subject, with additional entries where appropriate for series, joint author, editor, compiler, translator, etc. It would, of course, be freely supplied with all necessary cross references. Since the ideal is being described, let a descriptive annotation be added to the full bibliographical information which would be given.

Trade bibliography is one part of national bibliography, but of more restricted scope. It attempts to record those materials (usually books and pamphlets) which are available through the regular book trade. Most large encyclopedias and government publications, for example, are not ordinarily sold through bookstores—they are "outside the trade." Doctoral dissertations are not to be found on the shelves of the ordinary bookstore. The serial publications issued by business and industry as house organs, the publications of fraternal societies, of many learned societies, the research reports of laboratories and institutes, etc.—all these are not "trade items."

What this difference means in terms of bibliographical coverage of the publishing output in this country was illustrated by

171

the query put to John Cronin of the Library of Congress by *Library Journal* in 1959. That magazine was interested in knowing how much larger the figure for American books produced would be if, in reporting to UNESCO, titles beyond those in the trade lists were reported. It was Mr. Cronin's estimate that in 1959, if one included the, approximately 51,000 items registered in the Copyright Office and government publications at all levels of government (from the Federal to the local school district), the total would reach something like 1,140,000. That year we had reported 14,876 items—representing the trade books listed in *Publishers' Weekly*. Of course, a large part of the non-trade material is not of great interest to the smaller library—whether school, public, or college—but large libraries of all types, and small libraries with highly specialized collections, will find material of great importance appearing outside the book trade and not recorded in any trade bibliography. These libraries will not be able to rely solely on current trade bibliographies for identification and verification of titles, since their buying will range far beyond ordinary trade books to embrace a wide variety of remote or highly specialized materials. Although the authors have seen no later estimates on this subject, they see no reason for assuming that the proportion of trade to non-trade books has altered significantly since 1959 (although the total figures for both groups has risen considerably).

In studying a country's bibliography, it is desirable to try to see the pattern that exists among the various pieces, which, if put together, make up the total national bibliography. In the United States, for example, we have such bits and pieces as the *Catalog of Copyright Entries*, the Library of Congress catalogs, the *Monthly Checklist of State Publications*, the *Monthly Catalog of United States Government Publications*, *Dissertation Abstracts*, *Vertical File Index*, *CBI*, *Publishers' Trade List Annual*, *American Book Publishing Record*, etc. But we have no single source containing all types of materials, and the manner of presentation in the sources that we do have is not uniform. In addition, there is no assurance that even this variety of sources will pick up everything. Furthermore, the frequency with which these several parts of the American bibliography are published varies as much as the sources. This factor must be kept in mind in attempting to estimate the speed with which the national output is recorded (especially if one is concerned with early identification of current but obscure non-trade items). It is suggested that the student use American bibliography as his standard and compare it with British, French, and German national bibliographies, noting essential differences in an attempt to decide which country's method seems most useful.

American Bibliography

Variety appears in the retrospective coverage of American publishing due to the fact that different periods have been covered by different individuals or organizations with varying degrees of skill, time available for the undertaking, and differing convictions concerning what ought to be done and how material should be presented. Thus Sabin attempted to list not only books published in the Americas, but those about the Americas published elsewhere, and he presented the results alphabetically by author and anonymous title (largely). Evans restricted himself to books published in the United States and chose to arrange the titles chronologically by year of publication, with author-anonymous title and subject indexes. While both of these gentlemen provided considerable information about individual titles (Sabin's bibliographical notes are sometimes quite extensive), Roorbach and Kelly present a minimum of information, occasionally abbreviating the amount given to the point of near-uselessness. Shaw and Shoemaker attempted to fill the 1801-19 gap left as a result of Evans' death. They based their compilation on secondary sources as did Evans and Roorbach and Kelly. Shoemaker, using the same method of compilation, is moving beyond 1819 in an effort to provide more satisfactory coverage than that of Roorbach.

In addition to these bibliographies, one must remember the catalogs of out-of-print dealers, which are of great importance in retrospective searching (aimed at the purchase of out-of-print books). If the standard bibliographies represent infinite variety, these catalogs can only be described as "infinitest" variety. In arrangement, accuracy of entry and of information, care in description of items, extensiveness, adequacy of reproduction, and usefulness to librarians, these catalogs display a truly remarkable spread.

The field of current bibliography also displays a variety of approaches. *Publishers' Weekly* tries to list American titles published that week by trade publishers; the *Cumulative Book Index* provides a monthly approach to all publications in the United States (in whatever language) and to all books in the English language published abroad; *Publishers' Trade List Annual* and its indexes, *Books in Print* and *Subject Guide to Books in Print,* give another approach to American trade publications still in print, regardless of date of publication. The government lists its publications in the *Monthly Catalog* (not all of them), and paperbound books are represented in *Paperbound Books in Print.* Serial publications are listed in the Library of Congress' *New Serial Titles* (with holdings) as well as in the *National Union Catalog* (without holdings). There is overlapping of coverage among these various titles and varying manners of presenting the material, but the identification of currently issued trade books published in the United States (by reasonably active publishers) is not generally a major problem.

What all of this variety may detract from the efficiency of the librarian's efforts is certainly compensated for by the excitement, the mystery—sometimes; alas, the frustration—which is generated in trying to track down and identify some bibliographical culprit. The detective work going into the hunt is sometimes of a high order, and the ultimate discovery of the truth about a book sometimes approaches the kind of excitement and satisfaction which Balboa must have felt when he first viewed the Pacific. In the discussion of the individual bibliographies which follows, some of the surprises, puzzles, and eccentricities which lie in wait for the searcher will be detailed at greater length. Greater emphasis has been placed on current American bibliography because it is most used by most librarians, briefer treatment is given other types.

Current American Bibliography

For library selection and acquisitions purposes, coverage of current publishing actually begins before the publication of many of the titles which will eventually be recorded in the bibliographies. The librarian will have his attention called to forthcoming items by publishers' announcements sent to the library. These individual, scattered, and ephemeral broadsides, pamphlets, odd-sized sheets (arrayed in all the colors of the advertising psychologist's rainbow) are of great temporary utility. Once having served their purposes, however, they are disposed of expeditiously, disappearing from recorded bibliographic history via the wastebasket route. The selector's current bibliography begins at this point. An additional record of books to be published may be found in the announcement issues of such a magazine as *Library Journal* or such a publication as *Forthcoming Books*. When one shifts his attention to the record of books which have actually been published, he will find the most current and timely title is that of the book trade journal, *Publishers' Weekly*; its section called "The Weekly Record" is the first step in the permanent record of American trade bibliography.

(1) *Publishers' Weekly*. New York, Publishers' Weekly, 1872-

SCOPE

The "Weekly Record" aims at "prompt listing in full bibliographical detail of every book published in the United States"— to use *PW*'s own statement. This description of its scope is modified by a listing of the kinds of materials not included in the "Weekly Record": federal and state government publications; subscription books; dissertations; successive printings or impressions; serials, quarterlies, and other periodicals; and pamphlets under 49 pages.

ARRANGEMENT

The list is arranged alphabetically by author or title (where there is no author—as, for example, *World Almanac and Book of Facts*). At the risk of appearing to underestimate the capacities of the reader, may the authors point out that one cannot expect to find a book listed under both author and title. This is—to use another term—a listing by *main entry*. For those not familiar with cataloging terminology, this may not seem helpful, but for initiates it should fix the arrangement clearly and specifically. This particular point is being belabored here because it will reappear under each subsequent title. The reader will be expected to distinguish among various arrangements: author list; author and title; author and title and subject; title list only; etc. Sometimes a bibliography will be praised for listing under both main and added entries. This implied comparison with the dictionary card catalog should enable the reader to apprehend immediately the kinds of approaches afforded to individual items.

PW gives author, title, publisher, place, date (publisher, place and date will frequently be condensed in subsequent descriptions to one term: *imprint*), paging or volumes, size, whether illustrated or equipped with maps, tables, bibliographies, etc. (These will sometimes be condensed to *collation*, or the statement "full collation given.") A series statement appears, if appropriate. LC card number, price, frequently LC tracings (both Arabic and Roman numerals), and a brief descriptive annotation are given. (Appearance of the annotation is not invariable.) The author entry and descriptive cataloging information are taken from material supplied by the Library of Congress, while the annotations are supplied by *PW*, which remarks that its annotations are "intended to place, not judge, the books." Dewey classification numbers are given at the upper right hand corner of the entry.

FRANCESI, Wolfgang Ludwig, 1999-   301.158
   Crowds of power. Tr. from French by Starol Smith. New York, Imaginary Books Co., 2050 [c.2049] 612p illus. 49-8426 6.95
   1. *Political Science I. Smith, Starol, tr.* II. *Title.*
   Most of the above material first appeared in condensed form in *Madder Magaine.*

There are two uses of *PW* especially appropriate to our purposes. It is widely used as a selection device, and it is used for verification of titles requested for purchase. *PW* is frequently circulated to heads of subject divisions in a public library (departmental, college, or other subdivisions of a university library system), who check each weekly number for publications in their subject area. For their purposes, of course, it would be more convenient to have the weekly list arranged by subject, rather than by author. (The subject arrangement is accomplished each month in the *American Book Publishing Record*, the next title to be discussed.) But it is not an overwhelming task to read down the classification number at the upper right hand corner of each entry to pick out those books in the subject area for which one is responsible. Many of the titles may have been ordered before publication on the basis of publishers' announcements or review in Virginia Kirkus, but the weekly reading of *PW* provides a check against possible oversights. The student who is alarmed at the thought of using *PW* for selection (its annotations are only descriptive, not critical) is referred to that part of Chapter I in which "block buying" was discussed.

The second use is in the process of verification of order requests (described at length in Chapter X). For this particular purpose, of course, the alphabetical arrangement by author is most satisfactory.

A brief comment on the scope: we remind the reader that the reference to "every book published in the United States" quoted above really must be modified. A more accurate description would be "*PW* aims at including every *trade* book published in the United States." Trade bibliography is well covered, then, by *PW* on a weekly basis. Nothing so current exists for the recording of the total national output.

(2) *American Publishing Record.* New York, R. R. Bowker, Feb. 1, 1960-

SCOPE

A monthly cumulation of *PW's* "Weekly Record." Thus it is primarily a list of current American trade books.

ARRANGEMENT

The titles which had appeared in alphabetical order by author are now re-arranged under Dewey Decimal Classification numbers (by the Dewey number in the upper right hand corner). Following the classed order, there are two lists—fiction and juvenile—for such titles as could not be categorized by subject. (Please note the shortened form "classed arrangement." Wherever this appears in description of subsequent bibliographies, the authors mean that the titles included are classified by subject —although not necessarily by the Dewey Classification.) An index of authors and titles is also given, so that individual items can be located for verification. The information given in the entry and its format are identical with the entries in "The Weekly Record." Annual and five-yearly Cumulations.

(3) *Cumulative Book Index.* New York, Wilson, 1898-

SCOPE

CBI attempts to record two groups of publications: (1) all books produced by publishers in the United States, regardless of the language in which they are written and whether or not the item is available in the trade; and (2) all books in the English language appearing elsewhere in the world. Thus it attempts to be a national bibliography for the United States and a world bibliography of books in English. For the sake of emphasizing category No. 1, let it be noted that a book in the German language published in Milwaukee, Wisconsin, would be listed in *CBI*—a book in the German language, published in Leipzig, Germany, would not be listed in CBI. Do not—as individuals sometimes do—think of *CBI* as being solely a bibliography of books in English.

Omissions: two very large and important categories are not included in CBI—government documents and periodicals. Both of these categories are, of course, listed in other bibliographies. Other excluded categories include maps, sheet music, pamphlets, cheap and paperbound books (not *all* paperbounds!), tracts, propaganda, and what *CBI* describes as local, fugitive, and ephemeral materials. *CBI*'s term "Periodicals" includes newspapers as well as magazines. Note that films and phonorecords are also excluded. *CBI* is, therefore, adhering pretty well to the root meaning of bibliography—it is a list of *books*.

ARRANGEMENT

CBI lists books in a dictionary arrangement, with entries under author, subject, title, and where appropriate, such additional entries as editor, translator, joint author, illustrator, series, etc. There is one essential fact to bear in mind concerning these entries: full information is found under the *main entry* (usually author). This particular practice applies to many other bibliographies, and the librarian might well begin early to make an iron-bound habit of always consulting the main entry for any item located first under added entry. Much of the material found under main entry in *CBI* will be duplicated under all other entries, but such an important piece of information as series may not be given except under main entry. This is of great importance in order work to avoid duplication of items purchased on standing order for series, and the whole problem is discussed at greater length in the next chapter.

The dictionary arrangement makes use of the *CBI* very easy and reassuring, since it affords so many different approaches to the same item.

INFORMATION GIVEN

Under main entry, one will find author, title, edition statement where appropriate, price, publisher, date, LC card number, collation, and indication of the availability of Wilson cards. For titles in English appearing abroad, price is given in the currency of the country (25 kr, 66 s, 12s6d, Rs7.50 etc.). Where appropriate, price will be given for both British and American editions of the same title, affording an interesting opportunity for some trans-Atlantic bargain hunting. Generally speaking, full cataloging information is given (except size and place of publication).

SAMPLE ENTRIES

(A) **Francesi, Wolfgang,** 1964-1984.
　　Crowds of power; first translated into English in accordance with the original French ms. by T. L. Williams; with an introd. by the translator. 612p. $4.95 '84 Imaginary Books LC-84-493
(B) **Williams, Trevor Loper,** 1954-1984
　　(tr) See Francesi, Wilfgang. *Crowds of power*
(C) **Crowds** of power. Francesi, W. L. $4.95 Imaginary Books
(D) **Political Science**
　　Francesi, W. L. *Crowds of power.* $4.95 '84 Imaginary Books

HISTORY

CBI began publication in 1898. It was intended to be the current, continuing supplement to the *United States Catalog,* which appeared at intervals, cumulating *CBI* for those works still in print at the time of the publication of *U.S. Cat.* The last edition of the *U.S. Cat.* appeared in 1929, including books in print at that time. That edition also included those foreign titles which were regular importations of U.S. publishers and Canadian books in English not published in the U.S. It was with the 1928/29 volume (published 1930) that *CBI* expanded its coverage to all English language books published abroad.

COMMENT

A major bibliographical tool for American librarians, and the standard tool for many which cannot afford the very costly LC catalogs. Indeed, one British librarian has even asserted that the

major bibliography for British librarians is *CBI*. Remember that
CBI will attempt to record books outside the regular trade—
publications of societies and institutions, as well as privately
printed books. Thus its scope is wider than *PW* and *BPR*. Entries
in *CBI* are standard library entries—i.e., they will follow cataloging rules for entry. Note the special directory of publishers.
Inspect a run of *CBI* from its most recent issue backwards in
time to see how it cumulates its monthly volumes within the
year and what cumulations are made of the annual volumes into
the great, sprawling behemoths so familiar a part of the library
landscape.

(4) *Publishers' Trade List Annual.* New York, Bowker, 1873-

SCOPE

PTLA is a bibliography of American trade books, including
only those publishers who cooperate in the venture by furnishing
their catalogs. It is, further, an in-print list, that is, it contains not
only the titles published in a given year, but any titles published
previously which are still in stock at the publisher (and which
may have been published years earlier). Its scope is more restricted than *CBI*, resembling more closely the range of *PW*
and *BPR*.

Omissions: books published outside the trade, periodicals, government documents, and non-book forms are largely excluded,
unless a publisher includes them in his catalog, as in the case
with some periodicals. The major content, however, consists of
books, and one should not think of *PTLA* as attempting a
comprehensive coverage of periodical publishing in the United
States.

ARRANGEMENT

PTLA is a collection of publishers' catalogs and lists, in two
sections. There is the large alphabet of uniform-size catalogs,
arranged by name of publisher, occupying most of the bulk of
each edition. There is also a section on colored pages at the front
of the first volume containing lists by publishers of smaller
compass. An index to both lists heads the volume. If one checks
the name in the regular alphabet of catalogs and does not find a
catalog for that publisher, he ought to check the index before

concluding that the publisher is not represented—the particular list sought may be in the colored section.

Within the catalogs of individual publishers, arrangement is not uniform. Some catalogs are arranged alphabetically by author; some by author and title; some by subject. Some include out-of-print titles; some list titles in a series; some include advance listings. It is fruitless, therefore, to study one of the catalogs and hope to use it as a model of arrangement for other publishers. It seems most useful to fix in mind the fact that the catalogs vary in arrangement, and, when using a given catalog, to take a few moments to check on its arrangement.

Two indexes supplement the catalogs—*Books in Print* and *Subject Guide to Books in Print*. They will be discussed following *PTLA*.

SAMPLE ENTRIES

(A) *Crowds of Power*. Wolfgang L. Francesi. 2050 $6.95
This interesting book contains a discussion of the application of political power through mob action.
(B) Francesi, Wolfgang L. *Crowds of Power*. $6.95
(C) Francesi, Wolfgang Ludwig.
Crowds of Power. (c.2049) 612p. 49-9426 $6.95
This book contains a discussion of the application of political power through mob action.

The amount of information given in these three samples varies considerably, with B not even indicating the date of publication. Entry A gives the publication date, but C actually gives copyright date, as well as LC card number.

COMMENT

PTLA began in 1873, but there were no indexes to the catalogs until 1948, so that one would have to know the name of the publisher to locate an item in the volumes before that date. It does not serve, therefore, as a very useful retrospective national bibliography. (For studies of the output of a given publisher, of course, it is invaluable.) Its lack of indexes is not a serious blow to bibliography, for it is highly unlikely that the titles listed there would not be in the Library of Congress catalogs and—for the 20th century—also in *CBI*, since *PTLA* lists standard copyrighted trade items.

PTLA's major use is as an order department tool, rather than as a part of national bibliography in its broad sense. It enables

the library to find out what is available and how much it costs—
pragmatic details needed in ordering. This information can be secured from the indexes alone in most cases, and some libraries
may buy only them and not the collection of catalogs.

The statement made above—that *PTLA* will show prices and
what is available—must be qualified in the interests of accuracy.
Between the time that the catalogs are printed and *PTLA* is
received in libraries, prices sometimes change and books are
remainered by the publishers. This is not a fault to be laid at the
feet of the publisher of *PTLA*. One can only hope that eventually
most publishers will keep titles in print for a reasonable length
of time, and that they will hold to the prices listed in their catalog for at least the year covered by the catalog.

In using *PTLA* and its indexes, the librarian should keep in
mind that the entries do not follow the ALA rules for author
entry. This is a book trade list, and authors are given as they
appear on the title page—and hence as the books will be asked
for in bookstores. A book published under the pseudonym of
John Garnett (who is really our wondrous Wolfgang Francesi,
let us say) will be listed under Garnett. If a librarian recognizes
that a name is a pseudonym and hopes to save a trip on the cross
reference merry-go-round by going directly to the real name, he
will be disappointed. (Let it be hoped that he does not conclude
that the title is not in *PTLA!*)

PTLA is undoubtedly a tool of the greatest utility. Armed with
it and its indexes, the librarian can successfully dispatch most
current American order work (for trade books). With the addition of the *Subject Guide, PTLA* begins to resemble *CBI*, affording author, title, and subject approaches to the material. Certain
differences still exist, however: *PTLA* does not include coverage
of as many American publishers; it does not attempt to pick up
all books in the English language published outside the U.S.; the
amount of information given for each title—and the number of
approaches to it—are not identical with *CBI*.

(5) *Books in Print*. New York, Bowker, 1948-

SCOPE

Coverage is identical with *PTLA*, since this is simply one of the
two indexes to the collection of publishers' catalogs.

It consists of two parts: (1) an alphabetical list by author; (2) an alphabetical list by title (including titles of monographic series, as well as any other serial publications carried in the publishers' catalogs).

SAMPLE ENTRY

(1) From the author index:
   Francesi, Wolfgang L. *Crowds of power*. 2050 $6.95 Imaginary Books
(2) From the title index:
   Crowds of power. Wolfgang L. Francesi. $6.95 Imaginary Books

(6) *Subject Guide to Books in Print*. New York, Bowker, 1957-

SCOPE

Identical with *BIP*.

ARRANGEMENT

Entries are arranged under thousands of subject headings, consisting generally of regular Library of Congress headings (with some compression of highly complicated subdivisions).

SAMPLE ENTRY

POLITICAL SCIENCE
Francesi, Wolfgang L. *Crowds of power*. 2050. $6.95 Imaginary Books

(7) *Paperbound Books in Print*. New York, Bowker, 1955-

SCOPE

An in-print and forecast list for American paperbacks. Each succeeding issue has seen the number of publishers represented increase, with the number of titles listed also increasing.

ARRANGEMENT

Consists of monthly issues (subtitled "The Month Ahead") forecasting coming titles and quarterly cumulations of titles in print. Both the monthly issues and the cumulations are divided into subject, author, and title indexes. The information given in the two indexes is similar, and only samples from the cumulation will be given here.

SAMPLE ENTRIES

(A) From the Title Index:
   Crowds of Power. Francesi, W. 1.65 IB62 Imaginary Bks.
(B) From the Author Index:

Francesi, W. L. *Crowds of Power.* (Orig.) 1.65 (IB62) Imag.
Bks   (099)
(C) From the Subject Index:
               099 Political Science
          International Relations & Current
                 World Affairs
     Crowds of power. (Orig.) Francesi, W. L. 1.65 (IB62)
Imaginary Bks.

COMMENTS

One of the past complaints about the paperback trade was the
difficulty of obtaining a book you wanted, once its short day on
the newsstands had passed. With this in-print list, there is assurance that titles will be held in stock to a greater degree than was
true when the paperback trade was tied too completely to the
system of magazine distribution. The growing use of paperbacks
—as in education—will be facilitated by the continuance of this
work. At the same time, *Paperbound Books in Print* may also
stimulate that use further by allowing adequate access to desired
works.

(8) *Monthly Catalog of United States Government Publications.*
    Washington, Govt. Printing Office, 1895-

SCOPE

The *Monthly Catalog* attempts to list all government publications offered for sale by the Superintendent of Documents or
available from the various issuing agencies (even if not sold
through the Superintendent's office).

ARRANGEMENT

Each monthly catalog is an alphabetical listing by issuing
agency, with an index of subjects or titles. The subjects are frequently catch-words, brought into alphabetizing position by
re-arranging the title. An annual index is also supplied, made up
in the same way. All indexing is to the number assigned to the
item in each catalog, with the numbers running in regular serial
order from the beginning of the year to the end.

INFORMATION GIVEN

In addition to standard bibliographical material, the entry also
indicates where the item is to be purchased. Several symbols are
employed, to indicate that the publication is to be purchased
from the Superintendent, that it is to be ordered directly from
its issuing agency, that it is for official use only and not available

for purchase, etc. The LC card number and the classification
number in the Superintendent of Documents' classification
scheme are also given.

SAMPLE ENTRY

CIVIL AND DEFENSE MOBILIZATION OFFICE

3602 *Crowds of power,* by Wolfgang L. Francesi. 2050 ixx, 612 p.
il. (Studies in civil power, no. 14) * 6.95

L.C. card 49-8426   Y4Ec7:Em7/4/no.14
From the index:
Power, crowds of 3602

The Library of Congress Catalogs

The several catalogs of the Library of Congress make an excellent bridge between current and retrospective bibliography, since
even the most current issues of the author catalog are simultaneously current and retrospective. For libraries which can afford
the catalogs (about $5,100 up to 1968), they are the major
source of verification of titles. They also furnish a good contrast
between trade bibliography and the far wider-ranging national
bibliography. For the purposes of this discussion, the bibliographic separateness of the LC series of catalogs will be ignored
initially, and they will be considered as parts of one large
bibliography. Having surveyed the forest in this manner, we
shall then turn our attention to the individual trees in the LC
jungle.

SCOPE

The present catalogs are a universal list, including materials
published anywhere in the world at any time since the invention
of printing. In addition to showing those titles owned by LC for
which it has prepared cards, the catalogs include works not held
by LC, but owned and cataloged by other American libraries.
The types of materials recorded in the several parts of the catalogs include books and pamphlets, periodicals and other serials,
maps and atlases, music and phonorecords, films and filmstrips.
All are listed regardless of whether they are produced inside or
outside of the regular book trade. Thus the scope is very much
wider than *PW/BPR, PTLA,* or *CBI.*

ARRANGEMENT

The current (1968) catalogs are divided into 5 parts: (1) an
author catalog; (2) a subject catalog; (3) music and phonorecords; (4) motion pictures and filmstrips; (5) serial publications. Each of these separate catalogs is issued in a current series

which cumulates into volumes covering longer periods. Music and phonorecords, and motion pictures and filmstrips are gathered into the five-yearly cumulations of the author catalog.

Before describing the individual parts, a brief resumé of the development of this set of catalogs may be useful (or thoroughly confusing and demoralizing). The changes in title which have occurred in the original "main entry only" catalog reflected LC's expansion of its catalogs. Each part will receive its own description later, when it can perhaps be better understood with the history of the whole series in mind.

The catalogs began with *A Catalog of Books Represented by Library of Congress Printed Cards (Cards Issued from August 1898 Through July 1942)*, consisting of 167 volumes of photographically reproduced LC cards. This catalog listed all items only once—under main entry. It was primarily a book, pamphlet, and periodical list. The first supplement cumulated the years 1942-47 under the title *A Catalog of Books Represented by Library of Congress Printed Cards. Supplement. (Cards Issued from August 1942 through December 1947)*. Like the basic set, this was a "main entry only" catalog. Between this cumulation and the next 5-yearly supplement to the basic set, a change of title occurred (with the annual cumulation for 1949). This change was made because LC was about to begin issuing an addition to the catalog series, entitled *Library of Congress Catalog. A Cumulative List of Works Represented by Library of Congress Cards. Books: Subjects*. To distinguish between the two sets, the author catalog was renamed *The Library of Congress Author Catalog* for the duration of the current volumes, appearing in a more expanded form with the next supplement: *The Library of Congress Author Catalog. A Cumulative List of Works Represented by Library of Congress Cards 1948-1952*. In addition to the title change, a change in entry system (very important and most useful) was made: entries were now made for essential added entries (editor, joint author, etc.)

Before the appearance of the third 5-yearly cumulation (1953-57), two changes of title took place in the current supplements, reflecting a reorganization of the catalog. The first change altered the name from *The Library of Congress Author Catalog* to *The Library of Congress Catalog—Books: Authors*. (This change was made in January, 1953). The title was changed because three new parts of the catalog series had begun publication: (1) *Films;* (2) *Maps and Atlases;* (3) *Music and Phonorecords.* It was in 1953 that LC also began issuing *New Serial Titles,* which can be thought of as another "form" catalog to be added to the music and film sets. *Maps and Atlases* was short-lived, lasting only from 1953 to 1955.

In July of 1956, the title of the current volumes changed a second time, reflecting an expansion of the union catalog coverage of the author set. The third 5-yearly cumulation appeared as *The National Union Catalog; A Cumulative Author List Representing Library of Congress Printed Cards and Titles Reported by Other American Libraries, 1953-57.*

At the time of this writing (late spring 1968), the author set continues as the *National Union Catalog,* and the subject catalog and the separate catalogs for music, films, and serials continue to appear undisturbed.

The Author Series

(9) *A Catalog of Books Represented by Library of Congress Printed Cards (Cards Issued from August 1898 through July 1942).*

SCOPE: includes books, pamphlets, periodicals and other serials, but not motion pictures or filmstrips, since LC did not begin to issue cards for such materials until 1951. Music is not strongly represented (i.e., sheet music and music scores—one does find books on music or anthologies of music). The total number of items runs to about 4,250,000, with about 250,000 representing titles not held by LC, but for which copy was supplied by those libraries participating in LC's cooperative cataloging program. (Thus, even in this first catalog, a union catalog feature is present.) Inclusion is not restricted to materials produced in the United States, but includes work published anywhere—and at any time.

ARRANGEMENT: Listing is alphabetical *by main entry only,* that is, by personal or corporate author where there is one, or under title for serials, anonymous works, or wherever else appropriate under the ALA rules. This means, of course, that an item is listed only once, and one must have the correct main entry to find it.

SAMPLE ENTRY: (for book cataloged by LC)
    Francesi, Wolfgang Ludwig, 1999-
      Crowds of power. Trans. from the French by Starol
    Smith. New York, Imaginary Books, 2050 [c.2049]
      612 p. illus.
      Most of the above material first appeared in *Madder Maga-zine.*
      1. Political Science I. Title
    Library of Congress HQ 9875.F6   A49-8426

SAMPLE ENTRY: (for book cataloged by another library)
    Francesi, Wolfgang Ludwig, 1999-
      Crowds of power. Trans. from the French by Starol
    Smith. New York, Imaginary Books, 2050 [2049]
      612p. illus.
      Most of the above material first appeared in *Madder Maga-zine.*
      1. Political Science I. Title
    New York. Public library
      for Library of Congress   A49-8426

(10) *A Catalog of Books Represented by Library of Congress Printed Cards. Supplement. (Cards Issued from August 1942 through December 1947).*

Scope: This is the first 5-yearly supplement to the basic set, and there are no significant changes in scope, format, or arrangement, beyond the expansion of coverage of all forms of printed music. In 1943, LC began a more comprehensive cataloging program for music—although some cards had always been issued. One minor but interesting feature is the re-printing from the basic set of about 26,000 anonymous and pseudonymous titles, which had been listed in the basic set under author, but which are here realphabetized under title (identifiable by the black line drawn through the author entry).

Since there was no change in form of entry, no sample will be given here—it would be identical with the preceding entries.

(11) *The Library of Congress Author Catalog. A Cumulative List of Works Represented by Library of Congress Cards, 1948-52.*

SCOPE: This was expanded to include motion pictures and film-strips, when LC began issuing cards for such materials. This change began in the current supplements in 1951. The last two volumes of this set cumulated *Music and Phonorecords* entries and *Films*, whose arrangement will be described below, after the author set is finished.

ARRANGEMENT: a significant change was made in the former main entry listing. Beginning with this supplement, entries were made for essential added entries (editor, joint author, corporate body which might be thought to be the author of a book entered under personal author—and vice versa), which enables one to locate material more easily. These added entries are prepared especially for the catalogs and give only the more important bibliographical data.

(12) *The National Union Catalog; a Cumulative Author List Representing Library of Congress Printed Cards and Titles Reported by Other American Libraries, 1953-57.*

SCOPE: With the beginning of the National Union Catalog, the scope of coverage of titles cataloged by other libraries was very greatly increased. Whereas in the basic set only about one-seventeenth of the titles were those of cooperative libraries, in this first set over one-half are. About 500 libraries are represented. The coverage of this country's holdings are thus enormously increased. One special case: all serials included are those cataloged by LC; serial titles held by other libraries are reported in *New Serial Titles.* It is most important to note that a uniform cut-off date was employed. (It is really a uniform "start-off" date, but that term has never turned up in the authors' experience!) LC accepted cards for listing for all items published in 1956 or later. It did *not* print cards for older materials which might have just been purchased and cataloged by a cooperating library. If, for example, a library cataloged a 1475 title, this incunabulum would not have been reported in the *National Union Catalog.* Unfortunately, life can seem complicated at first glance, because, of course, this date does not apply to LC's own titles. Older works bought and cataloged by LC will appear in the *National Union Catalog.*

ARRANGEMENT: remains unchanged. But the information given now shows holdings of more than one library.

SAMPLE ENTRY

Francesi, Wolfgang Ludwig, 1999-
  Crowds of power. Trans. from the French by Starol Smith. New York, Imaginary Books, 2050.
    612p. illus.
    Most of the above material first appeared in *Madder Magazine.*
    1. Political science   I. Title
  HQ 9875.F6   301.158   A49-8426
  NNG IU   CMiC MoSU MiU NN IaU InU

(13) *The National Union Catalog 1952-1955 Imprints. An Author List Representing Library of Congress Printed Cards and Titles Reported by Other American Libraries.*

Although this title is out of chronological order of coverage, it has been put in at this point because it was issued after the preceding title. It is an extension backwards in coverage of date of publication, but is no different in scope or arrangement from the 1953-57 volumes, with one major qualification: it is restricted to monographs. There is some difference in appearance, since many of the cards are typed and the letters showing libraries holding copies are often at the side—but these are hardly major matters, since they in no way affect the content.

(14) *The National Union Catalog 1958-1962 Imprints* . . .

A 54-volume set, with no change in system of entry or in inclusions. Volumes 1-50 comprise the author list; volumes 51-52, the cumulation of *Music and Phonorecords*; volumes 53-54, the cumulation of *Motion Pictures and Filmstrips.*

(15) *[The National Union Catalog 1963-1967 Imprints]*

In June of 1967, the Library of Congress announced that it had contracted with Edwards Brothers of Ann Arbor, Michigan, to publish a 72-volume set of the *National Union Catalog* covering this period. The cumulation will list 1,210,000 entries. Publication is planned for the spring of 1969, with manufacture of the catalog scheduled for the fall and winter of 1968.

(16) *Current volumes*

At the time of this writing, the catalog continues with the multi-volumed annual cumulations for 1963 (5v.), 1964 (5v.), 1965 (7v.), 1966 (7v.), the quarterly cumulations Jan-March 1967 (2v.), April-June 1967 (2v.), July-September 1967 (2v.), the monthly volumes for October, November, and December 1967 (one volume each); and the January-March 1968 volumes (2v.) Thus a searcher in May of 1968 might have to consult *seventeen* separate places in looking for a title (say a title published in 1776, but not acquired by the Library of Congress until this year). And the next cumulation is not to appear for another year, by which time additional volumes will be added to the seventeen for search. (For those advocating the efficiencies of the book catalog—which must be up-dated by supplements—we offer this example as an indication that the book catalog does not solve *all* problems.) Some libraries, fortunate enough to be depositories of Library of Congress cards (and large enough to house the whole file), avoid this volume-by-volume search since they have all the cards arranged in one alphabetical file.

(17) *[The National Union Catalog. Imprints before 1955]*

In February of 1967, the American Library Association announced the selection of Mansell Information/Publishing Limited to publish the *National Union Catalog* of titles with imprints of 1955 and earlier. This catalog now exists as a file of more than 16 million cards at the Library of Congress. It shows the combined holdings of more than 2,000 libraries in the United States and Canada. The catalog will consist of 610 volumes, each planned for 704 pages. No date for completion of the project was announced. This catalog will provide a really magnificent tool for improved coverage of American (and other) bibliography.

The Subject Catalog

(18) *Library of Congress Catalog. A Cumulative List of Works Represented by Library of Congress Printed Cards. Books: Subjects. [1950-1954; 1955-1959; etc.]*

Includes those titles for which the Library of Congress has printed cards, covering books, pamphlets, periodicals and other serials, and maps, motion pictures, and music scores *through 1952*. (Motion pictures and music scores have their own subject indexes in their separate catalogs beginning with 1953. Maps were out for the brief span of the life of that separate catalog, and then were re-introduced into the subject catalog.) There is one very important limitation to keep in mind: only those items are included whose imprint date is 1945 or later.

ARRANGEMENT

LC cards (slightly abridged by omission of notes and tracings) are re-arranged under LC subject headings. Continued by quarterly and annual supplements, followed by quinquennial cumulations. Quarterly issues exclude belles-lettres and imprints issued before the current year being recorded. Annual cumulations include titles with imprint dates of 1945 or later if they were currently catalogued by LC.

SAMPLE ENTRY

POLITICAL SCIENCE
Francesi, Wolfgang Ludwig, 1999-
　　Crowds of power. Trans. from the French by Starol Smith. New
York, Imaginary Books, 2050.
　　612p. illus.
　　HQ9875.F.6　　　　　　　301.158　　　　　　　A49-8426

The Film Catalog

(19) *The National Union Catalog. A Cumulative List Representing Library of Congress Printed Cards and Titles Reported by Other American Libraries. 1953-1957. Volume 28. Motion Pictures and Filmstrips.*
Added title page:
Library of Congress Catalog. Motion Pictures and Filmstrips. A Cumulative List of Works Represented by Library of Congress Printed Cards. [1953-57; 1958-62; etc.]

The authors are sorry to have to present two titles for this one work, but a careful reading of these two titles will reveal the need for the added title page which LC inserts. The film catalog is not really part of the union catalog—it lists only works for which LC printed cards have been produced. But the cumulations are stuck on at the end of the cumulations of the *National Union Catalog*, becoming part of it. The added title page warns one that it is not identical in coverage.

SCOPE

Lists films and filmstrips, educational and commercial, for which LC cards have been prepared.

ARRANGEMENT

An alphabetical list by title of film (giving full information under title), with added entries for firms, and persons connected with the film (not actors and directors, but medical advisers, producers, distributors, and author of a published work on which a film is based). A subject index is appended. Continued by three quarterly issues, plus annual and quinquennial cumulations (the quinquennial cumulation becoming part of the *National Union Catalog's* 5-yearly cumulation).

SAMPLE ENTRY

Crowds of power. (Motion Picture) Futuristic Films, 2050.
   3 hrs., sd., color, 35 mm.
   Cinemascope. Color by Colortronics.
   Based on the study of the same title by Wolfgang L. Francesi.
   Credits: Producer, John Smith; director, Frank Smith; screenplay, John Smith, Jr.; music, Frank Smith, Jr.; film editor, John Smith III. *Cast:* Adele Smith, Robert Smith, Kipp Smith, Douglas Smith, John Smith IV.
   1. Political science. I. Francesi, Wolfgang L. Crowds of power.

ADDED ENTRIES

Futuristic Films, Inc.
   see *Crowds of power (Motion Picture)*
   Futuristic Films, 2050. FiA 50-5121
Jones, Elias H, 2010
   see *Crowds of power (Motion Picture)*
   Medical adviser, Elias H. Jones

ENTRY FROM THE SUBJECT INDEX

POLITICAL SCIENCE
   Crowds of power

The Music Catalog

(20) *The National Union Catalog. A Cumulative List Representing Library of Congress Printed Cards and Titles Reported by Other American Libraries. 1953-1957. Volume 27. Music and Phonorecords.*

Added title page:

Library of Congress Catalog. Music and Phonorecords. A Cumulative List of Works Represented by Library of Congress Printed Cards. [1953-1957; 1958-62; etc.]

Once again, the presence of a second title page tells us that although the separate catalog for music is cumulated into the polyennial cumulations of the *National Union Catalog*, it is not quite of a piece with it.

SCOPE

It includes entries for all types of music and phonorecords for which LC has prepared cards.

ARRANGEMENT

Primarily an alphabetical list of composers, with title entries for "anthology" records—e.g., "The Art of André Segovia," (all played by the same artist, but written by different composers); "Russian Folksongs" (various songs, not connected with any composers). Added entries are made for performers, performing groups, editors, and joint authors. A subject index, based on LC headings, is appended. Published semiannually, with annual and quinquennial cumulations (5-yearly cumulations issued as part of the *National Union Catalog*.)

SAMPLE ENTRY

Francesi, Wolfgang Ludwig, 1999-
   Crowds of power, a secular oratorio, with special obligato by Elias Jones.
   New York, Imaginary Music Co., 2050.
   295 p. 36 cm.
   1. Oratorios—since 1950—Scores. I. Jones, Elias. II. Title
M2050.F25C7   Music 256

FROM THE SUBJECT INDEX:

ORATORIOS
   Francesi, Wolfgang Ludwig, 1999-   *Crowds of power*
English

Serial Publications

(21) *New Serial Titles, 1950-1960. Supplement to the Union List of Serials, 3d ed. A Union List of Serials Commencing Publication after December 31, 1949.*

Includes serials which began publication in 1950 or later. The term *serial* includes monographic series as well as magazines and journals. Certain types of serials publications are omitted—newspapers, looseleaf publications, municipal government serial documents, publishers' series. It is published monthly, with annual cumulations. The annual volumes cumulate preceding annual volumes until the 5-yearly volume, when the cumulation starts over again. The first ten years, 1950-60, however, were cumulated into one alphabet.

An alphabetical list by main entry (most often by title, but sometimes by issuing body), showing which libraries hold runs, and indicating by symbols the completeness of the holdings in a general way (but not with the specificity of the *Union List of Serials*).

Crowds of Power. A quarterly devoted to political affairs. New
   York. v. 1, 2050-
        DLC 1-   MiU 1-

Two publications are available which classify the titles under subject. The first is a current supplement to *New Serial Titles*, issued monthly. It does not cumulate. A cumulated subject index to the set has been provided (for the 1950-60 and 1961-65) cumulations by the Pierian Press, which issued *Subject Index to New Serials Titles 1950-65* early in 1968. This makes available a subject approach to more than 200,000 serials, using some 1,800 subject headings.

Retrospective American Bibliography

(22) Sabin, Joseph *Dictionary of Books Relating to America, from its Discovery to the Present Time.* New York, Sabin, 1868-92; Bibliographical Society of America, 1928-36. 29 vols.

Sabin's work is one of the very important retrospective American bibliographies, listing about 250,000 editions (including those mentioned in the notes). As its title suggests, it is not limited to books published in America, but includes any dealing

with America. The period covered and the materials included are
not uniform throughout the set. Sabin tried to include materials
up to the date of publication of each volume. The twenty-first
volume (1929) restricted titles listed to those published not later
than 1876. In 1932, the cut-off date became 1860, and sermons,
government publications, and much local material were omitted.
After 1933, the date of inclusion dropped back to 1840.

Arrangement is primarily alphabetical by author. Anonymous
works, however, are listed alphabetically under title, under subject, or under place if they deal with a geographic entity (for
example, there are 582 items listed under New York). The information given for each title includes full title, publisher, place,
date, format, paging, and often contents. There are frequent
bibliographical notes, which are sometimes extensive. Other titles
by the author may be presented in the notes, references to a description or review of the item in some other work may be given,
and, in many cases, the names of libraries having copies are
listed.

In consulting Sabin, it is important to remember that his work
cannot be used with the same ease as the *CBI*. Many irregularities would have to be forgiven an author undertaking so mammoth a task single-handedly. Sabin himself remarked in volume
one: "Had the magnitude and extreme difficulty of the undertaking been presented to my mind in full proportions at the
outset, I should never have attempted it; and, indeed, I may
remark that I have more than once almost determined upon its
abandonment."

With this by way of introduction, consider some of the following examples of non-uniform presentation of material. Sabin
enters under the letter "A" the title *Abrégé de la révolution*, with
the cross-reference: "see Buisson." Under Buisson, one can find
the title listed, with fuller information as to what was on the
title page: *Abrégé de la révolution de l'Amérique* . . . Par
M.***, Américaine. If one looks under the pseudonym "M.***",
he will find a cross-reference to Buisson. Thus two expectations
are aroused by this example: (1) cross-references will be made
from the titles of pseudonymous works to the real author; (2)
cross-references will be made from the pseudonym to the real
author.

But, under Buisson, Sabin lists another title published by him under another pseudonym: *Nouvelles considérations* . . . par M.D.B.*** If one looks under the title *Nouvelles considérations* or under the pseudonym, he will find no cross-references to Buisson. Thus two titles by the same author are not treated in the same way.

Sabin also lists under title *Battle of New Orleans*, by a Citizen of Baltimore. If—on the basis of other examples of his procedure —one looks for a cross-reference from "Citizen of Baltimore" to this particular title, he will find none. Yet Sabin gives many cross-references under other pseudonyms beginning with the words "Citizen of."

He will also occasionally bury potentially interesting material under fairly useless entries. Under the title of a periodical, *Bulletin de la Société Philomatique*, he informs the reader that the volume for 1817 contains "Note sur une nouvelle espèce d'ours de l'Amérique du Nord, 'Ursus griseus', and Note sur le Wapité, espèce de cerf de l'Amérique septentrionale, by H. M. Ducrotay de Blainville." It might easily happen that a researcher would know the titles of these articles or even the author's name. If he looks under "Ducrotay de Blainville," "Blainville," "Note sur une . . .", "ours," "ursus," "Wapité," he will find nothing to lead him to the entry for the name of the periodical.

Admiral Vernon's *A New Ballad on the Taking of Porto-Bello*, issued with Vernon's name on the title page, is entered under title, not under Vernon nor under the place Porto Bello. It is true that the title can be found under Vernon's name; not, however, among the regular list of titles, but buried some 50 lines into the notes.

These examples are not given in an attempt to discredit or belittle Sabin's monumental work. It is intended, however, to caution the user of Sabin that he must not assume that an item is not in Sabin because it was not found in the place in which similar titles had been listed. As is the case with the British Museum *Catalogue*, if you don't find it in the first place you look, try four or five other approaches.

SAMPLE ENTRY

FRANCESI (W.) *Crowds of Power*. An Oration. Pronounced July 4, 1808. At the request of a number of the Inhabitants of the Town of Dedham and its Vicinity. In Commemoration of the Anniversary of American Independence. By Wolfgang Francesi.

. . . Dedham: Printed by the Imaginary Press. July 8, 1808. 8vo., pp. 16.
One hundred and twenty-five copies printed for Mr. J. Carson Francesi. Ten copies were printed on large paper for distribution to the friends of Mr. Francesi. M. +Another edition. Same title. *Philadelphia, Printed and Sold by William Metz, in Plymouth Alley,* 1810. 12mo., pp.24. The editor of the Bibliography of Americana calls this the second edition. I think it is the third.

(23) Evans, Charles. *American Bibliography; a Chronological Dictionary of All Books, Pamphlets, and Periodical Publications Printed in the United States of America from the Genesis of Printing in 1639 down to and including the Year 1820; with Bibliographical and Biographical Notes.* Chicago, 1903-34. 12 vols. Vol. 13, 1799-1800, Worcester, Am. Antiq. Soc., 1955.

As Evans' title indicates, this is a year-by-year listing of publications printed in the United States. The date in the title is misleading, however, since he did not complete the task he had assigned himself and had reached only the letter "M" for the year 1799 at the time of his death. The volume finishing 1799 and carrying the work through 1800 appeared in 1955. The chronological arrangement results in quite a different presentation from that of Sabin's alphabetical one. Evans believed that the chronological arrangement had proven "its perfect adaptability and superiority for reference" to an alphabetical one. That all those interested in tracing information about a particular title would agree with this judgment is doubtful. Some of the difficulties involved will be discussed in a moment, but at this point these remarks can be confined to the effect that this method of presentation has on the physical make-up of the individual volumes. If one arranges chronologically, it becomes imperative that some key be given for the searcher who is seeking a particular author's works. Evans was therefore forced to include an index of authors and anonymous titles in each volume. He further included a subject index, which enables one to gather the titles published in a given field. The subject approach is not afforded by Sabin (except, of course, to the degree that his listing under place and his listing of some anonymous titles under subject affords a subject analysis of his titles). Evans also furnished an index of printers and publishers in each volume.

For each title, he gives the standard information: author's full name, full title, place, date, publisher or printer, paging, size, and—in many cases—the names of libraries possessing copies.

A cumulated author and title index to all the volumes was published in 1959. It does afford a limited subject approach, since entries have been made for people, ships, and Indian tribes named in titles. But no systematic subject approach was attempted, so that it may still be necessary on occasion to use the subject index found in each volume. In using the subject indexes, it must be kept in mind that Evans was not employing a standard list of subject headings. In addition to the occasional scattering of materials which results from the lack of a standard list, there are other mysteries and difficulties to be encountered. Take, as a case in point, the following example: let us assume that a searcher is attempting to locate a certain title, which he assumes has been transcribed for him correctly. The title, as the inquirer transmitted it, is Offers Made by the Sachems of the Three Maquas Castles, to the Mayor . . . of Albany. Boston. What the searcher does not know is that the title really begins, not with the word "Offers" but with the word "Propositions." Not knowing the date, he dutifully searches through all the volumes under the title in the author-anonymous title indexes. He finds nothing. Being resourceful and reflective, he concludes that the title is suspect and probably garbled. He decides that he will use the subject indexes to locate the volume. But under what subject will he search? The word "castles" might well turn his mind entirely away from the personages concerned in making the offer, for who would associate castles with Indians? But the subject entry is "Indians," and, once located, it is clear that the keyword in the title for suggesting Evans' subject is "Sachems." But even here, one might assume that the sachems meant were politicians of the Tammany Society, doing business with a politician in Albany, rather than the chiefs of Indian tribes. Detective ability and careful thought might enable one to locate the item eventually, but the approach through Evans would not be an easy or a quick one. If one lacks the author's name, accurate title, or the date of publication, Evans should not be used until other sources had failed. But he lists titles which cannot be located elsewhere, and the bibliographic searcher will sooner or later either get accustomed to Evans' vagaries or at least resigned to them.

There are certain other problems which arise in part from his method in compiling. He began his compilation of the early volumes from catalogs upon which he placed considerable reliance. As a result, he describes many volumes which never existed, asscribes titles to the wrong authors, and makes many minor errors, as in matters of pagination.

These errors will be eradicated—and many titles not known to Evans added—in the new microform edition of Evans which has been undertaken by the American Antiquarian Society and the Readex Microprint Corporation (The Early American Imprints Project). This project will film the actual text of all of the non-serial titles represented in Evans. At the conclusion of the filming of the texts, the subscribers will receive the revised and enlarged edition of Evans in microprint. In addition, the cooperating institutions are undertaking the task of preparing a fourteenth volume for the set, which will include those titles discovered since Evans was published. These titles will be filmed and presented as a separate series following the completion of the Evans materials. (At the annual meeting of the Bibliographical Society of America in New York, January, 1968, Clifford K. Shipton reported that his revision of the original entries and the correction of errors was steadily progressing. He expected that this compilation, numbering some 40,000 entries, might be available late in 1968).

The presentation of the problems involved in certain kinds of searches in Evans and the knowledge that there are errors in his work might lead one to conclude that Evans is not of much value. This impression—if it has been given—must be corrected. For most searching, in which one knows author, title, and date, and in which one is only attempting to verify the information, Evans will present no major difficulties and remains a bibliographical tool of utmost value.

SAMPLE ENTRIES

1808   AUCTION
AD   VALUES
4700   FRANCESI, Wolfgang
          Crowds of Power. An oration, pronounced
          July 4, 1808. At the request of a number of the
          Town of Dedham and its Vicinity. In Com-
          memoration of the Anniversary of American
          Independence. *Dedham: Printed by the Imagi-*

From the Index of Authors:
  FRANCESI, WOLFGANG
    Crowds of power.   4700
From the classified subject index:
      POLITICAL SCIENCE
  Patriotism   4700, 5706, 6512

(24) Shaw, Ralph R, and Shoemaker, Richard H. *American Bibliography, a Preliminary Checklist, 1801-1819.*

This work closes a major gap in the chronological coverage of American publishing, which was left because Evans was unable to complete the task he had set himself. The bibliography was compiled from secondary sources, with the hope that libraries would report corrections and additions after the appearance of this preliminary edition. It consists of a series of annual volumes, arranged alphabetically by main entry. The entries are brief, with long subtitles omitted, main title sometimes shortened, and both imprint and collation abbreviated. Holdings are shown.

SAMPLE ENTRY

Francesi, Wolfgang
  Crowds of power. An oration . . . pronounced July 4, 1808.
  Dedham, Pr. by The Imaginary Press, 1808. 16p. DLC; MWA; NN
                                              15031

COMMENT

In 1965, Scarecrow Press issued a title index to the 20 volumes, giving references to the item numbers as the key. In 1966, Scarecrow issued a volume of corrections to the author list.

(25) Shoemaker, Richard H., comp. *A Checklist of American Imprints.* [For 1820-   ].

The first volume of this set (for 1820), announced that Shoemaker had projected a bibliography covering the years 1820-25, and planned coverage has been extended. He noted that most of the material for the later volumes was already on hand, and that work on them was in progress at the time of publication of the 1820 volume. The method of publication is identical with that of the Shaw and Shoemaker (Item no. 24). The volumes covering 1824 and 1825 are in press, and will be issued in 1969. The 1820-25 list will not include periodicals or newspapers.

Francesi, Wolfgang L.
   Crowds of power, or, A narrative of political experience,
adapted for the encouragement of arts and sciences and designed
especially for the instruction of children. Embellished with neat
copperplate engravings. Philadelphia, Ptolemy Philadelphus Publ.
Co., [1820] MWA   4391

(26) Roorbach, Orville. *Bibliotheca Americana,* 1820-61. New
York, Roorbach, 1852-61. 4 vols.

Roorbach's list begins with the year to which Evans intended
to come. It is by no means as full in its treatment of titles as
Sabin or Evans, nor is it always accurate. It is, in the main, an
alphabetical list of authors, with titles also given in the alphabet.
Not all titles are entered, however. Under "Abbess, The," one
finds the entry "by Mrs. Trollope. 2 v. 12mo. cl. 0 90 Harper &
Bros." Under the entry "Trollope", the information is cited again,
not quite as fully. "Trollope, Mrs. Abbess. 2 v. cl. 0 90 Harper
& Bros." However, under "Abbott, Jacob," his *Elements of Astronomy* is listed, but the title is not given under either "Elements" or "Astronomy, Elements of." Once again we are faced
with a lack of uniform practice. It is noteworthy that for the
Trollope and the Abbott items, no dates of publication are given.
Roorbach does not omit all dates but they cannot be counted
upon. His rule was to give dates for history, voyages, and travel.
As one can see from the entry for Mrs. Trollope's *Abbess,* the
amount of bibliographical information given is minimal, even to
the failure to give authors' full names. Roorbach also gives a list
of periodicals published in the United States. One peculiarity of
arrangement to be kept in mind is that he enters biography of
individuals under the name of the biographee, not under the
name of the biographer.

  (A) Author entry:
     Francesi, W. L. *Crowds of Power.* 8mo cl 0 75 Stringer '49
  (B) Title entry:
     Crowds of power. By Francesi 0 75 Stringer

(27) Kelly, James. *American Catalogue of Books Published in
the United States from Jan. 1861 to Jan. 1871.* New York,
Wiley, 1866-71. 2 v.

Kelly continues the recording of American publishing from Roorbach's closing date and gives much the same kind of brief information, with the difference that he regularly gives the year of publication. In addition to the main alphabetical author-title list, he supplies a valuable list of pamphlets, sermons, and addresses on the Civil War. He also appends to each volume a list of learned societies and literary associations with their publications. His two volumes include about 11,300 titles, excluding the appendix. He picked up some books published before 1861 which had been missed by Roorbach.

The extreme brevity of the statement of title page information occasionally leads to puzzles. Kelly gives the following cross-reference: "Abbot, Ezra see Alger." When one consults the entry "Alger," he finds that two Algers are listed: H. Alger, Jr., and W. R. Alger. There is nothing in the two title entries under each to connect either with Ezra Abbot. One might suspect that Ezra Abbott was a pseudonym used by Horatio Alger, Jr., or by W. R. Alger. Checking in other sources, however, will reveal that W. R. Alger's *A Critical History of the Doctrine of the Future Life* (which is all the information that Kelly gives) had an appendix written by Ezra Abbot (an extensive bibliography which was also published separately). The shortening of the title-page information leads into a blind cross-reference.

Both Roorbach and Kelly do not cover their periods completely, and they are often inaccurate and incomplete in presenting bibliographical data, but they represent the fullest lists for their periods and will list some titles not easily found elsewhere.

SAMPLE ENTRY

Francesi, W. L. *Crowds of Power.* 8vo. pap., 10cts. N.Y. Carters. . . . 1864

(28) *American Catalogue of Books, 1876-1910.* New York, Publishers' Weekly, 1876-1910. 15 vols.

The first volume of the *American Catalogue* intended to list all books in print and on sale to the general public as of July 1, 1876. The record included all reprints, importations kept in stock, those publications of learned societies which were for general sale, important government publications, and the law reports of the courts of the several states. The list excluded periodicals, sheet music, unbound maps, tracts and other low-priced pamphlets, local directories, and books composed largely of blank pages.

This catalog represents cumulations of the *Annual American Catalogue*, which was an annual cumulation of the titles appearing weekly in *Publishers' Weekly*. The annual volumes are largely but not entirely superseded by the cumulations. The cumulated volumes employed three different arrangements of the material: (1) through the 1890-95 volume, there were two volumes issued for each edition; one contained author and title entries, the other, subject entries; (2) the 1895-1900 cumulation bound both sections in one volume, but as separate parts; (3) the three succeeding cumulations combined authors, titles, and subjects in one alphabet.

In presenting the information, the author's full name is often not given, but initials are employed for first name and middle name. Title entries are usually restricted to novels, plays, poems, and juveniles, although some series titles, with contents given, are listed for those sets which were commonly quoted by title. The subject list is made up of catch-words from the titles, rather than being a standard list.

SAMPLE ENTRIES

Francesi, Wolfgang L. *Crowds of power*. Phil., Penn Pub. Co.,
  1899. c. 19p. S (Dramatic lib., v. I, no. 188) pap., 15¢
From the Author and Title Index:
Francesi, Wolfgang L. *Crowds of power*. '99 c. (D2) S.
  (Dramatic Lib., v. I, no. 188) pap., 15¢ . . . Penn Pub Co
Crowds of power. Francesi, W. L. 15¢ Penn
From the Subject Index:
Power.
  Francesi, W. L. *Crowds of power*. '99 15¢ Penn

(29) *American Book Prices Current, a Record of Books, Manuscripts, and Autographs Sold at Auction in New York and Elsewhere*. 1895-

This list of books, periodicals, manuscripts, autographs, broadsides, maps, and charts sold at auction is presented here as part of the retrospective bibliography because: (1) it will enable the librarian to arrive at some judgment concerning the prices at which desired out-of-print titles are offered. If a dealer offers a book for $100 which sold recently at auction for $5.00, the buyer might well beware. (2) The auction lists also serve as a supplement to the national and trade bibliographies for bibliographic details of an occasional title which may have slipped through the bibliographic net. It would certainly not be a place of first resort for the search, but may occasionally enable one to verify a title not listed elsewhere. Each entry gives author, title, edition, place, date, size, binding condition, date of sale, lot number, and price. The title has been selected as a sample of a type of compilation— Constance Winchell's *Guide to Reference Books* may be consulted for other American or British auction records.

SAMPLE ENTRY

FRANCESI, WOLFGANG LUDWIG
—*Crowds of power.* London, 1818. Sm 4to, 19th century mor.
  S Nov 17 (51) $50
  Anr copy. In 19th century lev mor, extra. S June 5 (97) £170
  Anr copy. Lacking the title leaf. In old calf, worn. Sold w.a.f.
  S June 5 (98) £6

British Bibliography

In the field of British bibliography, as in that of American bibliography, only a few of the major titles have been selected for consideration. The retrospective field is represented here by the general bibliographies of the British Museum's *Catalogue of Printed Books*, Watt, Lowndes, and Allibone. The short-title catalogs of Pollard and Wing are listed as examples of period bibliographies, while current bibliography is represented by the Whitaker and *English Catalogue* series and by the *British National Bibliography*.

(30) British Museum. Dept. of Printed Books. *General Catalogue of Printed Books. Photolithographic Edition to 1955.*

SCOPE

Like the Library of Congress catalog, it is a universal bibliography, but it represents the pre-1800 period more thoroughly than the LC catalogs do. It is a major tool for European retrospective searching, in addition to its paramount importance for British works.

ARRANGEMENT

It is primarily an alphabetical list by author. Subject approaches are afforded in several areas: (1) works about a person appear under his name; (2) many items are located under place name—see London, for example; (3) in treating anonymous titles, an effort is made to bring out the subject expressed in the title. Ordinary subjects (e.g., coal, war, health, etc.) are represented in the separate *Subject Index of the Modern Works Added to the Library*, which is not included in our list of titles for acquisition purposes.

HISTORY

The *Catalogue of Printed Books* was published from 1881-1900, and a *Supplement* was published from 1900-05. These catalogs represented accessions to about 1899. The catalogs were so heavily used that agitation led to a reprint of both (the *Catalogue* in 1946 and the *Supplement* in 1950).

In 1931, a new edition was begun, entitled *General Catalogue of Printed Books*, adding about 30 years' accessions. By 1954, the work had reached the letters DEZW- when mounting costs forced its discontinuance. The Museum announced that it would continue the alphabet by photocopying the reading room sheaf catalogue, and it entitled the new enterprise *General Catalogue of Printed Books. Photolithographic Edition to 1955*. When the alphabet was completed, the Museum swung round to the head of the alphabet and redid the A-Dezw volumes in the same manner. Production began in 1959, and the catalog was completed in 1966, running to some 263 volumes and containing over 4 million entries. An edition of 750 sets was published.

It is planned to keep the catalog current with annual supplements, which will cumulate into polyennial sets. These *Additions* began with 1963. No annual volumes are planned for the period 1959-62, as it is hoped that a decennial supplement covering 1956-65 will be published.

COMMENT

For librarians accustomed to searching the LC catalog, the BMC may seem difficult and may generate a sense of insecurity when a title cannot be located. The major difficulty in using the BMC arises from the fact that it uses rules of entry which do not coincide with American library usage. If an author—take as an example a woman—has published anonymously under three pseudonyms, under three different married names, as well as under her maiden name, all these works will be gathered together by American catalogers under the latest form of her name, with cross-references from alternative forms. American cataloging has long been convinced of the usefulness of the uniform author entry, whether for persons or corporate bodies. The BMC, on the other hand, prefers to take the book in hand as the ultimate source of main entry, rather than any information gathered from sources extraneous to the book. From the American point of view, the application of this rule can lead to a dismaying scattering of an author's work. Various titles by a given author, or even various editions of the same title, may have been published under the author's real name, under a pseudonym, and anonymously. Entry in the BMC would be made in three different places, sometimes without cross-references to tie the various entries together.

An inspection of the works of some of the famous English authors will reveal that this rule has been adhered to. Under Alexander Pope's name, a number of the editions of the *Essay on Criticism* will be found. Not all of the editions are listed here, for cross-references will send one to the entry "Essay," where the editions issued without Pope's name on the title page will be found. Similarly, the novels of Sir Walter Scott issued with his name on the title page are listed under Scott; those issued without his name on the title page are entered under title.

A second major difference arises in the treatment of anonymous titles. In standard American use, the entry for anonymous title is the first word of the title not an article. BM practice centers around catch-words, i.e., content revealed by the title, and there is a sequence of preferences for choice of catch-word. Any book naming or adequately describing a person, place, or object is catalogued under that name. If the book lacks such a person, place, or object, the first noun in the title is chosen as entry. Such a title as *Of and pertaining to the lately described and minutely analyzed perturbations* . . . would be entered under "Perturbations." This rule, of course, requires that the cataloger recognize the different parts of speech, which some might consider a most unreasonable requirement.

When the title contains no noun, BM will surrender and enter it under the first word not an article.

A third major difference arises from the definition distinguishing pseudonymous from anonymous works. According to BM usage, many items are treated as anonymous works which would be entered under pseudonym in American cataloging. The meaning of pseudonym is sharply restricted. Any book signed by a pseudonym of more than one word, which is (1) not made up like a real name; (2) not composed of a Christian name and an epithet; and (3) which is descriptive of the author, is treated as an anonymous work. Thus, a book whose title page gives "Farmer" as author, would be entered under the pseudonym "Farmer." If the title page gives "Northern Farmer"—ah! more than one word; not made up like a real name; not a Christian name plus epithet; descriptive of the author: treat as anonymous.

There are various refinements and subdivisions of these rules, but this general statement may suffice to warn the reader that in using the BMC he must not think in LC terms. In addition to the above, it is well to remember that BM uses form entries freely: congresses, periodical publications, ephemerides, dictionaries, encyclopedias, hymnals, etc. Another important practice is the habit of listing works about a person under his name.

The importance of this catalog, representing as it does the splendid collection of the British Museum, warrants effort on the part of the American librarian to become familiar with its procedures and practices. Perhaps, however, an anecdote will illustrate the unhappy truth that even long acquaintance with the BMC will not always produce intimate knowledge in every case. One of the authors went to consult the BMC recently and noticed a cataloger of some 25 years experience paging through the BMC, looking somewhat disconsolate. Upon being asked what was wrong, the cataloger explained that he had had to check up on a rather difficult pamphlet, had searched BMC long and hard, had finally located it. Some hours later, when preparing his final catalog copy, he noted that he had neglected to take down an item in the collation. Unfortunately, he had also failed to record the entry in the BMC under which he had located the title, and, on coming back to BMC, he could not find it again. Of course, it must be remembered that these difficulties occur only with certain types of titles, and that when one has the author, locating the title desired is simple.

SAMPLE ENTRIES

FRANCESI (WOLFGANG L.)
—*Crowds of Power*. An inquiry into their origin, growth, functions and future. pp. x. 282. Imaginary Books: New York and London, [1984.] 8°   08230.h.47

—[Another copy.] R.75.(6.)
—[Another edition.] pp. 305. J. Teulon: London, 2084. 12°
3455.b.75

(31) *British Museum. Dept. of Printed Books. General Catalogue of Printed Books. Additions.* 1963-

SCOPE

Shows holdings added to the library each year. Universal bibliography. No annual volumes for the period 1956 (when coverage of the *Photolithographic Edition* stops) to 1962, because a decennial index for that period is being published.

ARRANGEMENT AND ENTRIES

Same as the general catalog.

(32) Watt, Robert. *Bibliotheca Britannica; or, A General Index to British and Foreign Literature.* Edinburgh, Constable, 1824. 4 vols.

SCOPE

Includes some 40,000 authors. Although he includes non-British writers,' this is most useful as a supplement to the British Museum *Catalogue.* At the serious risk of belaboring the obvious, one may add that this work is not useful for works published after the 1820's. Like Allibone and Lowndes (to be discussed below), Watt is not a first place to go for anything. But if LC, and then BMC, fail—try Watt.

ARRANGEMENT

Watt's bibliography is divided into two sections: an author list, which gives biographical notes, a chronological listing of the author's works, and brief bibliographical details of each title. The second part is a list of subjects, with the various titles grouped chronologically under subject. The subjects are catchwords from the titles—not a standardized list of subject headings. Anonymous works are listed in this part of the bibliography only. Only brief title and date are given in the subject list. The full title is provided in the author section. In the subject list, the number and letter following the citation indicate the page of the author section on which the title will be found, with the letter indicating the section of the page.

Watt's general bibliography is divided into two sections: an

author list containing about 40,000 authors, which gives biographical notes, a chronological listing of the author's works, and
brief bibliographical details of each title. The second part is a
list of subjects, with the various titles grouped chronologically.
The subjects are catch-words from the titles—not a standardized
list of subject headings. Anonymous works are listed in this part
of the bibliography only. In the subject list, only brief title and
date are given, with full title in the author section. A number
and letter following the citation indicate the page of the author
section on which the title will be found, with the letter indicating the section of the page.

In addition to books, Watt analyzed the more important periodicals on art and science, such as the *Transactions* of the Royal
Society of London and of Edinburgh, the Linnaean Society, Hor-
ticultural Society, etc. His list is wider in scope than Lowndes,
which will be described below. Like both Allibone and Lowndes,
Watt is not the place to begin a search, but he will list titles not
found elsewhere, so that one may have recourse to him if the
British Museum Catalogue fails. Allibone's own comment on
Watt is perhaps an adequate summary: "Some late writers have
affected to depreciate the value of this work, because inaccuracies have not escaped the eye of the critic. Errors there are, and
some glaring ones, which can readily be excused in a work of
such vast compass, yet [it] will always deserve to be valued as
one of the most stupendous literary monuments."

SAMPLE ENTRIES

FRANCESI, WOLFGANG L., a learned Latin Philosopher;
was born in Rome, in the year 455, beheaded in prison, at Pavia,
October 23, 555, by order of Theodore, King of the Goths. He
wrote an Epic Poem, the hero of which was Noah, under the title
of the Noachides. Printed at Zurich, 1752, 1765, 1766. Translated
into English, by Jos. Collyer. Lond. 1767, 2ˈvols. 12mo.—His
Other Works were, *Crowds of Power*. Zurich, 1796.—*Of Homer*.
1799.—*Of Apollonius Rhodius*. 1799.

From the Subject Index:
POWER, CIVIL.—1796.   *Crowds of Power*.   384k

(33) Allibone, Samuel Austin. *A Critical Dictionary of English
Literature and British and American Authors, Living and De-
ceased, from the Earliest Accounts to the Latter Half of the
19th Century*. Containing over 46,000 articles (Authors) with

40 Indexes of Subjects. Philadelphia, Lippincott, 1858. 3 vols.
(Supplement, 1891. 2 vols.)

SCOPE

As the title indicates, Allibone included some 46,000 authors,
with another 37,000 included in the supplement. The authors are
largely British and American. His work was based on Watt (and
thus some of Watt's errors were perpetuated).

Chronological coverage extends (via the supplement) to about
the 1880's, but it is irregular, varying with the letter of the alphabet. The supplement also picks up earlier works missed by Allibone. As with Watt and Lowndes, its usefulness derives from the
fact that the out-of-the-way title, not listed by BM or LC, may
sometimes be found here.

ARRANGEMENT

An alphabetical author list, supplemented by the various subject indexes. Includes biographical information, a list of the
works, and often quotations from criticism of the author's work.
The 2-volume supplement was done by J. F. Kirk.

SAMPLE ENTRY

Francesi, Wolfgang L., b. in Jamaica, where his father was
island secretary; educated in England, returned to Jamaica in
1850; afterwards served in the Crimean War and the Indian
Mutiny and was made K.C.B. After his return to England, he
entered upon a successful literary career, writing books which
have been very popular. He was superintendent of the Kensington
School 1874-75 and has since resided in the colonies where he
has held appointments. Some of his works, having become rare,
command high prices with collectors. 1. *Songs of the Governing
Classes*, Lon., 1874, 18mo. 2. *Station Life in Jamaica*, Lon., 1869,
8vo; new eds., 1871, 1874, 1878, 1833.

"If grown-up people can be tempted, as doubtless they can, to run off
to the colonies in the way that school-boys are tempted by stirring narratives
of adventure to run off to sea, this must be a very dangerous book. Mr.
Francesi gives some express cautions on the subject, but the whole book is
very exhilarating . . . We find it full of singular interest and charm."
—*Spectator*, xli, 591.

3. *Crowds of Power*, 1860.

"It can make no pretence of being a finished study. Nor, for lack of
material, can it claim to be exhaustive. It may, however, be described as
trustworthy and straightforward."—*Sat. Rev.*, lv, 289.

(34) Lowndes, William Thomas. *Bibliographer's Manual of
English Literature, Containing an Account of Rare, Curious,
and Useful Books, published in or Relating to Great Britain
and Ireland, from the Invention of Printing, with Bibliograph-*

ical and Critical Notices, Collations of the Rarer Articles, and the Prices at Which They have been Sold. (4 vol., 1871, Bohn edition.)

SCOPE

About 50,000 titles are recorded, including only those Lowndes considered to be the principal works in their subject fields.

ARRANGEMENT

Alphabetical by author; also includes titles and catch-word subject entries. Often records prices at 19th century sales (which must not be confused with current value!) Like Watt and Allibone, supplements BMC.

SAMPLE ENTRY

FRANCESI, Rev. Wolfgang L. *Crowds of Power*; from the remotest Period to the Present Time. Felper, 1811. 2 vols. 8 mo.
This work has certain incidents not mentioned by the Duke of Chalfont in his *Arts of War*. An appendix contains charts and various notes by Capt. Basil Hall and a vocabulary of the Loo Choo language. An interesting and pleasing work, extremely valuable in its field.

(35) Pollard, Alfred W., and Redgrave, G. R. *Short-title Catalogue of Books Printed in England, Scotland, and Ireland, and of English Books Printed Abroad, 1475-1640.* London, Bibliographical Society, 1926.

SCOPE

Attempts to include all books published in England during its period (although it does not list books known to have been published, but for which no copies could be found). Its 26,500 titles have been estimated to include about 90% of extant titles and about 80% of extant editions.

ARRANGEMENT

Entry is alphabetical by main entry, giving brief title, size, printer, date, reference to entry in the *Stationer's Register*, and indication of libraries owning a copy. The first words of the title were accorded great respect in transcription, but following the opening words, extensive omissions might be made without indication. An *Index to the Printers, Publishers and Booksellers* was prepared by Paul G. Morrison and published in 1950.

COMMENT

The most comprehensive list for the period, and the bibliographer can only rejoice when he compares the ease of using the STC with the problems involved in attempting to do bibliographic work in such a title as the *Stationers' Register*.

University Microfilms (Ann Arbor, Michigan) has been engaged in filming STC items since 1937. Catalog cards have been prepared for each filmed item by the Catalog Department of the University of Michigan General Library.

In addition to the STC, there are a number of supplementary bibliographies, which grew out of STC, covering this period. Various libraries printed their holdings for the STC period, showing corrections to titles listed in STC and additional titles not shown in STC. The late Dr. William Warner Bishop published a *Checklist of American·Copies of "Short Title Catalogue" Books*, which showed holdings in about 120 libraries. A corrected and enlarged edition was published in 1950.

At the January, 1968, meeting of the Bibliographical Society of America, Katharine F. Pantzer, of the Houghton Library, Cambridge, Massachusetts, described her work of the past 18 years on the revision of the STC. Work has progressed to entry 23,817, or roughly 91% of the total. Publication is expected to begin about 1970.

SAMPLE ENTRY

Francesi, Wolfgang L. *Crowds of power*, etc. 4°. [Cambridge,] C. Legge, 1484. LC

(36) Wing, Donald Goddard. *Short-Title Catalogue of Books Printed in England, Scotland, Ireland, Wales, and British America and of English Books Printed in Other Countries, 1641-1700.* New York, Index Society, 1945-51. 3 vols.

SCOPE

A continuation of Pollard & Redgrave, bringing the coverage down to 1700. About 90,000 titles are listed, representing the holdings of more than 200 libraries.

ARRANGEMENT

Similar to Pollard & Redgrave. An *Index to the Printers, Publishers, and Booksellers* was prepared by Paul G. Morrison and published in 1955.

COMMENT

At the January, 1968, meeting of the Bibliographical Society of America, Wing described his plans for a revised edition, which he expects will cover an enlarged number of titles.

Since 1958, University Microfilms has been filming a selection of titles from Wing.

Francesi, Wolfgang L. *Crowds of power. Oxoniae typis & impensis Guil. Hall, prostant Venales apud F. Oxland & S. Pocock, 1684.* 8°. LT, O, C, LL, LGI; MH, NU

Current British Bibliography

Current British bibliography is covered by three different but parallel enterprises, two of them works of long standing, the third beginning in 1950. The oldest of the three is the *English Catalogue* series, which begins—in its current coverage—with the publication *The Publisher* (formerly *British Books*). This is a monthly magazine resembling *Publishers' Weekly. The Publisher* carries a monthly list of "Books of the Month."

(37) The *English Catalogue* itself runs along in two series (the past volumes forming an important retrospective bibliography): (1) the annual volumes, whose publication began in 1835; (2) the cumulated volumes, whose publication began in 1864. The first cumulation, based on the annual volumes, was issued by Sampson Low in 1853 (containing works published from 1837-52) and was called the *British Catalogue*. In 1864, however, he published the first volume of the polyennial *English Catalogue*, including books published from 1835-63. This list merged the contents of his *British Catalogue* and the *London Catalogue*, while adding a substantial number of titles, to make a total of 67,500 works. Before this volume appeared, Low had published an index to his *British Catalogue*, covering the years 1837-57. Subsequent volumes of catch-word subject indexes to the *English Catalogue* were published, covering the years 1856-89. No further subject indexes were published, as subjects were included in the *English Catalogue* beginning with the fifth volume. In 1914, a retrospective volume was published which covered the years 1801-36. This volume was compiled from similar sources and presented material in the same manner as the earlier Low catalogs.

A set published over such a long period contains, naturally enough, variations in the manner of presentation of the material. Generally speaking, it is an author list with catch-word subjects resulting from re-arrangement of the titles, with publications of learned societies and series entries usually listed in separate sections. Later volumes give more information, particularly after

the title-a-line system was abandoned (with volume 5). Some of
the 19th century volumes contain both author and title entries;
others only author and anonymous titles. In some volumes, biography is listed under both biographer and biographee; in others
under biographee only. Regularity of practice is also not always
observed in the earlier volumes. For example, in volume three,
the rule is given that title entry will not be used if the author is
known—but occasional titles, whose authors are known, are listed
both under title and under author. A complete checklist of each
volume's procedure (and exceptions therefrom) could be made,
but perhaps it is sufficient to warn the user of the retrospective
volumes to be wary of making only one check under one entry.
Resourcefulness in thinking of alternative entries will often be
rewarded by discovery of the item sought. Whatever its variations in practice, the bibliographer cannot help but look with
satisfaction on a set which carries a record of publication in an
uninterrupted flow for over 150 years, with no sign of an end to
its activities.

SAMPLE ENTRIES

Francesi (W. L.)—*Crowds of Power:* A Study of the Early Prin-
cipiate. Cr. 8vo. pp. 442, 3s. 6d. (*Univ. Tut. Series*)
Dodd, Jan. 94

Power, Crowds of, *Francesi* (W. L.) 3s. 6d ....*Jan.* 94

(38) The Whitaker series

Whitaker's bibliographies begin with *The Bookseller*, a weekly
trade magazine, containing articles on the book trade, news,
etc. Its bibliographic part consists of a list of publications for the
week, which is cumulated in the last issue of the month.
Whitaker's also issues a monthly classified list in *Current Literature*. Quarterly, *Whitaker's Cumulative Book List* appears,
cumulating into an annual volume. The author-title section cumulates the material in *The Bookseller;* the classified list cumulates
Current Literature. Polyennial cumulations complete the series.

In addition to this record of current publication, Whitaker also
issues an in-print catalog at irregular intervals, *British Books in
Print*, the equivalent of the American *PTLA*. Originally, it
was issued as a collection of publishers' catalogs. In 1936, however, it abandoned the catalog format and issued two parts:
author and title lists (the equivalent of *Books in Print*). In the
author list, entries are given under author, editor, translator, and
reviser. In the title list, catch-word subjects entries are also given

by inverting titles. Beginning with the 1967 edition, it will be
revised annually, rather than every four years.

SAMPLE ENTRIES

(A) *Whitakers Cumulative Book List*
   Crowds of power. (W. Francesi) D8.350 42/ Longmans Pol
   FRANCESI, W. L. Crowds of Power. D8.350. Ill. 42/ Long-
   mans (9.66) Pol
   Power, Crowds of (W. Francesi) D8.350 42/ Longmans Pol
(B) *British Books in Print, the Reference Catalogue of Current
   Literature*
   a. Author Index:
      FRANCESI, W. L. *Crowds of Power.* ('84) D8 350 42/
      Faber
   b. Subject Index:
      Crowds of Power. (Francesi) D8 350 42/ Longmàns
      Power, Crowds of (Francesi) D8 350 42/ Longmans

(39) *The British National Bibliography*

In 1950, the third of the current British bibliographies began
publication. Since its appearance, it has met with great praise
from American order librarians. Its bibliographic virtues are a
great satisfaction to the librarian seeking accurate information.
The material is based upon those titles received at the British
Museum for copyright purposes, but its editors have tried to expand its coverage beyond copyright items. Because of British
publishers' arrangements with non-British publishers, the list
includes publications issued in non-English-speaking countries,
and some American books simultaneously published in Britain.

BNB appears weekly, with monthly and quarterly indexes, an
annual volume, and polyennial indexes. Full bibliographical information is given, with many happy bonuses (translations are
listed with a note of their original title, publisher, and date of
publication; new editions have the date of the original or previous editions; series are listed; titles are identified as parts of
series). Arrangement is classified by the Dewey system, which
makes the weekly issues useful to the selector responsible for
given areas. The fullness of the indexes enables the order
searcher to find a given author or title easily. There is one difference from American practice which is worth remembering:
pseudonymous works are listed under the title-page pseudonym,
according to the rules for cataloging of the British Museum.

Cheap novelettes, music, maps, publications of the government
of Eire, and most British government publications are omitted.

Periodicals are listed at the time of their first issue and also on the first issue of a change in title.

In April, 1968, it was announced that the BNB had awarded a contract to a London firm to set up a computer system to produce full bibliographic records on magnetic tape. The system design will be compatible with the Library of Congress Project MARC (Machine-Readable Cataloging), which was launched in 1966. The BNB's MARC project will follow the United States' MARC II file structure (with appropriate additions for British usage). All British publications will be recorded by the BNB on paper tape for proofing and creation of a weekly MARC catalog. The system will be designed to print a BNB index, and a title index, of all BNB records added to the catalog each week.

SAMPLE ENTRIES

(A) From the Annual Volume:

320—Politics. General Works

FRANCESI, Wolfgang L.
Crowds of power. New York, Imaginary Books. 7/6. Oct [1984]. xii, 591p. *maps, tables.* 24 *cm.*
(Big Brother's University. Center for the Study of Political Control of Populations. Publications.)

(B) From the Index to the Annual Volume:

Crowds of power. See Francesi, Wolfgang L.

Francesi, Wolfgang L. *Crowds of power.* Imaginary Books, 7/6   320 (B84-21350)

Politics. 320

French Bibliography

This discussion of French bibliography has been limited to a small group of titles. Three general works (two catalogs of the Bibliothèque Nationale; Brunet's *Manuel*); two period bibliographies (Quérard's titles, covering 1700-1849, and Lorenz, 1840-1925), and two current bibliographies (*Biblio* and *Bibliographie de la France)* have been included. For our purposes of a general introduction to French bibliography, however, many titles have been excluded. Those interested are directed to the latest issue of Winchell's *Guide to Reference Books.*

(40) Paris. Bibliothèque Nationale. Dépt. des imprimés. *Catalogue général des livres imprimés de la Bibliothèque Nationale: Auteurs.* 1897-

As is the case in Great Britain and the United States, the catalog of the depository library of France is a major bibliography, not only of French works, but of books published abroad. It is not as comprehensive as either of the other two as regards type of materials covered, nor has the catalog ever been completed. Publication began in 1897 and by 1953, the letter "T" had been reached. In 1967, the volume covering "TURGAN-ULEY" was published, after 14 years in the "T's."

The early volumes are out of date, and there is no representation of the final letters of the alphabet. Thus, such an important French author as Voltaire is not represented. (He was not listed under his original name, Arouet, unfortunately.) Furthermore, this catalog consists of entries for *personal authors only*. There are no entries for corporate bodies, for anonymous titles, documents, serials, or society publications. There are no added entries for secondary persons or bodies which might be thought to be the author.

This situation obtains because, in the 1894 report of the Commission des Bibliothèques Nationales et Municipales (which had been charged with the task of examining the state of the catalogs of printed books of the Bibliothèque Nationale), it was suggested that a series of catalogs be prepared: (1) a list of personal authors; (2) a second list of anonymous works and general titles issued by corporate bodies; (3) a third list, which would treat of certain special categories of publications—budgets, reports, etc.—which would be primarily official publications of corporate bodies.

This full set of catalogs is far from realization. For a work whose author is known, however, and which happens to have been published before the date of publication of the volume into which it fits alphabetically, the catalog is very satisfactory, being characterized by very careful and accurate work. The fact that it is not complete, and that the early parts are so far out of date, requires a greater reliance on complementary works than is the case in the United States.

SAMPLE ENTRY

FRANCESI (Wolfgang).—*Foules de pouvoir*. Discours prononcé dans l'église métropolitaine de Nôtre Dame de Paris, le 13 juillet 1794, jour de la réunion annuelle des citoyens qui furent électeurs en 1789, en commémoration de la prise de la Bastille et de la conquête de la liberté, par W.-L. Francesi . . . —*Paris, Mame et fils*, 1794. In-18, 143 p., pl. et fig. $8y^2$. **51520**

(41) Paris. Bibliothèque Nationale. Dépt. des imprimés. *Catalogue général des livres imprimés: auteurs, collectivités-auteurs, anonymes.* 1960/64-   Paris, 1965-

SCOPE

For French works, includes all titles listed in *Bibliographie de la France* during the period, as well as any other titles cataloged by the Bibliothèque Nationale, whether or not the book was published during the 1960/64 period. (This would apply to books acquired by purchase or gift, rather than by legal deposit.) It includes not only those items listed in the *Bibliographie de la France's* general section, but also those listed in the parts devoted to theses, government publications, and auction catalogs. Foreign titles acquired by the Library would also be listed, regardless of date of publication. Periodicals are excluded, as there is a separate catalog of periodicals.

ARRANGEMENT

For the first time, corporate authors and anonymous works are included, which is a most happy enlargement of coverage. In addition to a wider array of main entries, the catalog includes secondary entries, where necessary, for joint authors, editors, writers of prefaces, translators, etc. Many title entries are also made for publications of corporate bodies.

Cross-references are supplied to aid in the identification of an author, especially where it is a corporate body which has a complicated name, or which has changed its name.

All these are presented in a single alphabetical list. Separate alphabets will be published for (1) Cyrillic; (2) Greek; (3) and Hebrew.

Note the many different formats for individual titles. What does this tell you about the method of publication employed?

SAMPLE ENTRY

FRANCESI (Wolfgang)
—**Foules du pouvoir,** par Wolfgang Francesi . . . —Rambouillet, l'auteur, 149 rue Madame de-Maintenon (Paris, impr. J. Grou), 1984. —In 4° (27cm), non paginé, fig., couv. ill., multigraphié.
18,50 NF

4°R. 9736 (1)

(42) Brunet, Jacques. *Manuel du libraire et de l'amateur de livres.* Paris, Didot, 1860-80. 9 vols.

Brunet's work is actually a universal bibliography of rare, important, or noteworthy books, but it is especially strong for French publications before the 19th century. His work has been highly esteemed as a prodigy of patience, exactness, erudition, and a monument of bibliography. The first five volumes are arranged alphabetically by author and anonymous title, while the sixth consists of a subject index, arranged according to Brunet's own bibliographical classification. The seventh and eighth volumes consist of supplementary lists and a subject index, while the ninth volume is actually not part of Brunet's list of titles, but Deschamps' dictionary of European cities and towns with their classical names, and, conversely, a list of classical place names with the modern European equivalent. The bibliography is selective. It serves, nevertheless, as an important supplement to the Bibliothèque Nationale's catalog. Brunet gives full bibliographical data, including author, title, place, publisher, date, size, and number of volumes. Notes which are often extensive give the record of editions and descriptions of important items (see the entry under the first Shakespeare folio).

SAMPLE ENTRY

FRANCESI (Wolfgang). *Foules de pouvoir,* en francoys, contenant quatre dialogues, fort antiques, ioyeux et facetieux. *Lugduni, apud Anisonios,* 1677. 4 part. en 1 vol. pet. in-12. [3924]

Ces dialogues sont composés à la manière de Lucien. C'est un ouvrage allégorique assez piquant. Malheureusement l'autorité crut apercevior, dans les allégories, des impiétés et des héresies condamnables, et le livre fut déféré au parlement de Paris, qui en ordonna la suppression, et fit mettre en prison le libraire Anison. L'édition originale a été supprimée avec tant de soin, qu'on n'en connaît, avec certitude, qu'un seul exemplaire vend 350 fr. Gaignol, et 1200 fr. La Chappelle, et qui est maintenant dan la bibliothèque de la ville de Versailles. Pourtant, le catalogue de feu M**** (des Plances), *Avignon,* 1778, in-8., p. 15, en annonce un autre, rel. en.*v.f.t.d. bords et bordures,* avec la fameuse vignette de la Pauvreté; mais cette annonce paraît s'appliquer à l'édition d'Amsterdam, 1732, dan laquelle on a reproduit le titre de 1677. Très-rares.

(43) Quérard, Joseph Marie. *La France littéraire, ou Dictionnaire bibliographique des savants, historiens, et gens de lettres de la France, ainsi que des littérateurs étrangers qui ont écrit en français plus particulièrement pendant les XVIIIe et XIXe siècles. Ouvrage dans lequel on a inséré, afin d'en former une*

Bibliographie nationale complète, l'indication 1° des réimpressions des ouvrages français de tous le ages; 2° des diverses traductions en notre langue de tous les auteurs étrangers, anciens et modernes; 3° celle des réimpressions faite en France des ouvrages originaux de ces mêmes auteurs étrangers, pendant cette époque. Paris, Didot, 1827-64. 12 vols.

This work consists of an author list, giving brief biographical notes concerning the authors, with the usual bibliographical data for the titles, plus bibliographical and historical notes. In addition, the last two volumes (besides giving additions and corrections) are a list of the pseudonymous and anonymous works of authors, under real name. The period covered runs from 1700 to 1826. Emphasis is on works in the field of literature, and so it is not actually a complete national bibliography.

SAMPLE ENTRY

FRANCESI, (Wolfgang) jurisconsulte, né à Dunkerque en 1741, mort à Paris, le 7 avril 1817.

—*Foules de pouvoir.* Paris, Laurens aîné, 18, 7, in-8.

Édition la plus précieux pour les gens de lettres, en ce que c'est la dernière revue par l'auteur, qui lui-même la nommait son édition favorite: on ne le trouve plus que par hasard. Il a été tiré quelques exemplaires de cette édition sur papier fin de Holland, qui sont très-récherchés des amateurs (20,000 a 30,000 fr.), ainsi que quelques-uns sur papier fort.

Après la publication de cette edition, l'editeur s'etant aperçu que plusieurs fautes s'étaient glissées dans le commencement du texte, se décida à faire réimprimer les sept feuilles A-G, dans lesquelles it fit des corrections et des augmentations qui nécessitèrent un changement dans l'ordre de la pagination. La table des pièces et celles des matières ne correspondent plus avec les pages changées. Cettes exemplaires son très précieux.

(44) Quérard, Joseph Marie. *La littérature française contemporaine, 1827-49. Le tout accompagné de notes biographiques et littéraires.* Paris, 1842-57. 6 vols.

This work continues his earlier title and is arranged on the same plan. Together the two titles cover 149 years, giving quite a range chronologically.

SAMPLE ENTRY

FRANCESI (Wolfgang), écrivain critique, conservateur de la Bibliothèque Mazarine, inspecteur de d'Académie de Paris, membre de l'Académie française.

—*Foules de pouvoir*, discours prononcés dans la séance publique tenu part l'Académie française, pour le réception de M. de Francesi, le 17 avril 1827. *Paris, de l'impr. de F. Didot*, 1827, in-4 de 36 p. —Autre édit. *Paris, de l'impr. de Béthune*, 1827, br. in-8.

M. Francesi a fourni au Journal des Débats un grand nombre d'articles de critique, signés A. Il avait quitté l'Académie par suite de tracasseries qu'on lui avait suscitées. Ses oeuvres sont pleine de frivoles argumentations, d'experience inexacts. Ses principales saillies sont puisées dan les lettres de madame de Sévigne.

(45) *Catalogue général de la librairie française.* Paris, Lorenz, 1840-1925. 34 vols.

This work, usually cited as Lorenz, is the major bibliographical tool of the 19th century, continuing the work of Quérard. It is hoped that supplementary volumes will be issued to bring the coverage to 1933, the year in which Biblio began publication. Since Lorenz was intended to be a practical, commercial tool, literary notes were omitted. The list is primarily alphabetical by author, with catch-word subject indexes. An important feature of the work is its linking together of various works by an author through cross references from later to earlier volumes.

SAMPLE ENTRY

FRANCESI (Wolfgang), professeur a l'Université du Michigan (États-Unis). (Voy. Tome xv, page 897).

—*Foules de pouvoir*. in-8. 1807. H. Welter. 25fr. La 1ʳᵉ édition à paru en 1897.

From the Index:

Politique; Brochures politiques.

Foules de pouvoir, par Wolfgang Francesi. In-8. 1897

(46) *Bibliographie de la France.* Paris, 1811-

This current weekly bibliography (whose retrospective volumes, going back to 1811, form a substantial bibliography, the usefulness of which is diminished by the lack of cumulations) is based on the official copyright list of the Bibliothèque Nationale and reflects the careful cataloging of that institution. Unfortunately, its format presents some problems. The publication consists of three parts: (1) "Bibliographie officielle," which records the books, pamphlets, and documents received for copyright, and which is supplemented by separate parts, issued at irregular intervals. These extra parts include the following sections: A—Periodicals; B—Engravings, prints, and photographs; C—Music;

D—Theses; E—Atlases, maps, and plans; F—Government publications. (2) "Chronique," consisting of notes and special features for the book trade. (3) "Annonces," publishers' announcements of new books, which are indexed cumulatively into *Livres de la semaine, Livres du mois, Livres du trimestre, Livres du semestre,* and *Livres de l'année.*

Since the titles are not listed until they have been cataloged, entries are often delayed for months after publication. Furthermore, the list does not include any works which have not been deposited for copyright. Because of its arrangement and delay, many order librarians have expressed a preference for the next title on the list.

SAMPLE ENTRIES
AUTEURS

(A)

  Francesi (W.) 2084

(B)   3. SCIENCES SOCIALES

  2084. FRANCESI (Wolfgang).

    —*Foules de pouvoir,* par Wolfgang Francesi.—Paris, Les belles lettres (Besançon, Neo-typo), 1960.—In-8° (24 cm), 16p., carte. [D.L. 12934-62]

    [8° Z.34266 (37)

      (Annales litteraires de l'Universite de Besançon. 37)

SAMPLE ENTRIES FROM SOME OF THE SUPPLEMENTS

(A) From "Périodiques"

N. SCIENCES JURIDIQUES, POLITIQUES,
ÉCONOMIQUES ET SOCIALES

  N2. POLITIQUE

    100. *Foules de pouvoir.* Mensuel. Dir. Wolfgang Francesi. N° 1, decembre 1960.—Guin, rue Lavoisier (impr. d'Auger). 45x32 cm. Le n° 0, 15 NF [D.L. 20-2-61]—N2b.

                                [Fol. Jo. 11708

(B) From the index to "Periodiques"

    Foules de pouvoir 100

(C) From "Gravures, Estampes, et Photographies"

I. AUTEURS
A. GRAVURES ET LITHOGRAPHIES

  1. FRANCESI (Wolfgang).

  —*Foules de pouvoir,* lithogr. en coul., vers 1961. [AA3

B. PHOTOGRAPHIES

  285. FRANCESI (Wolfgang)

  —100 phot.   [Oeuvre;—N.;—O.

(D) From the classified arrangement of "Gravures, Estampes," "etc."

II. CLASSEMENT PAR SUJETS
E. COSTUMES ET MOEURS

  510. *Foules de pouvoir,* album d'echantillons de tissus.—Paris,

Societe d'éditions de mode, 1962 et suiv. In-4°, fig.—N°1,
mars 1962.—Printemps 1962—Été 1963.

(E) From the section "Musique"   [Th. 231, in-4°
MUSIQUE
I. MUSIQUE INSTRUMENTALE
1. Francesi, (Wolfgang).
—*Foules de pouvoir*. [pour piano]. Nouvelle édition révue
par H. Vaillant.—Nice, S. Delgieu (1961). In-4°, 12p.
[D.F. 413]

B.N. [Vmg. 5965 (21)
Cons. [G. 9646 (21)
(F) From the section "Thèses"
Thèses 1961
VI.—LETTRES
Paris
4572. FRANCESI (Wolfgang).
—*Foules de pouvoir*. Recherches sur un region moins developpée,
vers 1854-vers 1871. Paris, Impr. nat., 1961.—24cm, 591p., fig.,
cartes.   [8° Lk. 1897
Thèse. Lettres. Paris. 1958

(47) *Biblio; catalogue des ouvrages parus en langue française
dans le monde entier*. Paris, Hachette, 1933-

The monthly *Biblio*, a world record of French language publications arranged in dictionary catalog style, lists titles sooner
than the *Bibliographie de la France*. *Biblio* uses the "Annonces"
and "Bibliographie officielle" of the *Bibliographie de la France*
as a base, but adds works published abroad and those which are
outside the copyright deposit. It is not as complete as *Bibliographie de la France* for non-book materials, but its convenience
of use leads many librarians to try it first for a desired item. The
annual volume cumulates the monthly list—with additions—in the
same dictionary arrangement,

SAMPLE ENTRIES
Foules de pouvoir (Coll. Histoire de la vie politique, 185)
FRANCESI, W. 58f. Gallimard
FRANCESI, Wolfgang
Foules de pouvoir (Coll. Histoire de la vie politique, 185).
17, 5 x 11. cxxxi,195p. Rel.: 58fr. ['66] Gallimard.
Reprod. de l'éd. orig., Bruxelles, Impr. Hayez, 1884.
POLITIQUE
FRANCESI, W. *Foules de pouvoir*. 58fr. '67 [i.e., '66]
Gallimard

Voir aussi: Anarchisme et anarchistes; Communisme; Constitutions; Democratie; Droit constitutionnel; Eglise et Etat; Elections; Etat; Fascisme; Legislation; Liberte; Monarchie; Opinion publique; Socialisme; et les subdivisions Politique et gouvernement et Vie politique aux noms de pays, p. ex.: Espagne—Politique et gouvernement.

German Bibliography

German bibliography can be divided into three periods: 19th century and earlier; 20th century before World War II; and post World War II, with its division of Germany into two nations. The 19th century and earlier is well covered by three works (the earliest bibliographies are not being considered in this general discussion): (1) Heinsius' *Allgemeines Bücher-Lexikon* (1700-1892); (2) Kayser's *Vollständiges Bücher-Lexikon* (1750-1910), and (3) the Hinrichs firm's series, including weekly (1842-1915), quarterly (1846-1914), half-yearly (1798-1915), and polyennial issues (1851-1912).

The 20th century period before World War II saw the assumption of the Hinrichs' series by the Börsenverein, the German book trade organization, and the supplanting of Heinsius and Kayser by the same publications. The weekly index, half-yearly, and five-year catalogs were continued, while the quarterly catalog was discontinued.

The second World War saw Germany divided into East and West Germany, each of which has attempted to publish bibliographies covering the total German output. In the German Democratic Republic, the Deutsche Bücherei at Leipzig and in the German Federal Republic, the Deutsche Bibliothek at Frankfurt-am-Main have both continued the publication of the weekly indexes.

(48) Heinsius, Wilhelm. *Allgemeines Bücher-Lexikon,* 1700-1892. Leipzig, 1812-94. 19 vols.

The first edition of Heinsius' work appeared at the end of the 18th century in four volumes (1793-98). It was based on publishers' and dealers' catalogs. The second edition (1812-13) revised and enlarged the first, in an attempt to make it more comprehensive and accurate. His fundamental principle of arrangement was to list alphabetically under author, when the author was known. His only exception was the listing of novels and plays in two separate sections under the chief word of the title even when author was known (although for the very famous authors, he made an exception to this exception and listed their works under their name in the author alphabet). When the author of a work—other than a play or novel—was not known, it was listed under the chief word of the title. He omitted engravings, maps, music, single sermons, dissertations, and ephemeral materials costing less than two groschen (unless they were by famous authors or important for other reasons). With the eighth volume (1823-34), the separate sections for plays and novels were discontinued. The period of coverage of the various volumes runs from four to seven years (excluding the basic four volumes, which covered the years 1700-1810). The long period of coverage—192 years—makes this a very extensive list, in spite of inaccuracies (of which Heinsius and his successors were aware. Heinsius complained bitterly of the inaccuracy of the publishers' catalogs themselves, on which he had to base his work, as well as of the cavalier attitude of some publishers toward the errors in their own catalogs).

SAMPLE ENTRY

F r a n c e s i, W. L., *M e n g e n der Kraft;* sinnreicher Aussprüche aus d. Geschichte d. ält. u. neuern Zeit; ein Lesebuch f. Grosse und Kleine. 8°. Magdeburg, Lauban, 725   —10

(49) Kayser, Christian Gottlob. *Vollständiges Bücher-Lexikon,* 1750-1910. Leipzig, 1834-1911. 36 vols.

Kayser runs roughly parallel to Heinsius for much of his period, with coverage beginning 50 years later and continuing 18 years longer. His work thus gives another long run of 160 years. Like Heinsius' work, this is primarily alphabetical by author, giving author, title, publisher, place, date, volumes, paging, series, and prices. Certain catagories of works—handbooks, dictionaries, etc.—are gathered together under the category, rather than under the name of the compiler. Eleven volumes of subject indexes were also published. Kayser is generally conceded to furnish greater detail with more regularity than Heinsius or

Hinrichs and is often found in order departments which have relegated those two sets to the stacks.

SAMPLE ENTRIES

(A) Francesi, Wolfgang, *Mengen der Kraft*. (iv, 395S.) gr.18. Wien, 905. F. Vahlen.

(B) Francesi, Wolfgang. *Mengen der Kraft* (XV, 494S.) gr.8. Berlin 855. H. Berthold.

(50) The Hinrichs'/Börsenverein series.

(1) *Hinrichs' Halbjahrs-Katalog* (1798-1915). The half-yearly catalogs consist of an alphabetical author list with subject indexes (catch-word subjects). In the period before World War II (1915-1944) when the Börsenverein took over publication, the title was changed to *Halbjahrsverzeichnis der Neuerscheinungen des deutschen Buchhandels*. The half-yearly catalog has been continued in the post World War II period by the West German *Halbjahrsverzeichnis*.

(2) *Wöchentlichis Verzeichnis* (1842-1915). In 1842, Hinrichs added this weekly index as a more current record of German publications. The weekly list was continued by the Börsenverein and by both East and West German bibliographies after World War II.

(3) *Vierteljahr-Katalog* (1846-1914). The chronological coverage was filled out further with the appearance of this quarterly catalog in 1846. It was discontinued when the Börsenverein assumed publication of the Hinrichs' series and has not been resumed subsequently.

(4) *Fünfjahrs-Katalog* (1851-1912). The five year cumulations of the Halbjahrs-Katalog were continued by the Börsenverein as *Deutsches Bücherverzeichnis* (1911-40), and are represented in the East German series as *Deutsches Bücherverzeichnis* and in the West German series as *Deutsche Bibliographie 1945-50*, etc.

SAMPLE ENTRY

(A) From the "Titelverzeichnis."

Francesi, Wolfgang: *Die Mengen der Kraft*. Roman. 5.Aufl. (111) 8° Lpzg, G. Messeburger, '11.   1.50d

(B) From the "Sachregister."

Kraft s.a. Kräfte.

Mengen der Kraft: Francesi

Current Bibliography

West Germany (German Federal Republic)
The Deutsche Bibliothek in Frankfurt am Main prepares the
Deutsche Bibliographie for publication. It attempts to list all
books published in Germany (in whatever language) and all
books in the German language published abroad. It is issued in
the following sequence:

(a) Weekly. *Reihe A.* A classified list with author and catch-
word subject indexes. Includes materials sold through the regular
book trade.

(b) Monthly.

   (1) *Verfasser- und Stichwortregister.* Author and catch-
   word index, cumulating *Reihe A.*

   (2) *Reihe B.* A list of materials outside the book trade.

(c) Bi-monthly. *Reihe C.* A listing of maps.

(d) Quarterly. Cumulated index to *Reihe A.*

(e) Semi-Annually. *Halbjahres-Verzeichnis:* cumulates *Reihe
A* and selected titles from *Reihe B.*

(f) Annually.

   (1) Cumulated index to *Reihe B.*

   (2) Cumulated index to *Reihe C.*

(g) Polyennially. *Deutsche Bibliographie. Bücher und Karten.*
Cumulates *Reihe A,* selected titles of *Reihe B,* and *Reihe C.*

SAMPLE ENTRIES

(A) From the polyennial cumulation

   Francesi, Wolfgang: *M e n g e n der Kraft.* 3.Aufl.–Karlsruhe:
   Krauss (1958). 85 Bl. mit Abb. 4°.

(B) From *Reihe B*:

   (a) From the monthly issue:

   #### 6. Politik, Wehrwesen

   156 **Frater,** Dedius. *Die Bundeswehr.* [Bonn, Welckerst. 11:]
   20 S. 8°

   Francesi, Wolfgang: *Die M e n g e n der Kraft.* s. Nr.
   195

   #### 14. Geschichte, Kulturgeschichte, Volkskunde

   195 **Francesi,** Wolfgang: *M e n g e n der Kraft.* (aus d. Engl.
   übertr. von Karl Lerbs.)–(Frankfurt a.M., Wien,
   Zürich: Büchergilde Gutenberg 1964.) 355 S. 8°

   (b) From the yearly index to the monthly volumes:

   Francesi, Wolfgang   195

East Germany (German Democratic Republic)

The Deutsche Bücherei in Leipzig prepares the *Deutsche Nationalbibliographie*, which attempts to include all books published in Germany (in whatever language) and all books in the German language published abroad. (Note the resemblance to a statement read previously.) It is issued in the following sequence:

(a) Weekly. *Reihe A; Neuerscheinungen des Buchhandels*, which lists books published in the regular book trade. Classified, with author and catchword indexes.

(b) Bi-weekly. *Reihe B; Neuerscheinungen ausserhalb des Buchhandels*. Includes materials published outside the regular book trade, such as dissertations and society publications. Classified, with author and catchword indexes.

(c) Quarterly. Separate indexes to Reihen A and B.

(d) Annually. *Jahresverziechnis des deutschen Schrifttums*. Cumulates Reihe A and B in two sections: (1) "Titelverzeichnis," listing works by author or title; (2) "Stich- und Schlagwortregister," listing works under catchword and subject.

(e) Polyennially. *Deutsches Bücherverzeichnis; Verzeichnis der in Deutschland, Österreich, der Schweiz, und im übrigen Ausland herausgegeben deutschsprachigen Verlagsschriften sowie der wichtigsten Veröffentlichungen ausserhalb des Buchhandels*. Cumulates the *Jahresverzeichnis*, listing works under author, anonymous title, and subject (in two sections).

SAMPLE ENTRIES

(A) From the "Titelverzeichnis."
    Francesi, Wolfgang: *Die M e n g e n der Kraft*. Epos in
        Spielszenen.—Wien: Rido-Verl. '55 90S. 8°   3.50
(B) From the "Stich- und Schlafwortregister."
    Kraft
        Francesi, W.: *Die Mengen der* ∼. '55

Guides to Bibliography

Besterman, Theodore. *A World Bibliography of Bibliographies.* . . 4th ed., rev. and enl. Lausanne, Societas Bibliographica, 1965-66.

Malclès, Louise-Noëlle. *Les sources du travail bibliographique.* Genève, Droz, 1950-58.

Totok, Wilhelm, and Weitzel, Rolf. *Handbuch der bibliographischen Nachschlagewerke.* 3. erw., völlig neubearb. Aufl. Frankfurt a.M., Klostermann, 1966.

U.S. Library of Congress. General Reference and Bibliography
Division. *Current National Bibliographies.* Washington, GPO,
1955.

Walford, Arthur J. *Guide to Reference Material.* 2d ed. London,
Library Association. v.1- 1966-

Winchell, Constance. *Guide to Reference Books.* 8th ed. Chicago,
ALA, 1967. [First Suppl., 1965-66. Chicago, ALA, 1968]

Bibliography

Besterman, Theodore. *The Beginnings of Systematic Bibliography.* London, Oxford University Press, 1936.

"Current Trends in Bibliography," *Library Trends,* April 1959.

Downs, Robert, and Jenkins, Frances. *Bibliography, Current
State and Future Trends.* Univ. of Illinois Press, 1967.

Growoll, Adolf. *Book Trade Bibliography in the United States in
the Nineteenth Century.* New York, Dibdin Club, 1898.

Growoll, Adolf. *Three Centuries of English Book-Trade Bibliography.* New York, Dibdin Club, 1903.

Larsen, Knud. *National Bibliographical Services; Their Creation
and Operation.* Paris, UNESCO, 1953. (UNESCO Bibliographical Handbooks, 1)

Malclès, Louise-Noëlle. *Bibliography.* (Translated from the
French by T. C. Hines) New York, Scarecrow Press, 1961.

Schneider, Georg. *Theory and History of Bibliography.* (Translated from the German by R. R. Shaw) New York, Scarecrow
Press, 1961.

UNESCO. *Bibliographical Services Throughout the World,* 1st-
annual report, 1951/52-

Wing, Donald T. "Interim Report on the Second STC." *Times
Literary Supplement,* 57:648, November 7, 1958.

Chapter X

Acquisitions

Introduction

Up to this point emphasis has been placed upon the selection of books and upon the problems involved in choosing the right book for a given collection. A second area to be considered in the building of a library book collection concerns the acquiring of the materials selected for purchase. This area raises a whole new set of problems: finding out whether the books are in print, where they are available if out-of-print, the best methods of purchasing, and the kinds of records necessary for controlling the order process.

In addition, a whole new dimension has been added to the problem of acquisitions by the phenomenal growth of library collections. Librarians are asking more frequently and more urgently, "Do we really need this book—or this whole catagory of books—or can a neighboring library accept the responsibility for certain materials?" This aspect of cooperation in buying among libraries will also be considered.

"The art of acquisition," according to Tauber, "combines the talents of the detective, the diplomat and the business man."

Organization for Purchase

No attempt will be made here to describe the acquisition system of any particular library. Instead, the various kinds of information needed to carry on acquisition work will be pointed out. Even the smallest library must exercise business-like

procedures in keeping essential bcok order records, and the
larger the library, the more complicated those records will be.
Nevertheless, certain records are common to both.

It is generally agreed that the work in any order department
is largely clerical (with approximately three clerks to one professional), although professional librarians are needed as well.
Since a large part of the staff is clerical, manuals of procedure
will expedite the training of personnel in an area where there is
considerable turnover. Certain characteristics should pertain to
all staff members whether professional or clerical: accuracy,
orderliness, resourcefulness, combined with speed, are among
the essential requisites.

Since material is acquired both by purchase and by gift and
exchange, these activities may be divided by method and han-
dled separately. Gifts and exchanges are frequently combined.
Another arrangement is by type of material, with separate sections for books, for serials, for documents. No matter how the
division of work is arranged, it is well to remember that only
simple and essential records should be kept.

Order Routines

Sources of materials to be ordered are various and differ from
one type of library to another. Suggestions come in from the staff
and readers, in addition to the titles approved during the
process of book selection. Replacements recommended by staff
and departments compose another source. There is usually a
want or consideration file (more elegantly referred to as the
desiderata file) in the order department. In college and university libraries, the faculty recommendations for purchase are an
important source of order requests. Once an order request has
reached the order department, whatever its source, the problem
is to verify the bibliographic information and to complete it if it
is deficient in necessary information. This first necessary step
comprises the searching of the title.

Searching is an activity in which both professionals and non-
professionals participate and in which the qualifications of the
detective play their part. A good knowledge of the details of
bibliographic form, of the national and trade bibliographies,
and—in the larger libraries, especially in college and university

libraries—foreign languages are essential. The searcher tries to verify the author's name (in good cataloging form), title, translator or editor (if any), publisher, edition, series (if any), number of volumes or copies, date, list price. This information is entered on the order card.

Let us take an order request through a large university system, since it will have the widest variation in records and practices and fragmentation of collections, as well as of sources of orders. Let us assume that a request for a group of titles has arrived from a professor in the history department. Before proceeding with the searching process, it may be enlightening to play the novelist and imagine how he gathered these particular titles. He reads therough his professional journals, noting titles and putting them down on slips (some of these notices, by the bye, may be announcements for books to be published at some future date; ordering a book not yet in print can cause some confusion in the order search). He reads the New York *Times*, the Lond *Times*, *Saturday Review, Harpers*, and again he busily notes titles and puts them down on order slips. (A dozen of his colleagues will be reading the same sources at the same time and noting many of the same titles, none aware, however, that others are doing the same thing.) He talks to various of his colleagues, perhaps at a national meeting, and they call titles to his attention which he hadn't seen. He puts down the names of the authors and transcribes the titles. He may not get quite the correct information, and he may not be aware of the fact that the titles are part of a series which the library has a standing order for as a series. Finally he decides to send his collection of titles over to the library to be ordered. He submits them first to his department chairman for approval, who initials them as a matter of course. The chairman doesn't keep a record of everything that each faculty member orders, so some of these titles may have been ordered in the past two weeks by someone else in the department—or, for that matter, by several other people.

The batch of requests arrives at the order department and is handed over to a searcher. The first thing the searcher does is to determine whether these titles are already in the library, or whether they are on order but have not yet arrived. It is at this point that the searcher may fall into one of the pitfalls which lie in wait for the unwary. The form of entry on the order slip may not be the form of entry under which the book is entered in the library's catalogs. The searcher may carefully search the official catalog (in the case of a large university library), may then consult the outstanding order file to see if it is on order, and may finally check on an orders-received file (which records those titles received but not yet cataloged). Since he is searching under the wrong entry, he will find no record of the book.

To obviate this chance of ordering a book which is already there, it may be thought advisable to verify the title and author first in one of the national or trade bibliographies, to determine that such a title actually exists and to discover what the correct main entry actually is. On the other hand, the library may decide that the number of cases in which such ambiguities arise is not great enough to justify verification of each title first. All titles would be searched in the library's records first, and then the residue, which had not been found, would be verified in the bibliographies. Some examples of actual order requests may illustrate the difficulties occasionally faced by a searcher in the effort to verify a title.

A recent order requested Churchill's *The Great Democracies.* This is actually volume four in his series on the history of the English-speaking peoples, which one university library had catalogued under the title of the set. No cards would be found for the individual titles. With Sir Winston there is no danger of failing to recognize the problem. But the monographic series, whose individual volumes are not analyzed by the library, offers splendid opportunity for duplicating titles. The history professor, who heard about a title at his national convention, might not have realized that this was part of a large series; he would order by author and title. The searcher would find no entry under author, if the library had elected not to analyze the series. He would therefore send the order through. When it arrived, there might be consternation created when it was discovered that this series was on standing order, and the library now had two copies of a title, where one would be sufficient. In large libraries, which order many of these series, the amount of duplication can become expensive.

A simpler example was the request for *Chinese Pottery and Porcelain,* Edinburgh, H.M. Stationers Office, 1955. This order request was not incorrect, merely incomplete. The searcher finally discovered that the entry was not under title, but rather under a corporate body: Edinburgh. Royal Scottish Museum.

Another not infrequent error is to cite a book under its sub-title, which is often more informative than the main title. A request for Carl Anton Dauten's *Fundamentals of Financial Management* turned out to be a request for his *Business Finance, the Fundamentals of Financial Management.* If Mr. Dauten were a very prolific author, the searcher might miss the title filed under B and assert that the library did not have it.

The following grab bag of actual order requests will furnish further illustrations of the problems which confront the helpless searcher.

As Requested	*As Verified*
National Education Association Education and the Self-Contained Classroom	Snyder, Edith Roach, ed. The Self-Contained Classroom
Sitashov, Iurii Mikhailovich	Shashkov, Iurii Mikhailovich
Jervis, T. B. Travels in Kashmir	Huegel, Carl Alexander Anselm Travels in Kashmir, with Notes by T. B. Jervis
Huckaby, Calvin	Huckabay, Calvin
D'Olanda, Francisco Dialoghi Michaelangioleschi	Hollanda, Francisco de I Dialoghi Michelangioleschi
Hyderabad State. The Freedom Struggle in Hyderabad	Hyderabad, India (State). Committee Appointed for the Compilation of a History of the Freedom Movement in Hyderabad. The freedom Struggle in Hyderabad

Sirotkovic, Jakov
  Economic Planning Yugosla-
  via

Sirotkovic, Jakov
  Privredno planiranje u Jugo-
  slaviji

Silvert, Kalman H.
  The Conflict Society; Reac-
  tion and Revolution in Latin
  America

Silvert, Kalman H.
  Reaction and Revolution in
  Latin America; the Conflict
  Society

Fet, Aff A.
  Polnoe sobranie stixotvorenij,
  biblioteka poeta osnovana M.
  Gor'kim sol'saja serija 2-Oe
  izdanie

Shenshin, Afanasii Afanas'evich
  Polnoe sobranie [etc.]

Khadduri, Majid
  Islamic Jurisprudence

al-Shafi'i, Muhammad ibn Idris
  Islamic Jurisprudence

Gadoffre, Gilbert
  Ronsard par lui-même.

Ronsard, Pierre de
  Ronsard par lui-même

Rosen, Joseph
  Reagent chemicals and
  standards

Rosin, Joseph
  Reagent chemicals and
  standards

Rothschild, Lionel Walter
  A Classification of Living
  Animals

Rothschild, Nathaniel Meyer
  Victor
  A Classification of Living
  Animals

Rubin, I. R.
  Jordi

Rubin, Theodore Isaac
  Jordi

Rousset, Camille Felix Michel
  L'Algerie. Paris, 1900-04.

Rousset, Camille Felix Michel
  Commencement d'une con-
  quête: l'Algerie de 1830 à
  1840. 2.êd. 1900

Corporate bodies cause more than their share of misery to the unhappy searcher. A request for American Institute of Accountants, *Accounting Terminology Bulletin* caused considerable trouble because the person requesting the serial did not realize— or did not indicate, at least—that it was published by the Committee on Terminology of the Institute. Its correct author was, therefore, "American Institute of Accountants. Committee on Terminology." In the case of a large institution with many, many subdivisions, all of which publish heavily, it may become difficult in the extreme to locate an item if the subdivision does not appear on the order card.

Sometimes a perfectly standard-looking order causes problems. A request for Clara Mae Taylor's *Foundations of Nutrition*, 5th ed., caused some perturbation because Miss Taylor turned out to be a later editor of a work which had been begun by someone else. The correct entry turned out to be Rose, Mary Davies (Swartz) 1874-1941. That author was dead by the time of the 5th edition, but the edition stayed under her name.

The ultimate—and, it is to be hoped, the unusual—difficulty that can be caused the harried searcher was described by the order librarian of one of the state universities. She described the arrival of a perfectly innocent-looking order: author, title, publisher, place, date—all complete and unsuspicious. A search was made, but the title could not be verified. Even the publisher could not be located. The order was returned with a request for the source of the title. Promptly, it returned with a citation to a legislative record. The journal was consulted: the data was all there as recorded. The title had been quoted by a legislator. Another search failed to reveal any information about the mysterious work. A letter was dispatched to the legislator, who finally wrote an embarrassed reply, explaining that he had needed a quotation to back up an argument, and that he had made up the title. This kind of request would probably be classified by the searcher among the "ghoulies, ghosties, and things that go bump in the night," from which one can only hope for deliverance.

Of course, these examples do not represent the bulk of order requests, which move through the order department without undue turmoil. But the large university library, which orders a substantial amount of foreign, peculiar, and unusual materials, far from the ordinary trade channels, affords the enthusiastic searcher much material against which he can match wits. One such dedicated soul remarked that it was the problems such as these that added zest to the task. Indeed, the detective work is sometimes of a high order.

To recapitulate: the searcher will check the order slip against the catalog to see if the library already has the title; he will check against the outstanding order file to see if it is on order but has not yet arrived; he will check against the orders received file, to see if it has arrived, but is not yet in the library's catalogs. If he does not find it in these sources, he will check the trade bibliographies to get full bibliographic and ordering information. It may be well to note that these various files do not all exist as separate entities in every library—various permutations and combinations of them are found. The order will then be sent on to the functionary who will choose the dealer for the various items being ordered.

Choosing the Dealer

This is an important step, probably second to the selection of the books themselves. Libraries have three primary sources for purchase of current books: publishers, bookstores, and wholesalers. Libraries do, in fact, buy from all three sources, but the greater part of public library purchasing is done through the wholesaler. The factors which are considered in deciding where it is most advantageous to buy are several: (1) Which gives the largest discount? (2) Which furnishes the speediest service? (3) Which will adapt his billing to local accounting requirements? (4) Which is most accurate in filling orders and most prompt in rectifying mistakes? These factors do not always reside in any one of the three sources, and in some cases speed may be more important than discount, accounting procedures may take precedence over all other considerations, accuracy may be more important than speed or cost. As a result, a given library may, on occasion, order from all three sources.

The great difficulty in ordering from multiple sources comes from the fact that this procedure increases the paper work considerably. Separate orders to ten different dealers mean ten separate letters, ten separate shipments, ten separate invoices, ten separate payments. Saving effected by shopping around and placing smaller orders at more favorable discounts may well be swallowed up by increased bookkeeping costs. Where speed in acquiring a title is the primary consideration (getting a reserve book for a college class which begins in five days, for example), nothing could be faster than walking across the street to the local bookstore and picking the book off the shelf. Here again, a more favorable discount may be sacrificed for the added service. The difficulty involved in placing all orders at a local bookstore (although this is done in some places because it is considered important to support local business) arises from the fact that bookstores with really large stocks of titles are few and far between. As the library moves out of the area of currently popular titles, its success in finding less popular items in the stock of the ordinary bookstore diminishes. In all questions of discounts, however, the librarian ought to face one issue squarely: should price be the only consideration, or should other factors—speed of acquisition, extra services furnished by the vendor, etc.—be taken into account? The cheapest purchase is not always the best bargain.

The wholesalers have seen their percentage of business with libraries increase greatly in the past twenty years. The advantage of dealing with the wholesaler is clear: the librarian places one order, receives one package, pays one bill, has only one person to deal with on service problems. The services offered to libraries by wholesalers has steadily expanded: special catalogs and lists have been compiled; pre-bound books will be supplied; notification as to the status of a book is made quickly; the special billing requirements of each library are observed. Generally speaking, wholesalers have shown themselves willing to provide any service which could be organized on a mass-production basis.

The mass-production requirement emphasizes the basic nature of the wholesaler's business. He buys multiple copies of large numbers of titles from many publishers. Because he buys large numbers of copies of individual titles from the publisher, he is able to afford a better discount than the publisher can give the individual library ordering only one copy. The wholesaler can also offer a better discount on that one copy because of his special system for handling orders. This is essentially the wholesaler's specialty, as it is not the publisher's. This means that the wholesaler's savings in handling orders—which allow him to give discounts—depend upon adherence to a routine, to something resembling an assembly-line treatment of orders. It is imperative, both for his good and that of his customers, that those doing business with him follow his procedures.

Wholesalers will follow library instructions for filling orders, and, for this purpose, they have prepared forms on which the libraries can give standard instructions according to which all their orders are to be treated. The following items suggest some of the complexities which the wholesaler is prepared to handle: (1) hold for 100 pound shipment; (2) make one complete shipment; (3) screen for rebinding; (4) rebind all juvenile books; (5) hold for bill; (6) duplicate bill; (7) triplicate bill; (8) quadruplicate bill; (9) see special instructions on billing; (10) extend each item; (11) bill alphabetically by author; (12) mail copy to second party (13) enclose bill; (14) bill each fund or department separately; (15) notarize invoice billed on our form; etc., etc.

All of these special cases can be dealt with because the instruction sheet is made part of the wholesaler's routine in handling all orders. It is important, therefore, that librarians do not deviate from their standard instructions casually and intermittently. Special instructions will interrupt the smooth flow of the routine, which will result in slower service.

Blanket Approval Plans

The "Greenway Plan" (Named for Emerson Greenway, Director of the Free Library of Philadelphia) was originally worked out with the J. B. Lippincott Company in the spring of 1958. It provided that the library would receive one copy of each Lippincott trade title in advance of publication—and for a nominal price. This would enable the library staff to review each title early and make its recommendation for purchase (or rejection) early enough so that books could be ordered in advance of publication. No return privilege was allowed, since the price was set so low that it would not justify the paperwork involved. Books not of interest to the library would be discarded—which would be cheaper than trying to arrange for their return. The plan was predicated on the assumption that the library would be purchasing multiple copies of many of these books, making it economically feasible for the publisher to send all titles. As an indication of what "multiple copies" can mean in a metropolitan library, let the order of one such library be introduced as an example, even though an unusual one: it bought 900 copies of a certain best-selling novel.

The plan was extended, by the Free Library, to cover other publishers. Other libraries also began to arrange contracts with publishers for the same purpose. In 1968 one public library, serving approximately 400,000 people, had contracts with some 22 publishers, but in addition, it used four jobbers and ordered from a total of 840 different suppliers.

Large academic libraries were also interested in finding some method like the Greenaway Plan to meet some of their postwar acquisitions problems. Such libraries, however, are much less likely to be concerned with buying multiple copies of titles. They are generally interested in buying single copies of a large number of titles—many outside ordinary trade publishing channels. At the same time, they face a high rate of increase in acquisitions (they added twice as many titles in 1966 as in 1960) and they are feeling the impact of federal funds which enlarged their acquisition budgets. They have become painfully aware of the increasing cost of operating libraries (with the salaries of librarians and the cost of materials rising faster than the rate of inflation of the economy as a whole). In addition, many new colleges are being founded, and they need "instant libraries;" similarly, many former colleges have been changing to universities, with a new diversity of programs demanding expanded library facilities.

A growing tendency to use "blanket-order" approval plans became evident by the mid-1960's. A wide variety of such plans are available and all of them tend to send to the library materials by categories, rather than individual titles which have been evaluated and selected by the library in advance, and for which it placed specific orders.

One of the early plans was the blanket order plan of the Association of American University Presses, which ships (on

approval) all books published by the member presses in the
subjects selected by the library. Many libraries of large academic institutions had discovered that they were buying substantially all of the titles issued by the University presses, and some
have gone to blanket purchase (not blanket order on approval,
with intent to return some titles) of all the titles of university
presses. The reduction in cost of bookkeeping is estimated to
exceed by a factor of many times the cost of the small number of
titles which would not have been purchased. This process, as
was suggested in Chapter I, has been distressing to some libraries, but it is fair to point out that some of the most outspoken of the critics have been librarians of smaller institutions,
which would not be buying on the wide scale of the large
research libraries.

Another example is the service offered by one supplier of
scientific and technical books. The library may specify the subjects it wants, the publishers, and the level of education aimed
for. The dealer also furnishes LC cards without additional cost,
allows full return privileges, and even offers (at an additional
charge) MARC format cataloging information on punched cards
or tapes. In this case, too, books are shipped on or near publication date, the number of personnel needed as compared with the
title-by-title ordering system is reduced, and selection can then
be done with the book in hand. The larger discounts make it
economically feasible to discard the book rather than to attempt
to retain it.

The argument for blanket ordering goes as follows: If a large
library would ordinarily buy 90 to 100 books obtained on blanket order (assuming an average cost for current American
nonfiction trade books at $8.00) the books obtained on blanket
order would cost $800.00. If they were selected individually and
only 90 were bought, the cost for books would be $720.00 and
there would be a saving in book funds of $80.00. If blanket
ordering saved labor costs of $2.00 per title, which is probably a
conservative estimate, the saving in labor cost for acquisition
work would be $200.00, minus the $80.00 spent on books not
wanted, or a net saving of $120.00, even if the unwanted books
were given to a library in an underdeveloped country or otherwise discarded. This calculation would, of course, vary with the

average cost of books, with the average percentage of titles really needed for the collection, and with the average saving in labor effected by blanket ordering. Furthermore, it must be recognized that the scales are commonly weighted on the side of blanket ordering by the well-known fact that it is commonly easier to get additional money for books than it is to get the additional funds required for selecting and processing them.

One of the areas the student interested in acquisition work should investigate is the variety of plans available—with a view toward deciding the size and type of library for which each would seem suited.

Preparing the Order

Systems of ordering will differ from library to library, and the procedure outlined here is given as one example, not to be construed as the only possible method. When full bibliographic information has been secured, the order cards should be arranged alphabetically by author—or, in the case of exceptionally large orders, by publisher—and the order sheets typed in duplicate.

A letter is typed to the dealer, with a carbon copy for library files. This letter should be businesslike and should deal with the order only. Any information about other matters, such as bills or the returning of part of a previous order, should not be dealt with in this covering letter. The only information to be added is the reason for a "rush" request, if one is needed. Such requests should be kept to a minimum.

The order list is then typed. Care should be taken to arrange and space the items in such a way that the order can be filled easily. The prime factor is clarity. Items for inclusion should be entered in the following order: author, title, edition, place, publisher, date, series, binding (if other than cloth), list price. It is advisable to leave one inch margins on each edge of the paper. If more than one copy of a book is ordered, the number of copies should be entered at the left of the author's name (this may vary, of course, with the kind of order form used).

When the books are received, the invoice should be compared with the books and with the order card at the same time, in order to detect any error in price, discount, or edition requested. The date of receipt, date of the bill, and net cost per copy should be entered on the order card, which has been withdrawn from the outstanding order file and will now be filed in the orders received file (or its equivalent, if the library has some other division of records). The book is then marked with whatever data the particular library includes and is sent on to the catalog department. In the meantime, the various financial records will be altered. In the case of a university library, the particular department's financial records will be charged with the cost of the book, the bills will be approved for payment, the various records will be filed in their appropriate places.

An alternative method involves the use of multiple. copy forms, sometimes called "fanfolds." They are 3 x 5 slips with inter-leaved carbons, or made of the carbonless copying paper. With such forms, more than one copy can be made simultaneously. In a large system, the number of copies may be considerable. For the purpose of introducing certain order terms—and also to illustrate certain of the points which represent problems— we will take the reader through such a set of slips, warning him that this particular form is not introduced as a model, but merely as an example.

The particular form we will follow involves the typing of 10 slips in the fanfold. (That is, of course, only one typing is done on an electric typewriter, with the machine making 9 additional copies simultaneously.) The slips consist of the following: (1) outstanding order file—on white; (2) fund slip—tan (3) encumbrance release—green; (4) dealer purchase order—yellow; (5) dealer report slip—pink; (6) claim slip—orange; (7) official catalog—pink; (8) public catalog—pink; (9) labelling guide—white; (10) arrival notice—green. May we hasten to remark that the various colors are means of quick identification and a help in sorting—but we are by no means attempting to prescribe these particular colors for the individual type of slip! We suspect that a library might survive if its outstanding order file slip were yellow instead of white, its fund slip green instead of tan, etc., etc.

The following disposition is made of the slips when the order has been typed: (1) the dealer purchase order and dealer report slips are shipped off to the dealer as the order. (2) The fund slip is filed in the fund record, as an indication of the amounts charged against the fund but still outstanding. (3) The outstanding order slip—and all remaining slips—are filed in the outstanding order file to await arrival of the book.

The front of all slips would be identical (except for the legend at the bottom of the slip naming it and two additions to the encumbrance release slip). Bibliographic information is given (author, title, publisher, place, date, series, volumes), and in addition the following items are called for: order number; name of the fund on which the book is being purchased; name of the dealer; name of the library in the system to which the book is going; name of the person recommending purchase; date ordered; catalog number and item number, if the book was ordered from an o.p. catalog; estimated price.

Let us follow the dealer purchase order and dealer report slips along their path. The front, as was remarked in the preceding paragraph, would contain the same information as all other slips. But the back of the dealer purchase order would contain instructions to the dealer (these would vary widely from library to library, of course). The following legends appear on the sample we are using:

> Invoice: Bill in DUPLICATE, referring to order number. Bill items on same FUND on one invoice (Fund is directly under order number on reverse side of this form.)
>
> Shipping: Send accompanying report slip inside front cover of book; show full order number on all packages. Address shipments to:
>
>> Order Department
>> X Library
>> Z City, State
>
> Report: Report slip is enclosed for your convenience in reporting on orders that can not be filled.
>
> Series: If an item is part of a series and we have not so indicated, please report on pink slip before sending.

The instructions on billing is an area in which dealers have to accustom themselves to great variation. Many libraries associated with state or city governments—or school boards—are bound by rigidly prescribed accounting rules which may demand notarized invoices, thirteen copies—the fourth of pink vellum, the sixth and eighth upside down, etc., etc. Sometimes dealers seem to prefer to ignore all instructions and proceed as they choose. No doubt excessively complicated systems may irk them considerably.

The report slip is most important to the library, but the dealer may not find it very impressive, and books may return without the slip. Of course, they can be identified by searching the outstanding order file, but on occasion the main entry under which the book is ordered may be in error, and if no report slip comes back, it may take some time to find where the outstanding order slip was filed. Note especially the last instruction concerning series. This is an effort to avoid the duplication caused by ordering under author and title a book which is in a series the library gets on standing order. If the library has failed to discover that the book is part of a series, it needs to know— and woe betide the careless searcher!

The front of the report slip—identical with all others. The legends on the verso of the slip:

If Book is Not Available Return This Slip to:
Order dept, X lib, etc.

——Sold; order cancelled.

——Not yet published

——Out of Stock at publisher   Due——— { —Order cancelled

                                      —Will send

——Out of print, order cancelled

——Please confirm order:

      1. Author's correct name is:
      2. Series:

——Other

Perhaps the terms are reasonably self-explanatory, but it may be well to run straight down the list. "Sold; order cancelled"—is clear enough, and the order cancelled will cause the library to withdraw the outstanding order slip. "Not yet published"—ah yes, the problem of people sending in orders for books which have only been announced for publication. The dealer then has the option of cancelling the order, or of holding it until the date of publication and sending. He also indicates the same options if the book is out of stock, but the publisher will reprint at a given date: dealer either cancels, or holds order and fills it when publisher prints. Of course, if he cancels in either of the two cases, the library will have to re-initiate the whole business after the appropriate date. "Out of print, order cancelled." Clear enough. The "Please Confirm Order", however, is more interesting. Something is not in accord between the library's searchers and the dealer's searchers. If the library has ordered it under a different name (corporate body instead of personal, personal instead of corporate, or some person other than the real author), it wants to know, in the event that it already has the book under the form the dealer has discovered. And, as was remarked a moment ago, any large system which orders many series on standing order wants to be informed if its searching has not identified a given book with its series.

To return, however, to the slips waiting in the library's files. The outstanding order file slip will not only furnish a record of the book's "outstanding" state, but will also serve to prevent undesired duplication of titles. The official and public catalog slips will be used to file into those catalogs when the book arrives, pending full cataloging. The labelling guide will go to the labellers' desk along with the book to instruct them as to the call number to be put on the spine. The arrival notice will be sent to the person who recommended purchase of the book, to let him know it is now in the library. Many libraries might not prepare the catalog and labelling records at the point of writing up the order, but it does allow those forms to be prepared with the one, original order typing.

The encumbrance release slip and the fund slip are part of the accounting system, before whose general majesty (and mystery) the present authors tremble. But the need to make some comment on these arcane business rites is clear, and so we will forge ahead into the unknown. The encumbrance release slip has two items added to its front: the date received and the cost of the item (which replaces the estimated cost originally charged against the fund). The estimated cost had appeared on the fund slip, originally filed under the fund name to show emcumbrances. When the item is paid, it is the amount on the encumbrance release slip which is used, and the fund slip is discarded.

There are occasions—rare, we trust—when that little transfer of figures does not get made, with startling results. One librarian received his departmental library's annual budget in July, and one month later, he was informed that he had no more money left. This came as a great surprise, since he had hardly ordered anything. The longer he thought about it, the more agitated he became, and he finally descended on the startled order department like a ten ton truck gone wild. The matter did not take long to clear up, for it was a simple slip, perhaps resulting because of summer heat, compounded by vacations and people filling in at jobs. The librarian had ordered several hundred items whose cost had been estimated at $7.00 each, since they could not be verified. When they arrived, they turned out to be 25 cent pamphlets. Alas, the order clerk took the $7.00 from the original fund slip, ignoring the 25 cents on the encumbrance release slip and promptly wiped out this year's allotment. (It was as easily restored.)

The last slip in the batch is the claim slip, calmly waiting in the outstanding order file against the day when it is discovered that a book which was ordered has not arrived. The verso of the claim slip contains the following legends:

We have not as yet received the title indicated on the reverse side of this slip. Please report by checking the appropriate box below. If the title has already been sent, please do not duplicate shipment.

☐ Shipped on
☐ Not yet published. Due   Will send.
☐ Out of print. Cancelling.
☐ Out of print. Searching
☐ Out of stock. Will send
    (Please give approximate date if possible.)
☐ Sold. Cancelling
☐ Other:

Various forms are available from commercial firms supplying

libraries. The individual library may also find it necessary to devise its own forms to take into account local procedures and files. It is hoped that this brief run through one possible arrangement has not proved too devastating.

The acquisitions department, with its many business routines, is one of the first places likely to be considered for automating or even computerizing operations. The whole system of ordering has been computerized in some libraries, which claim reasonably satisfactory results (preceeded, usually, by some startling "bugs" in the system). If one thinks of the information that has been typed on order slips, he can quickly see that it could just as readily be typed on a key-punch keyboard, giving a record that could be transferred to the memory banks of a computer. It would also be relatively simple to assign a code number to each supplier of books and then to store the address of each dealer in the computer. Punched cards for each order, coded by dealer, could then be fed into the computer, which would prepare order requests by dealer and could simultaneously keep the accounts for each transaction by encumbering the separate funds coded into the cards and later debiting them for the actual amount spent. It could even stuff and seal the envelopes it prepared. Periodically, the computer would report exactly which books were on order and the status of each order; it could be programmed to write claim notices for items which had not arrived, report which items had been claimed and when, and it would keep all accounts current. Such a system, let it be noted again, is not one which "might" some day be operative; it has been done, more or less routinely, for several years.

Out-of-Print Titles

The ordering of books which are out-of-print presents a more complicated picture than the ordering of current trade books. There are two general aspects to the problem of acquiring o.p. books. One involves the search by the library for a specific title which it wishes to acquire. The other involves searching the catalogs sent to the library by various o.p. dealers to see if anything is being offered which the library would like to buy.

To attempt to find a specific title in the o.p. market resembles the children's game of "Button, Button, Who's got the

Button?" There are hundreds of o.p. dealers, and it is difficult to find which one has any given title at a particular moment. It is true that these dealers send copies of their catalogs to libraries, but the search through masses of the catalogs looking for a prticular title can be tedious indeed. And it is also unfortunately true that the titles listed in a given catalog will soon be sold (at least the desirable titles will be), so that holding this year's catalog for next year's searching is not liable to produce satisfactory results. The library can take other steps to obtain the individual title. It can send the order to a dealer who specializes in that type of material, in the hope that he will have it in stock or will be able to obtain it. There are also various searching services, which will search for requested titles. Thirdly, there are publications in which libraries can advertise lists of titles wanted. Out-of-print dealers can then submit bids for those titles which they have in stock.

The second aspect of the o.p. business in libraries consists of checking dealers' catalogs for titles which the book selector thinks might be desirable. The items checked are then searched in the library catalogs to see if the item is already in the collection. If any are not, they are then ordered from the dealer. This procedure has its own special problems. The arrangement of dealers' catalogs and the amount of bibliographic information which they give varies greatly. Occasionally the catalogs are not arranged in any order, but are assembled helter-skelter—all subjects intermingled, no alphabetizing by author. Sometimes dealers are not very precise in differentiating one edition from another; some are very brief in identifying the author—occasionally giving only an initial for the forename—and title—which is sometimes shortened until one cannot be sure that it is really the title wanted. In addition, the description of the condition of the book may be misunderstood, since a term like "good condition" is not very precise and may mean different things to the dealer and to the librarian. Speed in searching is essential, for the titles desired may be sold by the time the dealer receives the library's order. Some libraries send immediate requests to reserve a title until their order machinery can be set in motion.

There is another difficulty involved in dealing with the o.p. trade, but it is one which can only be mentioned, since there

seems little which can be done about it. The same title may be
advertised in several different catalogs over a period of a few
months at considerably different prices. A librarian may be
somewhat disconcerted to see the book—which he has just
purchased at $10.00—advertised by another dealer for $3.00. But
the prices of o.p. books, one can only conclude—are not regular
and fixed: they represent the value which the book has in the
eyes of the dealer. If a book seems over-priced, the library can
always wait. But if it has long wanted the book, it may run the
risk of seeing the next advertisement of it ask an even higher
price.

One source of information about the second hand book trade
is the *AB Bookman's Yearbook*, issued annually by the *AB
Bookman's Weekly* (itself a organ of the antiquarian trade). The
section of the *Yearbook* called "The O.P. Market" contains a
directory of specialist and antiquarian booksellers, with a subject index. Bowker's *American Booktrade Directory* contains a
state by state, city by city, listing of bookstores, including
secondhand shops, with information on specialities.

Gifts

Gifts are a valuable source of enriching the library's book
collection. They usually take the form of books, although dona-
tions of money for purchase of materials are sometimes made.
The gift of money poses a few problems as the usual procedure
of book selection will be followed in its expenditure. In theory,
at least, the same book selection principles should be applied to
gifts of books and other materials as are applied in the library's
own selection. This is sometimes difficult as the human factor,
in the person of the donor, enters into the picture, and the
librarian may have to adopt his role as diplomat. Most librarians
prefer to accept only gifts which have no strings attached. The
no-string-attached rule can avoid all sorts of difficulties which
may arise because the donor wishes to insist on various kinds of
restrictions. He may demand that no markings be put on the
bindings; he may ask that the gift collection be kept intact as
one unit—perhaps in its own special quarters; he may refuse to
allow the library to dispose of any titles which are duplicates of
titles already in the library; he may oppose the discarding of any

material which the library feels does not meet its standards of selection.

The librarian should be free to decide whether all or part of the gift should be integrated into the collection, discarded, exchanged, or sold. The donor should trust the librarian's judgment, for certainly rare items will be respected and treated as such. Gifts can be an important source for rare, unusual, or expensive items which the library budget cannot afford, but it is also true that the offerings of gifts may include much material which would only prove a burden to the library. Libraries have on occasion refused a gift collection because the cost of processing the materials exceeded the worth of the collection. Certainly there is need in every library of a policy regarding the acceptance of gifts. If such a policy does not exist, much duplication and added expense in handling materials may occur.

Patrons of the library, as well as members of Friends of the Library organizations, have proved effective sources for substantial gifts. When a gift is received, it should be acknowledged promptly. Various forms may be used, according to the importance of the material. An exceptional gift warrants a personal letter from the librarian or the president of the library board. It sometimes happens that a donor gives a series of books over a period of time which are marked with special book plates. In that event, some member of the order department may have the responsibility for seeing that the plates are prepared and that they are properly inserted in each of the items of such a collection as it arrives (the collections are often memorial in nature).

The alert librarian should also be on the look-out for free materials from various sources. Publications such as *Public Affairs Information Service Bulletin, Vertical File Index,* and *Publishers' Weekly* list free pamphlet material. It is possible to request that the library's name be put on the mailing lists of various government and private offices, organizations, and institutions which send free publications.

Duplicates and Exchanges

Duplicate material tends to accumulate in every library. These are often sorted into different categories for disposal: (1)

discards—books which are worn out and are only fit to be sold as waste paper; (2) duplicates which may be sold because their condition is satisfactory; (3) exchanges, which comprise those which the library can exchange with some other library to acquire materials not in the library. Exchanges involve the development of some method of trading duplicate materials with other libraries. The term "exchanges" also refers to the process by which libraries connected with institutions which publish their own materials exchange these publications for the works produced by other institutions (as, for example, the exchange of one university's publications for another, which is done on a wide scale, involving international as well as intra-national exchanges). It is important that a businesslike procedure for exchanges be set up, allocating the work to one department, preferably to acquisitions. In actual practice, it has sometimes been made the responsibility of the reference or circulation departments.

The United States Book Exchange was established in 1948 as an outgrowth of the American Book Center for War Devastated Libraries. The American Book Center had been created by the national library associations to build up foreign library collections from duplicate books and periodicals supplied by American libraries. The USBE acts as a pool for participating libraries who want to dispose of duplicate materials of value to research in return for other materials which they do not hold. It is the one centralized place where a participating library may send its duplicate materials with the least amount of labor and with the certainty that they will be utilized in the best possible way. This service is proving an excellent means of exchanging materials on both a national and an international basis.

Exchanges may also be facilitated through dealers and through certain associations of special libraries, such as the Medical Library Association, the American Association of Law Libraries, and the American Theological Library Association. The United Nations Educational, Scientific, and Cultural Organization's Library Division also promotes international exchange and maintains a clearing house for publications, which acts as a center for information about materials available. The *UNESCO Bulletin for Libraries* regularly contains a section listing materials available on exchange from foreign libraries.

Cooperative Acquisitions

The discussion of exchanges leads naturally to a consideration of cooperative acquisition. It is only one step from the USBE and UNESCO's efforts to facilitate exchanges to cooperative efforts in the collecting of materials, making them available through union catalogs, and storing little used materials in regional depositories. Although librarians have acknowledged the need for cooperation for at least fifty years, the tremendous growth in research collections has made it increasingly important. Fifty years ago, there were only four or five American libraries with collections of more than a million volumes. Now there are between 25 and 30. The larger libraries have become, the more librarians have realized that no library can hope to acquire everything published in every field. The need for dividing responsibility for acquisitions in various subjects has grown more acute. The change in the psychology of the librarian, however, from the gatherer of materials to the cooperator with other libraries and librarians is a difficult one to accomplish.

Some librarians still maintain a fairly isolationist attitude toward this matter of cooperation for legal, financial, or psychological reasons. They may admit that in theory librarians feel the strong professional pull of Zusammengehörigkeitsgefühl (which is supposed to characterize professional groups), but they point out that they are legally obligated to serve their own communities and are not really authorized to serve outside interests. Others point out that being helpful can become very expensive. One library printed a catalog of a special collection it had, which used to be used by a small but steady number of researchers. The distribution of the catalog led to wide-spread knowledge of the holdings of the collection. Now the library has to have one full-time person just to see that all the requests for photostating and microfilming are fulfilled. Some of the larger university collections find the economic burden of supplying books on interlibrary loan a substantial one. Finally, some librarians feel that the substitution of cooperative acquisitions for local purchase is a mark of deterioration of library service. They may agree that we will be forced to substitute getting the book by interlibrary loan for having it available immediately to the user, but they will not agree that this is the equal in terms of immediate and satisfactory service.

And still efforts at cooperation go forward. The constant growth of areas of research, the expansion of fields to be covered, and the expansion in the actual production of material make cooperation necessary. Learned societies with their journals, the publications of scientific laboratories, the expanded program of publication of research by the government: all these have increased the wave of published materials to tidal proportions. The limitations of physical space as well as financial resources add to the librarian's problems in attempting to cope with the flood of printed processed, and near-print materials.

Union catalogs and interlibrary loan through actual circulation of materials or reproduction of copies by photography have been developed in an attempt to make the best use of exisiting resources. Regional union catalogs have appeared across the country: the Pacific Northwest Bibliographic Center, Seattle (1948), the Bibliographic Center for Research, Denver (1934), the Union Catalog at Western Reserve University Library, Cleveland, the Union Library Catalog of the Philadelphia metropolitan area, and the Union Catalog of the Library of Congress. The appearance of the *National Union Catalog* of the Library of Congress is an outstanding achievement in cooperation. It is hoped that interlibrary loans within contiguous regions will develop from its use.

Cooperative acquisitions programs in the matter of purchasing materials in certain subject areas have been in effect for a good many years. In Chicago, the John Crerar Library, the Chicago Public Library, and the Newberry Library agreed on areas of development at least 60 years ago and have maintained the agreement. Other local agreements have been reached in New York City, in the Bay Area of San Francisco, in the Raleigh-Durham-Chapel Hill triangle of North Carolina, and elsewhere. The Farmington Plan was established in 1949 with the objective of assuring that one copy at least of every important foreign publication would be stocked in some American library, listed in the *National Union Catalog,* and available for photoreproduction or interlibrary loan. Certain subject areas were assigned to cooperating libraries. A recent study of the plan has been made which reveals both the effectiveness and the limitations of the plan. Fortunately, it is flexible enough to allow procedures to be altered to meet changing needs.

Smaller libraries in various areas have contracted with larger ones to benefit from cooperative purchasing and processing. With the implementation of the Library Services Act, there is a more definite trend toward cooperative purchasing of library materials. Various ALA committees also contribute toward the development of cooperative acquisitions.

Since micro-copying is expensive, libraries have often worked out cooperative methods of purchasing and use. For example, the Association of Research Libraries' Foreign Newspaper Microfilm Project makes available to approximately 50 libraries the currently filmed files of about 150 selected foreign newspapers. This project maintains a central file from which the subscribers may borrow. Stanford points to this project as a notable example of "genuine cooperative acquisitions among a sizeable group of libraries for joint purchase and shared ownership of selected materials without costly duplication of copies."

Another form of cooperation which has appeared as a result of the rapid rate of increase in the size of research collections is the cooperative storage library. These libraries relieve the individual member library of the pressure of constantly increasing holdings; they also provide a central collection upon which all members may draw for more extended research materials than any one could hold. Cooperative storage libraries were first proposed about 1900 by William Coolidge Lane, librarian of Harvard. His proposal was supported by President Eliot, but opposed by the faculty. (It has been suggested that part of its failure must be attributed to an unfortunate choice of terms: the storage facility was proposed as a place for "dead" books.) Although discussed from time to time, it was not until the 1940's that the New England Deposit Library was opened as "a regional bibliographic research center for little used books." (Which, one must admit, sounds more impressive than a storage warehouse for dead books.) Charter members included the Massachusetts State Library, Boston Public Library, Boston Athenaeum, Boston College, Boston University, Massachusetts Historical Society, Massachusetts Institute of Technology, and Harvard University.

The Center for Research Libraries, organized in 1949 under the name "Midwest Inter-Library Center" and located in Chicago, was established to supply Midwestern universities with storage space for little used materials as was the New England Deposit Library. But the Center for Research Libraries has undertaken two other activities not practiced by the New England library. It attempts to eliminate duplication of storage holdings by discard, and it attempts to fill in gaps in the collections of the member libraries by purchase, thus providing a centralized location for new acquisitions not held by any of the member libraries. An important program was the purchase by the center of all titles abstracted in *Chemical Abstracts* which were not in any member library.

Thus, as collections grow in size and as the range of materials being published constantly increases, the need for effective cooperation grows ever more acute. One major challenge to the great research libraries in the next few decades may well be the development of an effective method of cooperation in acquisitions and in utilization of all materials by some system of interlibrary cooperation. In the public library field, the standards of 1956 were based on systems of libraries, not on the smaller individual library. Here too, the implementation of the standards will depend on the development of cooperation among libraries, if not in county or regional library systems, at least in cooperative efforts. To achieve cooperative acquisitions programs, cooperative storage programs, county and regional library systems, and not lose library service of a high order of quality is a central problem in facing this challenge to the ingenuity of librarians.

Bibliography

"Building Library Resources through Cooperation." Ralph T. Esterquest, Issue Editor. *Library Trends*, v. 6, no. 3, January, 1958.

"Current Acquisition Trends in American Libraries." Robert Vosper, Issue Editor. *Library Trends*, v. 3, no. 4, April, 1955.

Downs, Robert B. "Cooperative Planning in Acquisitions." *Southeastern Librarian*, Fall, 1956, p. 110-115.

Drury, Francis K. W. *Order Work for Libraries*. Chicago, ALA, 1930.

Goldhor, Herbert, ed. *Selection and Acquisition Procedures in Medium-Sized and Large Libraries.* (Institute, U. of Ill. Grad. Sch. of Lib. Sci., Nov. 11-14, 1962. Champaign, Ill., Illini Union Bookshop, c. 1963. Allerton Park Institute, no. 9)

Jacob, E. D. "Use of T.A.A.B. in Out of Print Book Searching." *College and Research Libraries* 17:16-18, January, 1956.

Tauber, Maurice F. *Technical Services in Libraries.* N.Y., Columbia University Press, 1954.

Wulfekoetter, Gertrude. *Acquisition Work: Processes Involved in Building Library Collections.* Seattle, University of Washington Press, 1961.

Appendix A

Three Statements on Book Selection

The Library Bill of Rights

The Council of the American Library Association reaffirms its belief in the following basic policies which should govern the services of all libraries.

1. As a responsibility of library service, books and other library materials selected should be chosen for values of interest, information and enlightenment of all the people of the community. In no case should library materials be excluded because of the race or nationality or the social, political, or religious views of the authors.

2. Libraries should provide books and other materials presenting all points of view concerning the problems and issues of our times; no library materials should be proscribed or removed from libraries because of partisan or doctrinal disapproval.

3. Censorship should be challenged by libraries in the maintenance of their responsibility to provide public information and enlightenment.

4. Libraries should cooperate with all persons and groups concerned with resisting abridgment of free expression and free access to ideas.

5. The rights of an individual to the use of a library should not be denied or abridged because of his race, religion, national origins or social or political views.

6. As an institution of education for democratic living, the library should welcome the use of its meeting rooms for socially useful and cultural activities and discussion of current public questions. Such meeting places should be available on equal terms to all groups in the community regardless of the beliefs and affiliations of their members, providing that the meetings be open to the public.

(Adopted by Council June 27, 1967)

The Freedom to Read

A statement prepared by the Westchester Conference of the
American Library Association and the American Book
Publishers Council
May 2 and 3, 1953

The freedom to read is essential to our democracy. It is under attack. Private groups and public authorities in various parts of the country are working to remove books from sale, to censor textbooks, to label "controversial" books, to distribute lists of "objectionable" books or authors, and to purge libraries. These actions apparently rise from a view that our national tradition of free expression is no longer valid; that censorship and suppression are needed to avoid the subversion of politics and the corruption of morals. We, as citizens devoted to the use of books and as librarians and publishers responsible for disseminating them, wish to assert the public interest in the preservation of the freedom to read.

We are deeply concerned about these attempts at suppression. Most such attempts rest on a denial of the fundamental premise of democracy: that the ordinary citizen, by exercising his critical judgment, will accept the good and reject the bad. The censors, public and private, assume that they should determine what is good and what is bad for their fellow-citizens.

We trust Americans to recognize propaganda, and to reject obscenity. We do not believe they need the help of censors to assist them in this task. We do not believe they are prepared to sacrifice their heritage of a free press in order to be "protected" against what others think may be bad for them. We believe they still favor free enterprise in ideas and expression.

We are aware, of course, that books are not alone in being subjected to efforts at suppression. We are aware that these efforts are related to a larger pattern of pressures being brought against education, the press, films, radio and television. The problem is not only one of actual censorship. The shadow of fear cast by these pressures leads, we suspect, to an even larger voluntary curtailment of expression by those who seek to avoid controversy.

Such pressure toward conformity is perhaps natural to a time of uneasy change and pervading fear. Especially when so many of our apprehensions are directed against an ideology, the expression of a dissident idea becomes a thing feared in itself, and we tend to move against it as against a hostile deed, with suppression.

And yet suppression is never more dangerous than in such a time of social tension. Freedom has given the United States the elasticity to endure strain. Freedom keeps open the path of novel and creative solutions, and enables change to come by choice. Every silencing of a heresy, every enforcement of an orthodoxy, diminishes the toughness and resilience of our society and leaves it the less able to deal with stress.

Now as always in our history, books are among our greatest instruments of freedom. They are almost the only means for making generally available ideas or manners of expression that can initially command only a small audience. They are the natural medium for the new idea and the untried voice from which come the original contributions to social growth. They are essential to the extended discussion which serious thought requires, and to the accumulation of knowledge and ideas into organized collections.

We believe that free communication is essential to the preservation of a free society and a creative culture. We believe that these pressures towards conformity present the danger of limiting the range of variety of inquiry and expression on which our democracy and our culture depend. We believe that every American community must jealously guard the freedom to publish and to circulate, in order to preserve its own freedom to read. We believe that publishers and librarians have a profound responsibility to give validity to that freedom to read by making it possible for the reader to choose freely from a variety of offerings.

The freedom to read is guaranteed by the Constitution. Those with faith in free men will stand firm on these constitutional guarantees of essential rights and will exercise the responsibilities that accompany these rights.

We therefore affirm these propositions:

1. *It is in the public interest for publishers and librarians to make available the widest diversity of views and expressions, including those which are unorthodox or unpopular with the majority.*

Creative thought is by definition new, and what is new is different. The bearer of every new thought is a rebel until his idea is refined and tested. Totalitarian systems attempt to maintain themselves in power by the ruthless suppression of anv concept which challenges the established orthodoxy. The power of a democratic system to adapt to change is vastly strengthened by the freedom of its citizens to choose widely from among conflicting opinions offered freely to them. To stifle every non-conformist idea at birth would mark the end of the democratic process. Furthermore, only through the constant activity of weighing and selecting can the democratic mind attain the strength demanded by times like these. We need to know not only what we believe but why we believe it.

2. *Publishers and librarians do not need to endorse every idea or presentation contained in the books they make available. It would conflict with the public interest for them to establish their own political, moral or aesthetic views as the sole standard for determining what books should be published or circulated.*

Publishers and librarians serve the educational process by helping to make available knowledge and ideas required for the growth of the mind and the increase of learning. They do not foster education by imposing as mentors the patterns of their own thought. The people should have the freedom to read and consider a broader range of ideas than those that may be held by any single librarian or publisher or government or church. It is wrong that what one man can read should be confined to what another thinks proper.

3. *It is contrary to the public interest for publishers or librarians to determine the acceptability of a book solely on the basis of the personal history or political affiliations of the author.*

A book should be judged as a book. No art or literature can flourish if it is to be measured by the political views or private lives of its creators. No society of free men can flourish which draws up lists of writers to whom it will not listen, whatever they may have to say.

4. *The present laws dealing with obscenity should be vigor-*

ously enforced. Beyond that, there is no place in our society for extra-legal efforts to coerce the taste of others, to confine adults to the reading matter deemed suitable for adolescents, or to inhibit the efforts of writers to achieve artistic expression.

To some, much of modern literature is shocking. But is not much of life itself shocking? We cut off literature at the source if we prevent serious artists from dealing with the stuff of life. Parents and teachers have a responsibility to prepare the young to meet the diversity of experiences in life to which they will be exposed as they have a responsibility to help them learn to think critically for themselves. These are affirmative responsibilities, not to be discharged simply by preventing them from reading works for which they are not yet prepared. In these matters taste differs, and taste cannot be legislated; nor can machinery be devised which will suit the demands of one group without limiting the freedom of others. We deplore the catering to the immature, the retarded or the maladjusted taste. But those concerned with freedom have the responsibility of seeing to it that each individual book or publication, whatever its contents, price or method of distribution, is dealt with in accordance with due process of law.

5. *It is not in the public interest to force a reader to accept with any book the prejudgment of a label characterizing the book or author as subversive or dangerous.*

The idea of labeling presupposes the existence of individuals or groups with wisdom to determine by authority what is good or bad for the citizen. It presupposes that each individual must be directed in making up his mind about the ideas he examines. But Americans do not need others to do their thinking for them.

6. *It is the responsibility of publishers and librarians, as guardians of the people's freedom to read, to contest encroachments upon that freedom by individuals or groups seeking to impose their own standards or tastes upon the community at large.*

It is inevitable in the give and take of the democratic process that the political, the moral, or the aesthetic concepts of an individual or group will occasionally collide with those of another individual or group. In a free society each individual is free to determine for himself what he wishes to read, and each group is free to determine what it will recommend to its freely associated members. But no group has the right to take the law into its own hands and to impose its own concept of politics or morality upon other members of a democratic society. Freedom is no freedom if it is accorded only to the accepted and the inoffensive.

7. *It is the responsibility of publishers and librarians to give full meaning to the freedom to read by providing books that enrich the quality of thought and expression. By the exercise of this affirmative responsibility, bookmen can demonstrate that the answer to a bad book is a good one, the answer to a bad idea is a good one.*

The freedom to read is of little consequence when expended on the trivial; it is frustrated when the reader cannot obtain matter fit for his purpose. What is needed is not only the absence of restraint, but the positive provision of opportunity for the people to read the best that has been thought and said. Books are the major channel by which the intellectual inheritance is handed down, and the principal means of its testing and growth. The defense of their freedom and integrity, and the enlargement of their service to society, requires of all bookmen the utmost of their faculties, and deserves of all citizens the fullest of their support.

✻   ✻   ✻

We state these propositions neither lightly nor as easy generalizations. We here stake out a lofty claim for the value of books. We do so because we believe that they are good, possessed of enormous variety and usefulness, worthy of cherishing and keeping free. We realize that the application of these propositions may mean the dissemination of ideas and manners of expression that are repugnant to many persons. We do not state these propositions in the comfortable belief that what people read is unimportant. We believe rather that what people read is deeply important; that ideas can be dangerous; but that the suppression of ideas is fatal to a democratic society. Freedom itself is a dangerous way of life, but it is ours.

Endorsed by: American Library Association Council, June 25, 1953

American Book Publishers Council, Board of Directors, June 18, 1953

Not Censorship But Selection
By Lester Asheim

(Reprinted from *Wilson Library Bulletin,* September 1953)

There is an amusing word game with which many of you are familiar in which the object is to trace an action, a point of view, or a characteristic through the gamut of its connotations from the most to the least acceptable. The point of the game is that the most admirable aspect of the characteristic is always assigned by the speaker to himself, whereas the least attractive aspect is taken to be that which characterizes somebody else. Thus, "I know the value of a dollar; he is miserly." To many, the title of my paper would seem to reflect a similar tendency. *I* select but *he* censors.

When librarians discuss the matter among themselves, they are quite satisfied with the distinction between censorship and selection, and are in smug agreement that the librarian practices the latter, not the former. Non-librarians are less disposed to be so generous in their interpretation of the librarian's action. Thus in its article on censorship, the *Encyclopedia of the Social Sciences* points out that "Libraries and booksellers have sometimes undertaken to censor books, declaring that they would not circulate books 'personally scandalous, libelous, immoral, or otherwise disagreeable,'" and Morris Ernst is even more outspoken:

> The subterranean censorship may appear in the public library as well. ... Do public libraries attempt to supervise the tastes of their readers by making it a fixed policy not to buy "objectionable" books? It is a simple expedient and has often been applied. The public librarian often has the plausible excuse that as the funds of a library are limited, he

must pick and choose, and naturally the more "wholesome" books are to be preferred. He insists that he is exercising not censorship but the prerogative of free selection. Nevertheless, the character of this choice is often suspicious.[1]

Clearly, in these two quotations, any deliberate bar against free access to a book is designated "censorship," and it does not matter that the control is enforced by the librarian rather than by a postal authority, or a pressure group. Does the librarian really have any grounds for claiming that there *is* a difference?

Our concern here, of course, is not with cases where the librarian is merely carrying out an obligation placed upon him by law. Where the decision is not his to make, we can hardly hold him responsible for that decision. Thus, the library which does not stock a book which may not be passed through customs or which is punishable by law as pornographic, will not be considered here. The real question of censorship versus selection arises when the librarian, exercising his own judgment, decides against a book which has every legal right to representation on his shelves. In other words, we should not have been concerned with the librarian who refused to buy *Ulysses* for his library before 1933—but we do have an interest in his refusal after the courts cleared it for general circulation in the United States.

What is the Difference?

Yet, in its practical results, what is the essential difference to the patron who cannot get *Ulysses* from the library because the customs office refused it admission to the United States, because the librarian decided not to buy it, or because a local pressure group forced its removal from the shelves? In each case, he is deprived of access to a particular piece of communication through the action of someone else. Can we seriously make a case for our claim that in the first and third instances censorship was operative, but in the second instance, the librarian was exercising selection, not censorship?

The first instance illustrates censorship in its purest and simplest form: a work is banned from the entire country by legal action. If this is the characteristic of censorship, then the librarian is not a censor, for he does not go to law to enforce his judgment—and he does not because he has no intention of denying access to the book through any channel but that of his own agency. He does not say (as the law says), "This book shall not be circulated." He says only. "*I* will not circulate it."

The third instance illustrates censorship in its impurest and most complex form: a work is banned from an entire community by the extra-legal pressure of a small segment of the community. Again, it is the scope of the ban which distinguishes the second and third instances: the librarian controls only the content of his own institution; the pressure group attempts to control the content of all institutions, whether under their jurisdiction or not.

Limited Span of Control

But the allegedly limited span of the librarian's control is not a sufficient virtue to absolve him of any suspicion of censorship action. The local pressure group, after all, is also limited in its effectiveness; a ban in Boston does not affect the rest of the nation or even the state of Massachussets. But it is considered to be censorship nevertheless, and if an effect on a single community is sufficiently wide to qualify rejection as censorship, we must recognize that in many communities the library is the only real agency for the circulation of book materials and that the ban in the library is, in effect, a ban which operates on the community as a whole. If we accept the range of its effectiveness in its community as the key to censorship action, we are forced into the position of saying that when the small town library fails to purchase an expensive book of limited scholarly interest, that is censorship, but when a large city library rejects a book of minority political opinion, that is not. Most of us would suspect, I think, that just the reverse is the truth.

But why? If the results of the action are the same, wherein does the difference lie? Can we actually claim—seriously—that the reasons, the motives, the causes are different, and that this difference is sufficient to justify the distinction between the rejection which we will call selection and the rejection which we will call censorship? I think we can—and I think that even the patron who is deprived of the book is affected differently when the motive is selection rather than censorship. To use a far-fetched analogy, a man who has his leg amputated in order to save his life is in a different situation from a man who has his leg amputated by a sadistic doctor who performs the operation through psychotic compulsion rather than scientific requirement. The end result is the loss of a leg in each case—but these are different kinds of things nevertheless—and the "victim" of the loss knows the difference.

It may be objected that even though this be so, there is still the problem of whether the doctor knows the difference and if he does, whether he can be relied upon to admit it. Will he not rationalize his action in terms of the acceptable reasons? Will not the doctor insist that the amputation was necessary to keep the body healthy even as the librarian now claims that the rejection is necessary to keep the collection strong?

The answer to these questions is well known; each of us is familiar with man's ability to paint himself in the most flattering colors. But that good motives are sometimes claimed by those who have no right to them does not mean that therefore no good motives are possible. We have said that they are possible and that they are the key to the distinction between selection and censorship. We have said also that we cannot rely solely on stated claims to guide us to that key. Our problem is complicated by the fact that we are forced to check what a man says against his actions.

Well, the action with which we must deal is the rejection which occurs in the library. Librarians do not deny that rejection occurs, but they claim that the ideal of absolute equality for all books is unattainable even supposing it were desirable. To demand that all books be equally accessible is to demand that all books occupy the same place on the same shelf—a physical impossibility. And as soon as we defer to the laws of physics and place each book in a different place, we shall start having some books less accessible than others and shall be—in a sense— discriminating against the least accessible.

Physical Problems

But let us suppose that we recognize that equal accessibility is unattainable, why should not all books be available at least? Again we run into physical impossibility—no library in the world is large enough to house even one copy of every printed publication. Nor is the difficulty merely physical, as any practicing librarian knows from bitter experience. Long before we are allowed to test the physical limits of complete availability we are brought up short by financial limits (implicit already in the physical in that among the many things we cannot afford to buy is the needed space). So complete representation of every title ever published is an idle dream. Consequently some titles will not be purchased, and that is rejection.

Many librarians would say that, in such a situation, that is also selection, and they would like to stop the discussion at that point. Since we can't have everything, since we can't afford all of the things that might be purchased, it is necessary to select, the reasons are financial and physical, and that—they would like you to believe—is that. It would be dishonest to pretend, however, that financial considerations are the only ones which shape the judgment to purchase or reject. The librarian also feels an obligation to select in terms of standards—and there are some books that he would not buy even if money were no problem. Unfortunately, some of our standards are sufficiently subjective, sufficiently vague, and sufficiently imprecise to serve the uses of the censors as well as of the selectors. Merely to cite the standards does little to prove our claim that ours is not a censoring function.

Intent of the Author

One of our standards, for example, is the presumed intent of the author and the sincerity of his purpose. This is a valid standard certainly, but only a subjective judgment can be made concerning it. There is a very real danger, almost impossible to combat, that a point of view with which the reader is in agreement will seem to be more sincerely held than one with which he disagrees. When a book attacks a basic belief or a way of life to which we are emotionally attached, its purpose will seem to us to be vicious rather than constructive; dangerous rather than valuable; deserving of suppression rather than of widespread dissemination. Some of the most notorious instances of censorship have been based upon the assumption that the writer's purpose was pornographic or treasonable—and I think we must concede that the censors in most of these cases really believed that ideas which offended them so deeply must of necessity have an ignoble motivation.

Literary excellence is a second criterion to which most librarians would subscribe, but again the judgments are essentially subjective, although more precise indicators can be established to test literary quality. A reader who does not like a book usually considers it to be badly written; conversely a book whose ideas please him will seem to be one which is written well. We have plenty of evidence that the readers of books which have little or no critical acceptance—the rental romances and the moral tracts—consider them to be very well written indeed. Try to convince an Edgar Guest devotee that his poetry is poor, or that the poetry of Dylan Thomas is better; try to make a case, to a constant reader of the Lutz books, that there is stronger moral fibre in a book like *Catcher in the Rye*.

There is an added complication here—and that is the high incidence of books which are not written well but which do have literary standing. The Dreisers, the Farrells, the James Joneses fall down on some of the simplest basic rules for good writing, yet most librarians accept them as deserving additions to a library collection. To many of our patrons it seems that the library's choice of works is based, not upon literary excellence but upon the amount of sordidness, iconoclasm, and obscenity that can be crammed within the covers of a single book. Why is it, they ask, that the librarian always finds a "dirty" book to be better written than a "wholesome" one?

Still another criterion for selection is the presumed effect upon the reader, and here again we have only our guesses, based upon our own individual subjective reaction. And here again, we have a standard which is the basis for most of what we should all be agreed may properly be called censorship. What other reason is there for censorship than the assumption that the condemned book will have a harmful effect upon its readers—or at least on some of them? That we know nothing about reading effects really, that no solid studies exist which prove that books have a bad effect upon readers is of very little use in a battle against censorship. If we have almost no evidence that books are harmful, we have less that they are not, and it is quite understandable that those who favor censorship should advocate wariness against materials which may be harmful. If you don't know whether a bottle contains poison or not—I paraphrase a standard argument—it is better not to drink from it.

Time and Custom

Lastly, librarians agree with the courts that the time, and the custom of the community, are important elements to be considered in judging the value and effectiveness of a book. Such a standard, however, is a strong support for censorship which would stultify the development of a literature and the propagation of thought and ideas. Almost all of the great classics have been the books which said something new, or said something differently, ahead of or not in step with the custom and traditions of the community. This is the standard which fires a Whitman from his job and forces a Galileo to recant.

If we are agreed that the standards employed as touchstones by the librarians are essentially the same as those used by the censor, the distinction between selection and censorship will have to be found in the *way* the standards are applied. The honorable surgeon and the sadist both wield a knife, but in the framework in which they perform their operations and the premises on which they base their actions lies the key to the distinction between them. The atmosphere in which the decision is reached to reject a book tells us more than the mere fact of rejection, the high-minded excuses the rejector makes public to justify it, or the standards against which he allegedly weighs his decision.

Negative or Positive?

The major characteristics which makes for the all-important difference seems to me to be this: that the selector's approach is positive, while that of the censor is negative. This is more than a verbal quibble; it transforms the entire act and the steps included in it. For to the selector, the important thing is to find reasons to keep the book. Given such a guiding principle, the selector looks for values, for strengths, for virtues which will overshadow minor objections. For the censor, on the other hand, the important thing is to find reasons to reject the book; his guiding principle leads him to seek out the objectionable features, the weaknesses, the possibilities for misinterpretation. The positive selector asks what the reaction of a rational intelligent adult would be to the content of the work; the censor fears for the results on the weak, the warped, and the irrational. The selector says, if there is anything good in this book let us try to keep it; the censor says, if there is anything bad in this book, let us reject it. And since there is seldom a flawless work in any form, the censor's approach can destroy much that is worth saving.

An inevitable consequence of the negative approach is that it leads to the use of isolated parts rather than the complete whole upon which to base a judgment. Taken out of context and given a weight completely out of keeping with their place in the over-all work, single words and unrelated passages can be used to damn a book. This technique has been typical of many of the most notorious instances of censorship: the major theme, the total purpose, the effect of the work as a unified whole have been ignored in order to focus on a word or phrase or sequence. In other words, four letters have outweighed five hundred pages.

Nor is this failure to view the relevancy of the parts to the whole an outmoded one; it was in 19—not 18—53 that an official censor went on record publicly to the effect that he does not distinguish between a nude in a work of art and one in any other context. "It's all"—and I quote—"lustful to me." The censor who starts with such a premise will inevitably find much that is offensive, because that is what he is seeking and because he is abnormally susceptible. The phenomenon is not a new one, nor is the suspicion which logically follows: whether a mind so oriented does not bring more dirt to the book than was original-ly there.

The negative orientation, which seeks reasons to ban rather than to preserve, also leads to the judgment of books by external rather than internal criteria. The censor need not ask what the book has to say, what values it has to contribute, what—within the covers of the book itself—is the material which will be lost if the book is suppressed. He can ask, instead, what kind of a husband and father is the author; of what nation is he a citizen; what are his political affiliations, what magazines does he read; what is his color, his race, his religion? And if present circum-stances cannot lead to a rationalization for the ban, he can go into the past—what has the writer ever done with which I am in disagreement? The book is not judged on its merits as a book at

all; it is used as a stick to beat its author for personal deviations
whether they are reflected in the book or not.

Internal Values

The selector, on the other hand, judges by internal values.
Since it is the book with which he is concerned, it is the content
of the book that is weighed, not the table manners of the
publisher or the sartorial orthodoxy of the author. By extension,
then, the librarian, if he is truly a selector and not a censor, does
not succumb to irrelevancies—introduced either by the prejudices
of his own background or the pressures of his library's patrons.
He admits the right of the reader to take issue with the writer,
but he is swayed by arguments only where they have relevance
to the book itself, and to the book as a whole.

It is important to note here that, whether they annoy us or not,
some pressures are legitimate and our patrons have every right
to exert them, *so long as they are pressures on opinion, not on
the expression of opinion.* So long as the opposing point of view
may be expressed, the reader has a right to reject it, to take issue
with it, and to try to convince others of its falsity. Unfortunately,
the methods taken to convince others often introduce elements
which limit by intimidation the freedom to arrive at an honest
judgment on the merits of the case alone—as when the police
authorities threaten to find fire hazards in a theater which
shows a film to which they are opposed. Strictly speaking the
police have not censored—they have merely expressed their
opinion of the film in question, and it is the theater owner who
refuses to show the film. But the values in the film have not
been the basis of his decision; irrelevant pressures have been
exerted, and it is the use of such irrelevant pressures that has
given a bad name to all pressures and has led many advocates of
free speech to seek retaliatory limitations on the freedom of
special interest groups.

Irrelevant Threat

Fortunately in most library situations, the implied and irrelevant threat is seldom used to dictate selection policy. But many
librarians have been known to defer to anticipated pressures,
and to avoid facing issues by suppressing possible issue-making

cause . In such cases the rejection of a book *is* censorship, for the book has been judged—not on its own merits—but in terms of the librarian's devotion to three square meals a day. Do not misunderstand me—I am as devoted as any to the delights of the table and a roof against the rain. But these considerations should not be mistaken for literary criteria, and it is with the latter that the librarian-as-selector is properly concerned.

Finally, the selector begins, ideally, with a presumption in favor of liberty of thought; the censor does not. The aim of the selector is to promote reading, not to inhibit it; to multiply the points of view which will find expression, not limit them; to be a channel for communication, not a bar against it. In a sense, perhaps, it could be said that the librarian is interfering with the freedom to read whenever he fails to make some book available. But viewed realistically, the librarian is promoting the freedom to read by making as accessible as possible as many things as he can, and his selection is more likely to be in the direction of stimulating controversy and introducing innovation that in suppressing the new and perpetuating the stereotype. That is why he so often selects works which shock some people. The books which have something new to say are most likely to shock and consequently may not readily find another outlet through which to say it. The frequent forays of the censors against the libraries is heartening evidence that selection and censorship *are* different things.

Liberty or Control

Selection, then, begins with a presumption in favor of liberty of thought; censorship, with a presumption in favor of thought control. Selection's approach to the book is positive, seeking its values in the book as a book, and in the book as a whole. Censorship's approach is negative, seeking for vulnerable characteristics wherever they can be found—anywhere within the book, or even outside it. Selection seeks to protect the right of the reader to read; censorship seeks to protect—not the right— but the reader himself from the fancied effects of his reading. The selector has faith in the intelligence of the reader; the censor has faith only in his own.

In other words, selection is democratic while censorship is

authoritarian, and in our democracy we have traditionally tend-
ed to put our trust in the selector rather than in the censor. We
treasure our freedom and we trust those who demonstrate a
similar desire to protect it, although we are sometimes deluded
for a time by those who only profess a devotion to our liberties.
While we are willing to defer to the honest judgment of those in
special fields whose knowledge, training, and special aptitude
fit them to render these judgments, we demand that those to
whom we delegate such authority shall demonstrate the virtues
which are the basis of that trust. In the last analysis, this is what
makes a profession: the earned confidence of those it serves. But
that confidence *must* be earned, and it can be only if we remain
true to the ideals for which our profession stands. In the profession of librarianship, these ideals are embodied, in part at least,
in the special characteristics which distinguish selection from
censorship. If we are to gain the esteem we seek for our profession, we must be willing to accept the difficult obligations
which those ideals imply.

Notes

1. Morris L. Ernst and William Seagle. *To the Pure ... A Study
of Obscenity and the Censor.* New York, Viking, 1928. p. 101

Appendix B

Library Book Selection Policies and Procedures

Selected from a List Prepared for the ALA
Book Selection Work Conference, July 2-3, 1955

Authority
Final authority for the determination of policy in the selection
and acquisition of materials is vested in the Library's Board of
Trustees.

—The New York Public Libary

Responsibility
Ultimate responsibility for book selection, as for all library
activity, rests in the Director, who operates within the framework of policies determined by the Board of Trustees.

—Enoch Pratt Free Library

The privilege and responsibility for selection of books and
other library materials for purchase, belongs to every member of
the staff. This is based on the assumption that no one person,
nor few persons, can know enough about all subjects, nor the
reading needs and desires of all people, to be qualified to
assume all responsibility for book selection.

—Oklahoma City Public Library

It is considered desirable to insure maximum participation of
professional staff members in the reviewing process. Wide reading of books is encouraged despite the delay involved since an
informed staff contribute immeasurably to intelligent use of the
book collection.

—New York Public Library

Community Analysis

Formulation of book selection policies necessarily begins with the examination of the community, of the organization and the existing collections of the library, and of the services which the library is expected to perform.

—Queens Borough Public Library

Objectives

Not only the library's responsibilities but also its objectives must be considered as a part of the basis for selection of materials.

—Peoria Public Library

The book selection policy is intended to implement the general objectives of the public library. The purpose of the selection process is to obtain expertly selected books and other materials to further the library program of giving information, reference assistance, and help to those engaged in educational pursuits, as well as to provide general home reading.

—Washington, D.C., Public Library

Criteria (basic)

In general the library's policy has been to purchase the best books which satisfy the clientele of the library within budget limitations, with no obligation, except in special departments, to provide research material, though frequently doing so incidentally. The established criteria for all fields include:

A. Permanent or timely value
B. Accurate information
C. Authoritativeness
D. Clear presentation and readability
E. Social significance
    Fundamental values are defined in terms of human relationships:

    1. *Individual* information, education, and recreation
    2. *Group* responsibility in the family unit, the vocational and economic fields, as citizens in a democracy and relation to the international scene.
F. Eliminate the unimportant, the cheap and trivial, the delib-

erately distorted, sensational or offensive, particularly in the fields of religion, sex hygiene, racial prejudice, political ideologies and fiction.

G. Present both sides of controversial issues: labor-management, planned parenthood, Communism, etc.

H. Balance special group interests with general demand, e.g., books in foreign languages.

I. Include books of doubtful value occasionally for their time-liness, such as campaign biographies, flying saucers, or a book of fiction about which curiosity has reached fever heat. They are discarded when they have served their purpose.

J. Some books may be restricted for minors too immature to see them in their proper perspective. Proselyting books are not considered public library material. Textbooks are not bought as textbooks. Dreambooks, magic, hypnotism fail to serve the purpose of the public library. Representative books, such as *Mein Kampf* and the *Communist Manifesto* are included where they have historical significance and bring into the open the ideologies which democracy seeks to combat.

The primary obligation of the library is to uphold the doctrine of freedom of speech and of the press. We sub-scribe to the American Library Association's Bill of Rights that censorship of books "that would establish a coercive concept of Americanism must be challenged ... in mainte-nance of (the library's) responsibility to provide public information and enlightenment through the printed word." In administering this policy the library tries to keep a true balance between its duty to make available honest presenta-tion of both sides of every public question, and its determi-nation not to allow itself to be used as a propaganda agency by the enemies of our form of government.

K. Collector's items as such are not purchased.

L. Format may be a deciding factor. Possibility of rebinding is considered, as well as type and legibility

M. Price may also be a deciding factor.

—Carnegie Library of Pittsburgh

Certain general criteria are followed by all selectors: (1) the

author's reputation and significance as a writer; (2) the importance of subject matter to the collection; (3) scarcity of material
on the subject; (4) timeliness or permanence of the book; (5)
appearance of title in special bibliographies or indexes; (6)
authoritativeness; (7) reputation and standing of the publisher;
(8) price; (9) availability of material elsewhere in area.

—Indianapolis Public Library

Adult Book Selection

Points considered in adult book selection are literary, educational, informational, and recreational value; authority and effectiveness of presentation; qualities conducive to critical
thought and understanding; and available funds and space.
Contemporary and popular authors are included, as well as
those who have demonstrated enduring worth. Titles are selected on the basis of the content as a whole and without regard to
the personal history of the author. In the case of controversial
questions, variety and balance of opinion are sought whenever
available.

—New York Public Library

Controversial issues

The public library asserts its right and duty to keep on its
shelves a representative selection of books on all subjects of
interest to its readers and not prohibited by law, including
books on all sides of controversial questions. Books on any
subject, if published by reputable and well-known publishers
and sold without restriction in bookstores, are properly admitted
to the public library. The public library has no right to emphasize one subject at the expense of another, or one side of a
subject without regard to ·the other side. It must carry the
important books on all sides and all subjects.

—Chicago Public Library

Labeling

The library will not indicate, through the use of labels or
other devices, particular philosophies outlined in a book. To do
so is to establish in the reader's mind a judgment before the
reader has had the opportunity to examine the book personally.

—Denver Public Library

Fiction

New fiction considered for purchase is read on approval, with the exception of some twenty authors such as Ernest Hemingway, John Steinbeck, etc. It must satisfy the basic criteria of excellence and social significance. Best sellers are considered on individual merits, as are inferior works of a standard popular author.

—Carnegie Library of Pittsburg

Semi-and Pseudo-Scientific Materials

Special care is necessary in the purchase of books in those borderline areas of science in which subject matter or treatment is not recognized by reputable scientific authority ... the following "rules of thumb" are helpful in dealing with questionable scientific, health, and borderline material: author (reputation, professional or academic position, other publications, etc); publisher (whether book is privately printed by author, a bookshop or a small unknown press, or whether notice gives only P.O.box); source (whether sent unsolicited by author, distributor, or propaganda organization, especially when accompanied by high-pressure sales letter); content and purpose (whether authoritative, in accepted tradition of handling the subject matter; whether book attempts to examine the subject objectively); literary style (character of vocabulary and style—whether nebulous, full of abstract or unusual jargon); typographic format (quality of paper, press-work, bindery—general impression of book as a book). While all of these factors may help to "spot" the pseudo-scientific, in the last analysis final decision on a questionable book must be based on expert opinion.

—Enoch Pratt Free Library

Sex

The library purchases books about sex for such users as social workers, clergymen, physicians, teachers, parents, young people contemplating marriage, newly married couples, and adolescents. An effort is made to obtain only material that is authoritative, sane, and up-to-date. However, extremely scientific and technical works are usually not added to the collection.

—Washington, D.C., Public Library

Recreational Reading

It is, of course, difficult to define the term "recreational reading." It might be said to be that reading which is done in one's leisure time, for pleasure only. However, the same book, or type of book, does not give pleasure to everyone. It may be fiction to some, travel for others, biography or history for still others. Therefore, the library, as a public institution, feels that it should try to have a well-rounded collection of recreational reading to satisfy these different desires, always with the understanding that this reading material will be the best of its kind that can be selected.

—Indianapolis Public Library

Non-Fiction

Non-fiction is chosen with the same care as fiction, and the general criteria of selection are used. Staff members with special fields of interest, experience, or study are asked to read and make recommendations for books in these fields.

—Indianapolis Public Library

Religion

Since we are a public library we strive to maintain an impartial recognition of all religions while specializing in none.

—Newark Public Library

In the literature of religion, more perhaps than in any other class, library selection must be broad, tolerant, without partisanship or propaganda, yet consistently directed toward the choice of the best books as regards authority, timeliness, and good literary quality.

—Cincinnati Public Library

Children's Books

The basic policy of book selection for children is to choose the best new books and replace and duplicate the older titles which have proved their worth. The selection includes books for recreational reading, inspirational books of lasting value, and books of information covering a wide range of knowledge that will satisfy the child's natural curiosity and widen his interests.

Each book is judged on its own merits; it is considered also in relation to the collection as a whole and in relation to the children for whom it is intended.

It is the policy of the children's department to read every book purchased, with the possible exception of some technical, in which the choice is made from authoritative book reviews and from a knowledge of the reliability of the author.

—Indianapolis Public Library

Selection for Young People

The ultimate aim of the library work with young people is to contribute to the development of well-rounded citizens of their own country and the world. To this end, readable adult titles are selected that are keyed to the young people's needs and interests, as well as books that will tend to open up new interests in cultural, economic and social fields. Some titles written specifically for young people are naturally included in the collection, and children's titles are occasionally duplicated. Since readers of 'teen age vary widely in ability and background, the books selected for them will of necessity vary in content and reading difficulty, but all titles are purchased in the hope that they will lead to continued reading in adult fields on as high a level as possible for each individual.

—Enoch Pratt Free Library

Book Selection Aids

Ideally every book added to the library should be read before purchase by a librarian with trained judgment, knowledge of the library's present resources, and acquaintance with the requirements of local readers. Where circumstances make such reading impossible or unnecessary the staff makes skilled use of selection aids, such as basic general lists, current general lists, special bibliographies for reference books and particular subject materials, and book reviewing journals. While book reviews are a major source of information about new books they are not followed blindly. No one publication is relied upon exclusively; furthermore, the critical opinions of reviewers are checked against each other.

—Washington, D.C. Public Library

[Excerpted from the California Library Association *Freedom Kit*]

Book Selection Policy
Free Public Library, Bloomfield, N.J.
September, 1956

The place of the public library in the community

It is the function of the public library in America today to provide the means through which all people may have free access to the thinking on all sides of all ideas. The public library has become a practical demonstration of the belief in universal education as a life-long process. It is the responsibility of the library to provide books and other media of communication for people of all ages and give guidance in their use. It must offer opportunity and encouragement to individuals and groups:

1. to educate themselves continuously;
2. to keep abreast of progress in all fields of knowledge;
3. to maintain freedom of expression and a constructively critical attitude toward all public issues;
4. to be responsible members of the community, the country and the world;
5. to develop greater efficiency in the performance of their work;
6. to discover and develop their creative capacities for and powers of appreciation of arts and letters;
7. to use their leisure time in the enjoyment of reading.

The Bloomfield Public Library philosophy and policy

The Bloomfield Public Library subscribes to the book selection principles contained in the Library Bill of Rights, adopted by the American Library Association in 1948. [Adopted by the Board of Trustees, 1953] It is keenly aware of the necessity for careful evaluation and selection of materials. It believes that ideas, intelligently presented, are powerful forces for good and that ideas, carelessly presented, may work against the public interest. It seeks materials which are accurate, objective and sincere and diligently avoids those which are consciously sensational. In fulfilling its responsibility, the library strives to include:

1. Source material which documents the past,
2. thoughtful interpretations of the ideas of the past,
3. a record of the times which is of current interest and provides material of future historical significance. This includes books which present conditions and mores and those which reflect varying trends of thought.
4. personal accounts and papers, memoirs or other writings of personal opinion on a subject of interest. Books in this area are counter-balanced by expressions of other and contrary opinions if they are available.
5. contemporary and standard works for recreation and leisure. This category includes the novel and other writings of a more ephemeral nature, which draws public demand because of a certain timeliness, surface originality and fashion.

The selection and acquisition of books is based on four controlling factors:

1. the community;
2. the individual merit of each book;
3. the library: its existing collections, budget and services,
4. common sense.

Community factors

There are two prime factors which have a direct bearing upon the selection of books: the people themselves; other institutions where library books are available for public use.

1. The People

In selecting books for the Bloomfield Public Library we must first consider the people we serve and the general aspects of the community as a whole. Bloomfield reflects the fusion that is America: there are different races, creeds, nations represented; it presents contrasts of taste, opinion, education. It is the home of scholars, artists, the small business man, those who came to

America yesterday and those whose roots grew in this country many years ago.

To serve a community of this variety in which the politician, scientist, industrialist, housewife, Senior Citizen, kindergartner and professional sportsman meet each other at the Public Library, there must be a collection of books, broad in subject, comprehensive in viewpoint, with wide latitude in reading levels. There must be books for the reader's serious study and books which will satisfy his personal needs for recreation and leisure.

2. Other libraries.

Other libraries where book collections are available for public use affect the book selection in limited but interesting areas and ways. For example, for special use, the company libraries of Bakelite Corp., Schering Corp., etc., supply a book or item of information too specialized for public library purchase but necessary to the inquiring borrower. The public library, on the other hand, works closely with these companies to supply answers to questions which highly specialized libraries do not have. This cooperation was begun some years ago, with the public library taking the initiative and serving as the catalyzing agent. It has proved highly successful for all concerned.

Another profitable experiment was begun during World War II, when gasoline was scarce and when war workers needed information for their jobs that could be secured only from library books. It was the interchangeable system of Bloomfield, Glen Ridge and Montclair Public Library borrowing privileges. In many cases, duplication of expensive items has been avoided because one of the cooperating libraries has had a need to buy the item for its shelves.

The merit of the book

The basic principles outlined below apply to all acquisitions whether purchased or donated (although the following statements are written with specific regard to books, the same criteria are applied to magazines and other reading materials not in book form):

1. Factual Materials

It is impossible to classify all fields of knowledge represented in books, define them and establish a firm guide or standard by which each book may be indisputably accepted or rejected. A book may not be judged solely on its literary merit or else we should lose some of our most valuable human documents. Nor can a book be judged solely on its scholarship for we must provide reading for the hours of relaxation and leisure. Therefore, the book selector must endeavor to penetrate further, must judge impartially and evaluate critically:

a. the degree of accomplishment of purpose
b. the authority and competence of the author
c. comprehensiveness in breadth and scope
d. sincerity and fundamental objectivity
e. clarity and accuracy of presentation
f. potential usefulness
g. relation to existing collection
h. importance as a record of the times
i. relative importance in comparison with other books on the subject.

2. Books for Leisure

As leisure time has increased throughout the country, the importance of leisure time activities has increased in an even greater proportion. Never in our history have so many people had so much free time to devote to activities of their own personal choosing. The library assumes as one of its major responsibilities the provision of suitable reading materials for this increased free time. The leisure reading of the library's public is influenced by the many factors which affect the personal life of each individual: educational background, the degree of specialization, profession or occupation, living conditions, and many others. Recreational reading may be either fact or fiction, poetry or drama. The range may be from the simple and ephemeral to the scholarly. The library must take all these aspects into consideration and select for all interests, judging the books as competently as possible on the following qualities:

a. vitality
b. artistic expression
c. originality and imagination
d. honesty and integrity

e. sustained interest

f. sympathy and conviction

g. consistency in characterization

In evaluating books, the selector must be alert to experimental style or treatment which may portend a new literary trend.

The Library

The several internal library factors influencing selection of books are: budget, space, the content of the present collection, the organizational structure of the library system.

1. Budget, space, etc.

The books selected and purchased must obviously come within the budgetary allowance and there must be sufficient space available to house them properly.

2. Organizational Structure of the Bloomfield Public Library

The organizational structure of the Bloomfield Public Library system is designed to bring books close to the homes of the people and to do this in as economical a fashion as possible. This is partly accomplished by the central location of the library building, and partly by the services of the bookmobile.

Basic Policies Concerning Selection and Evaluation
of Materials for Compton Secondary School District
(California)

I. In our Democracy, public education has the commitment of interpreting and making more meaningful the "democratic way of life" as a part of our American Heritage. Public Schools have to assure the following as their specific responsibility:

Provide learning situations in which constructive citizenship and democratic procedures may be experienced by pupils through individual and group activities.

Provide qualified personnel, who will promote faith and confidence in American institutions, American ideals, and processes of American democracy, to select materials and conduct activities.

Provide materials that will develop critical thinking, objective evaluations, and aesthetic appreciation suitable to the maturity level and activities of pupils.

II. Selection and evaluation of materials

A. Materials, as used in this policy statement, may be defined as:

1. Instructional material—material used to develop the curriculum according to the basic course of study at the levels of maturity of the pupils.

2. Library material—material used to support and enrich the curriculum and selected for the personnel of the school in which the library is located.

B. Selection of material, because of changing and enlarging curriculum and the publishing of new materials, is a continuous process, therefore:

1. Materials are selected by qualified representative personnel consisting of teachers, librarians, coordinators, and administrators through individual and committee study and recommendations.
2. Materials are selected by personal and/or committee examination of material and from recommended and authorized bibliographies or lists of materials.

C. The following evaluative criteria are used:

1. Materials are essential and appropriate for development of the subject.
2. Materials are factually accurate and objective in presentation.
3. Materials are contributing to literary appreciation or have aesthetic value.
4. Materials are selected because of the content and emphasis on the entire work.
5. Authors are competent and qualified in the field.
6. Materials on controversial issues are represented by both sides of the issue in an objective way.

III. Since opinions may differ in a democracy, the following procedures will be observed in recognizing those differences in an impartial and factual manner.

A. Citizens of the school community may register their criticism with the School Authorities and directed to the Board of Education.

1. All criticism must be presented in writing. The statement must include specific information as to author, title, publisher, and page number of each item to which objection is being made.
2. The statement must be signed and identification given which will allow proper reply to be made.

B. The Board of Education through the School Authorities will appoint a committee of school personnel to re-evaluate the materials being questioned and to make recommendations concerning it.

1. The committee shall consist of one teacher representative from each of the Junior High Schools, two teacher representatives from each of the Senior High Schools, one qualified librarian, and one school administrator.

2. The School Authorities may call in representative citizens of the school community for consultation.

(This report was accepted and approved Nov. 9, 1954, by the Board of Trustees of the Compton (Cal.) Union High School District. Exerpted from the California Library Association Freedom Kit)

Library Objectives and Book Selection Policies
Detroit Public Library—September 1954

(Exerpted from "The Public Library—an Educational Institution?" by Ralph A. Ulveling, Director, Public Library, Detroit; Library Resources and Technical Services, Winter, 1959)

The people of Detroit are a heterogenous group of nearly two million people with widely-differing interests, educational backgrounds and native ability. Behind or beside all of these is a mass of industrial and similar organizations, having book needs that are quite as definite as the book needs for individuals. For all this vast assemblage, the Detroit Public Library is the common book center to which they turn, with the full expectation that books and other material suitable to their individual needs will be available when required.

To function adequately in such a situation, the Detroit Public Library must operate as two distinct but coordinated libraries: The Home Reading Services and the Reference-Research Services.

a) The Home Reading Services provide the books for general non-specialized readers, then, through stimulation and guidance, promote their use, to the end that children, young people, men and women, may have opportunity and encouragement for their fullest development as individuals, as members of a family, as citizens. Since this service is concerned with the best personal development of people through existing knowledge, rather than with the refinement and extension of knowledge itself, its purpose in selecting books is to choose the best and the most usable that are available at varying levels.

b) The Reference-Research Services have the responsibility for preserving knowledge in its most comprehensive sense, and for maintaining open avenues for the exercise of intellectual freedom of inquiry. To carry this out, they must provide the usual as well as the obscure, the scholarly, and even the socially, economically, religiously, or politically unorthodox materials necessary for research.

The Library in choosing books applies certain standards as to quality of writing, accuracy, completeness, and integrity of the writer. In approving each title under consideration, these standards must vary, depending on the availability of materials and the availability of funds. With all the exigencies that can and do develop in the course of years, the excellence of a book selection policy will depend less on carefully defined criteria for judging books than on:

1) The careful practices established to sift and resift books under consideration for purchase, and later to reconsider any title which either the staff or the reading public feels may have been misappraised, and

2) A carefully selected staff of librarians having integrity and professional judgment of such degree that, within their field of service, they merit the same confidence accorded the doctor, the lawyer, and the art curator in their respective fields of service. But not every member of the public will agree with every decision made. The best evidence of the policies being pursued and to be pursued is in the record of the past.

Organization for Book Selection
Detroit Public Library

The Book Selection Department function of the Detroit Public Library is defined in the Library's organizational chart as follows:

> Making recommendations to the Director concerning general book selection policies after consultation with the Service Directors; making available, through approval copies, books and other materials that should be considered for inclusion in the Library's collection; establishing with the aid of committees ... lists of titles of books, periodicals and other materials approved for purchase ... ordering all books, pamphlets, films and phonograph records at the lowest possible cost to the Library by making agreements with the book trade for discounts; disposing of gifts and exchanges.

All orders, approval and firm, are processed through the Book Selection Department which performs a correlative function for the Reference and Home Reading Services.

Procedure for Selection of Books for Reference Services

Department Heads, assisted by their staffs, make the decisions for inclusions. No inter-departmental meetings are held since subject specialization minimizes their usefulness.

Procedure for Selection of Books for Home Reading Services

Each new title received in the Library is examined for potential use in Home Reading collections, and books of general interest are directed to a professional staff member for reading, reviewing and recommendation for inclusion.

The selection process for Home Reading Services functions

through two committees: a "Small Committee" composed of two of three Branch Librarians, plus one or two general assistants whose background, experience, and book knowledge give them an understanding of the institution's aims and responsibilities, and a "General Book Committee" composed of the heads of all Home Reading Service agencies.

The time requirements of the Small Committee are so heavy—a minimum of twenty hours a week of staff time—that members serve on a rotating basis. Current books, together with staff and professional reviews, are exhibited for one week in the Book Examination Room. Committee members and the Chief of Book Selection individually consider all books before taking group action to recommend each title for inclusion. A weekly list is then compiled for blanket ordering which briefly annotates fiction and all titles not accepted. Books on which opinion is sharply divided are held for presentation at the General Book Committee meeting, and the members of this committee make the ultimate decision on acceptance.

The General Book Committee meetings are held on alternate Fridays. Although Department Heads are present and may contribute to the discussion of the books, voting on selection of titles is restricted to the heads of the Home Reading Agencies since the meeting is not concerned with the acquisitions of the Reference Departments. Members of the Small Committee present the books, lead discussion of them, and give their recommendations. It functions only as an advisory committee. The final decision is vested in the General Book Committee, which is a large group reflecting many viewpoints. Though these meetings are basically for decision making purposes, they are an aid in providing information needed for book purchasing by the individual agency heads and in informing all of the total book intake into the Home Reading Services.

Since great importance is placed on the staff member's written and oral reviews, each staff reviewer is expected to:

Read the book conscientiously.

Look up information about the author and his work.

Make pertinent comparisons to other books in the field.

Make a short statement of theme or subject.

Indicate the author's purpose, treatment, sincerity and degree of achievement.

Indicate potential readers.

Write an honest, concise and reliable evaluation of the book based on personal judgment.

Refrain from reading printed reviews before reviewing books.

Inasmuch as all members of the professional staff share in the book reviewing necessary for the Library, new personnel in their orientation session are advised as follows:

"Book reviewing by professional staff members is a privilege and a responsibility. One should do it conscientiously and promptly, not as a staff assignment, but as part of the broader assignment and responsibility assumed when one chose and prepared for the career of librarianship. Do not consider reviewing as an infringement on your personal time. You have chosen a profession, not a skilled vocation, and the demands of a profession are not always confined within an eight hour day . . . Fundamentally, a good librarian must like to read and should be willing to read. It cannot be a sacrifice for him, it must be a primary function of his profession."

BOOK SELECTION POLICY
Los Angeles Public Library
(Adopted by the Board of Library Commissioners, August 22, 1956)

Adult Books

Objectives
It is the responsibility and aim of the Los Angeles Public Library to provide circulating material and reference service to meet or supplement the needs of Los Angeles city residents of all ages. For this purpose, representative materials are selected and maintained for general information, education, occupational and industrial uses, and the enjoyment and enrichment of leisure time.

Responsibility
Initial responsibility for book selection lies with the heads of the subject departments at the Central Library, who specialize in their respective fields. After approval for acquisition, titles may be selected by branch librarians or other designated staff members for inclusion in individual branch collections.

Final responsibility for book selection rests with the City Librarian, who operates within a framework of policies adopted by the Board of Library Commissioners.

General factors influencing book selection
The unique character of the City of Los Angeles, with its varied neighborhoods, cultural groups, and new areas in the process of development, makes tremendous demands upon the library. As a public agency, the library attempts to meet and anticipate

reasonable community needs, within the limitations of budget, space, and availability of materials in the area.

Criteria
Judgments of experts, of professionally trained staff members, and of qualified book reviewers in national and international magazines, provide a balance of opinion as the basis for selection. Though a variety of criteria is used for each subject, final decision is based on the value of the material to the library and its public, regardless of the personal taste of the selectors. These standards apply equally to materials purchased and those accepted as gifts.

Special aspects of book selection
The collection may include: works of an authentic genius, within the realm of his specific contribution, regardless of his moral or political reputation; works of potential historical significance, regardless of political or social variance; key books in fields that represent an aspect of belief or opinion which has not been completely authenticated; certain books whose language or content may restrict their use to the mature reader. Variety of opinion is represented whenever available.

Interpretation of policy
Questions concerning the scope and policies of an individual collection may be discussed with the librarian in charge of the department or branch. Complaints or comments on policies should be addressed in writing to the City Librarian.

Juvenile Books
Books are provided for children in the City of Loss Angeles through the public library and the schools.

It is the aim of the public library to meet the needs and diverse interests of the individual child from infancy through junior high school, by providing a well rounded, wisely selected collection of books which will encourage in him a love of reading and an appreciation of the values gained from reading the best in books.

On the other hand, the schools provide books and related materials which support the teaching program. In a broad sense this includes subject material covering a wide variety of subjects.

Responsibility for the selection of books

Book selection in the public library is the joint responsibility of the Department of Work with Children, which initiates and coordinates the book selection process, and of the children's librarians throughout the system, who read and evaluate the books before purchase.

While, in the final analysis, the responsibility for the decision as to which books are to be included in the library's collection is that of the Director of Work with Children, who works under the supervision of the City Librarian, each children's librarian shares and contributes to this decision.

After the books are approved it is the responsibility of the children's librarian in each library unit to select those which, within the limits of need and book budget, meet the reading interests of the children served by that unit.

Criteria

All books for children should be authentic in fact and feeling, straightforward in presentation, unbiased in point of view, and within the child's ability to comprehend. This is especially important in books dealing with religions, peoples, races and governments, which should inform by stated fact rather than by implication.

In order to recognize these qualities the children's librarian utilizes her professional training and experience, her knowledge of children and children's books, the opinion of qualified reviewers, and the standards established by the Children's Book Evaluation Committees of the Los Angeles Public Library.

Special aspects

As the Los Angeles City Schools and other local educational institutions supply textbooks and related materials for students, it is not the province of the Los Angeles Public Library to provide texts for school use. However, certain textbooks are included in the collection for the value of their informational content.

Readers used as basic texts in the primary grades of the Los Angeles City Schools are purchased in limited quantity and issued to parents for use with children. Other readers, through the third grade, are purchased to give the young child an opportunity for extensive reading on his grade level which will give him added skill in reading and the satisfaction of accomplishment. Emphasis is placed, however, upon the selection of appropriate books, other than school readers, for his independent reading.

Interpretation of policy

As each children's librarian shares in the process of book selection, so she, as a member of the group, supports the principles of this selection. When criticism is made of the inclusion of books in the collection, it is heard objectively and referred for decision to the Children's Librarians as a group, the Director of Work with Children, and the City Librarian, who interprets the library's book selection policies which have been adopted by the Board of Library Commissioners.

General Information

Policy. Initial selection of books and other materials, whether acquired by purchase or gift, is made by the Central Library departments, Young Adult Services and Children's Services in accord with the Library's book selection policy (described elsewhere). The selection process is continuous and involves most of the Library's professional staff, who review and evaluate new books and re-evaluate books already in the collection.

After a title has been selected for Central Library it may be added to branch collections by purchase at regular order meetings, scheduled or special replacement orders, or by gift. Branches also occasionally acquire material by transfer from other branches or the Central Library.

Book selection for the branch is the responsibility of the Branch Librarian in consultation with the branch professional staff. Adult books are selected by the Branch Librarian under the guidance of the Regional Librarian. Young Adult books are chosen by the Branch Librarian under the guidance of the Regional Librarian and upon recommendation of the Young Adult Librarian. Juvenile books are chosen by the Children's Librarian under the guidance of the Regional Children's Librarian or the Regional Librarian.

Lists and suggestions are provided by the professional staff of the Office of the Adult Book Coordinator and the Coordinators of Young Adult and Children's Services who consult and work with Subject Department Heads, Regional Librarians, Regional Children's Librarians, and various evaluation committees.

Preliminary Selection

Adult Books. As a preliminary step in new book selection, Subject Department and branch staff members are asked to write reviews of some new fiction titles, and non-fiction in fields where individual Librarians have special knowledge or interest. The staff of the Adult Book Coordinator's Office also reads and reviews books.

Young Adult Books. Books received from publishers (gifts or approvals) by Young Adult Services, or considered suitable by the Book Selection Committee are sent to Librarians in Central Library Subject Departments and branches to be read and considered for purchase, or are read by the staff of Young Adult New Book Order List.

Juvenile Books. Books received by Children's Services are sent to Children's Librarians to be read and considered for purchase. Books accepted are listed on the Juvenile New Book Order list which is compiled by the Staff of Children's Services and Senior Children's Librarians.

ORDERING

New Book Titles

Policy and General Information. Only those new titles being purchased by the Central Library Subject Departments are available for branch purchase. A Book Selection Committee composed of the Adult Book Coordinator, Coordinator of Young Adult Services, and a Regional Librarian examine books being purchased by the departments, discuss them with the Subject Department Heads, consult published and staff reviews, and select the books to be included on the Adult and the Young Adult New Book Order lists. The Book Selection Committee also designates which books will be reviewed orally. A committee composed of the staff of Children's Services and Senior Children's Librarians makes the selection for the Juvenile New Book Order list.

Bi-weekly (adult and young adult) and monthly (juvenile) order meetings are held at the Central Library. Available new books are displayed with reviews attached. Other books on the order lists are represented by reviews and/or copies of earlier editions. Books are also available for inspection on the day preceding the order meeting.

At the adult order meeting, attended by Branch Librarians and Librarians-in-charge of sub-branches, the Subject Department Heads and the Coordinator of Young Adult Services present oral reviews of selected books on the order lists. Branch Librarians check the items desired and make final decisions after a regional meeting where purchases are discussed with the Regional Librarian and the other Librarians of the region.

At the juvenile order meetings, attended by Children's Librarians and Librarians-in-charge of sub-branches, Children's Librarians and the staff of Children's Services present oral reviews of selected books on the order list. Children's Librarians check the items desired and make final decisions after a regional meeting where purchases are discussed with the Regional Children's Librarian or the Regional Librarian and the other Librarians in the region.

New Books on Display

General Information. The Adult Book Coordinator and the Coordinators of Young Adult and Children's Services arrange to have the new books on the lists displayed in the Assembly Room in Central Library on the day preceding as well as the day of the order meeting. Branch Librarians, Young Adult Librarians and Children's Librarians examine and evaluate the books on display on the day preceding the order meeting. As schedules permit, other professional staff members examine the books also.

Order Meeting.

General Information. Branch Librarians and Librarians-in-charge of sub-branches, or Children's Librarians and Libarians-in-charge of sub-branches meet in Assembly Room, Central Library at 9:00 A.M. and examine books and reviews until meeting begins.
Subject Department Heads and the Coordinator of Young Adult Services present oral reviews of specially selected books on the Adult and Young Adult New Book Order lists. Children's Librarians and the staff of Children's Services review selected items on the Juvenile New Book Order list. Books may be selected for oral reviews because of these circumstances or combination of circumstances: (1) The content or quality is not obvious in a short examination, (2) the unusual treatment of the subject, (3) the outstanding literary style, (4) controversial or questionable aspects. The reviewer indicates the value of the book in relation to similar books on the same subject and compares them with other editions.

BOOK SELECTION POLICY
LOUISVILLE FREE PUBLIC LIBRARY
(SEPTEMBER 1968)

A. *Adult Materials*

1. The library endorses the *Library Bill of Rights* as adopted by the American Library Association.

2. The library does not purchase or accept as gifts, materials dealing with the subject of hypnotism on a "how-to-do-it" basis. We will provide materials on its historical background and its uses, however.

3. The library does not purchase cartoon books except in rare cases of certain special editions.

4. The library exercises great care in selecting for purchase, books on the subjects of self-medication and legal advice.

5. Controversial books, i.e., "sexy" items or books with a plethora of scatalogical expressions, are designated for shelving in the stacks in order to avoid offending unaware browsers.

6. The library reserves the right to designate any material for restricted use or special handling, specifying that an item be for reference use only, for placement in the bookstacks rather than on the open shelves, or as seven-day material.

7. The library makes an attempt to build certain special collections:

   a. *Kentucky History.* This collection is housed in the Kentucky Room of the main library. It is composed of materials by and about Kentucky and Kentucky citizens. None of the material circulates. The Kentucky Room is a division of the Reference Department.

   b. *Negro Collection.* This collection is housed at Western Branch Library. It is composed of material by and about the

Negro. Some of the material circulates. Periodicals relative to the Negro, regardless of whether or not they are indexed, are kept at Western Branch. This branch attempts to compile a collection of materials by and about Negroes. Indexed periodicals in this collection may be duplicated in the Reference Department.

c. *Confederate Collection.* This collection is housed in the bookstacks in the main building.

d. *Reference Collection.* This collection is housed in the main library as a separate department. It is a non-circulating collection, avaiable for use in the library during regular library hours. This collection attempts to hold all representative, standard tools and sources for use by the entire system. Most of the materials may not be duplicated in branch libraries.

f. *Art-Reference Collection.* This collection is housed in the Kentucky History Room and consists of expensive and unusual items. All are listed in the main catalog and available on request for building use only.

8. Generally, the library does not purchase text books except in cases where no other material on a given subject exists or where the demand of the patrons is greater than can be met by the existing collection.

9. Religious material purchased or accepted as gifts must be of a general nature. Material designed to be used for proselyting is not suitable for the library's collection.

10. The library may purchase paperback editions of items which are in great demand. It is understood that no cataloging treatment will be given to such items. However, paperback editions of out-of-print items frequently are bound and cataloged.

11. Westerns, mysteries and science fiction are purchased in limited quantities, and librarians are urged to make such purchases in remaindered stock in order that the greatest amount of this material can be obtained by the smallest expenditure from funds.

12. Special requests or recommendations by patrons are always accepted for consideration. Acceptance of such a request or recommendation does not mean that the library is obliged to purchase an item.

13. No book may be purchased by any agency if it has not been approved at a book-selection committee meeting or appeared on the book-selection truck and personally examined by the librarian of the agency for which it is ordered.

14. Certain publishers' books are received automatically by the library either on an on-approval basis or under the Greenaway Plan. The library is obliged to accept at least one copy of all Greenaway books, but it is under no obligation to place these books in the collection.

15. While the library is sympathetic to the needs of students, it is not the primary responsibility of the library to provide curriculum centered materials for them.

16. Addition of a book to the library's collection in no way represents an endorsement of any theory, idea, or policy contained therein.

17. Branch reference collections should be maintained to meet the "ready" reference type of requests rather than "research" encyclopedias, dictionaries, and, in the major branches, *Reader's Guide* should meet most needs. Special indexes, current news services, loose-leaf services, and special reference works are not purchased by branches.

Branches are also expected to maintain a vertical file of free and inexpensive materials to meet reference needs. In addition, many branches have a need for such items as the Reference Shelf series.

Reference requests which cannot be met with available materials, or which require resources beyond those found in the branch, should be directed to the Reference Department of the Main Library.

18. *Indexed Books:* Titles included in the *Essay and General Literature Index* are automatically purchased by the Circulation Department.

B. *Book-Selection Policy: Juvenile*

1. The Children's Department of the library endorses the *School Library Bill of Rights* as adopted by the American Library Association insofar as it is applicable to public libraries.

2. Although the library is sympathetic to the needs of students, the library does not accept as its chief function the responsibility to provide textbooks or curriculum-related materials for the users of the library.

Index

Index

Index